GREG PAK   GIANNIS MILONOGIANNIS   IRMA KNIIVILA

RONIN ISLAND ™

VOLUME THREE
A NEW WIND

Published by

BOOM! ™
STUDIOS

Ross Richie .... CEO & Founder
Joy Huffman .... CFO
Matt Gagnon .... Editor-in-Chief
Filip Sablik .... President, Publishing & Marketing
Stephen Christy .... President, Development
Lance Kreiter .... Vice President, Licensing & Merchandising
Arune Singh .... Vice President, Marketing
Bryce Carlson .... Vice President, Editorial & Creative Strategy
Kate Henning .... Director, Operations
Spencer Simpson .... Director, Sales
Scott Newman .... Manager, Production Design
Elyse Strandberg .... Manager, Finance
Sierra Hahn .... Executive Editor
Jeanine Schaefer .... Executive Editor
Dafna Pleban .... Senior Editor
Shannon Watters .... Senior Editor
Eric Harburn .... Senior Editor
Matthew Levine .... Editor
Sophie Philips-Roberts .... Associate Editor
Amanda LaFranco .... Associate Editor
Jonathan Manning .... Associate Editor
Gavin Gronenthal .... Assistant Editor
Gwen Waller .... Assistant Editor
Allyson Gronowitz .... Assistant Editor
Ramiro Portnoy .... Assistant Editor
Kenzie Rzonca .... Assistant Editor
Shelby Netschke .... Editorial Assistant
Michelle Ankley .... Design Coordinator
Marie Krupina .... Production Designer
Grace Park .... Production Designer
Chelsea Roberts .... Production Designer
Samantha Knapp .... Production Design Assistant
José Meza .... Live Events Lead
Stephanie Hocutt .... Digital Marketing Lead
Esther Kim .... Marketing Coordinator
Breanna Sarpy .... Executive Assistant
Amanda Lawson .... Marketing Assistant
Holly Aitchison .... Digital Sales Coordinator
Morgan Perry .... Retail Sales Coordinator
Megan Christopher .... Operations Coordinator
Rodrigo Hernandez .... Operations Coordinator
Zipporah Smith .... Operations Assistant
Jason Lee .... Senior Accountant
Sabrina Lesin .... Accounting Assistant

RONIN ISLAND Volume Three, December 2020. Published by
BOOM! Studios, a division of Boom Entertainment, Inc. Ronin
Island is ™ & © 2020 Pak Man Productions, Ltd. Originally
published in single magazine form as RONIN ISLAND No.
9-12. ™ & © 2020 Pak Man Productions, Ltd. All rights reserved.
BOOM! Studios™ and the BOOM! Studios logo are trademarks
of Boom Entertainment, Inc., registered in various countries
and categories. All characters, events, and institutions
depicted herein are fictional. Any similarity between any of the
names, characters, persons, events, and/or institutions in this
publication to actual names, characters, and persons, whether
living or dead, events, and/or institutions is unintended and
purely coincidental. BOOM! Studios does not read or accept
unsolicited submissions of ideas, stories, or artwork.

BOOM! Studios, 5670 Wilshire Boulevard, Suite 400, Los
Angeles, CA, 90036-5679. Printed in China. First Printing.

ISBN: 978-1-68415-623-8, eISBN: 978-1-64668-035-1

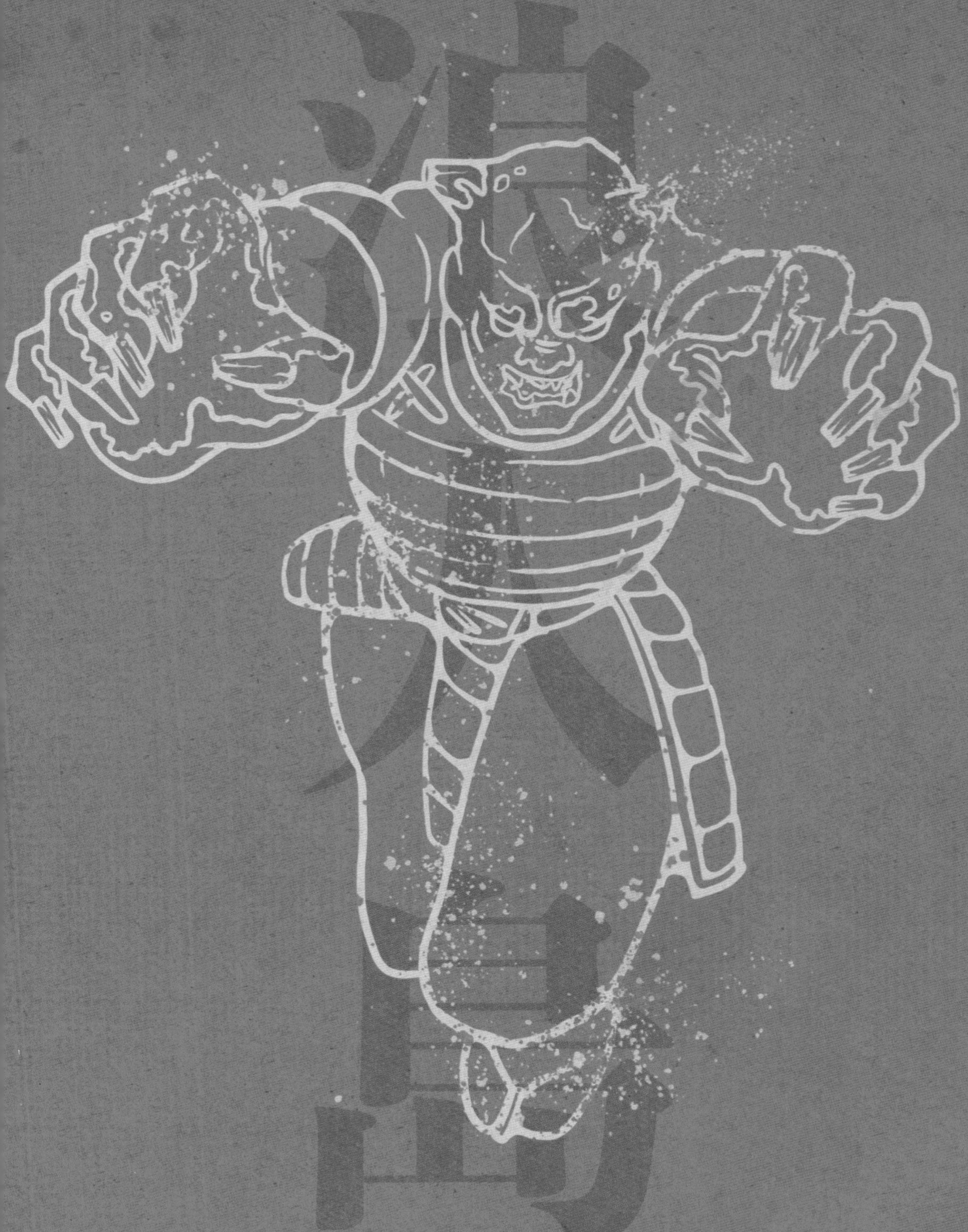

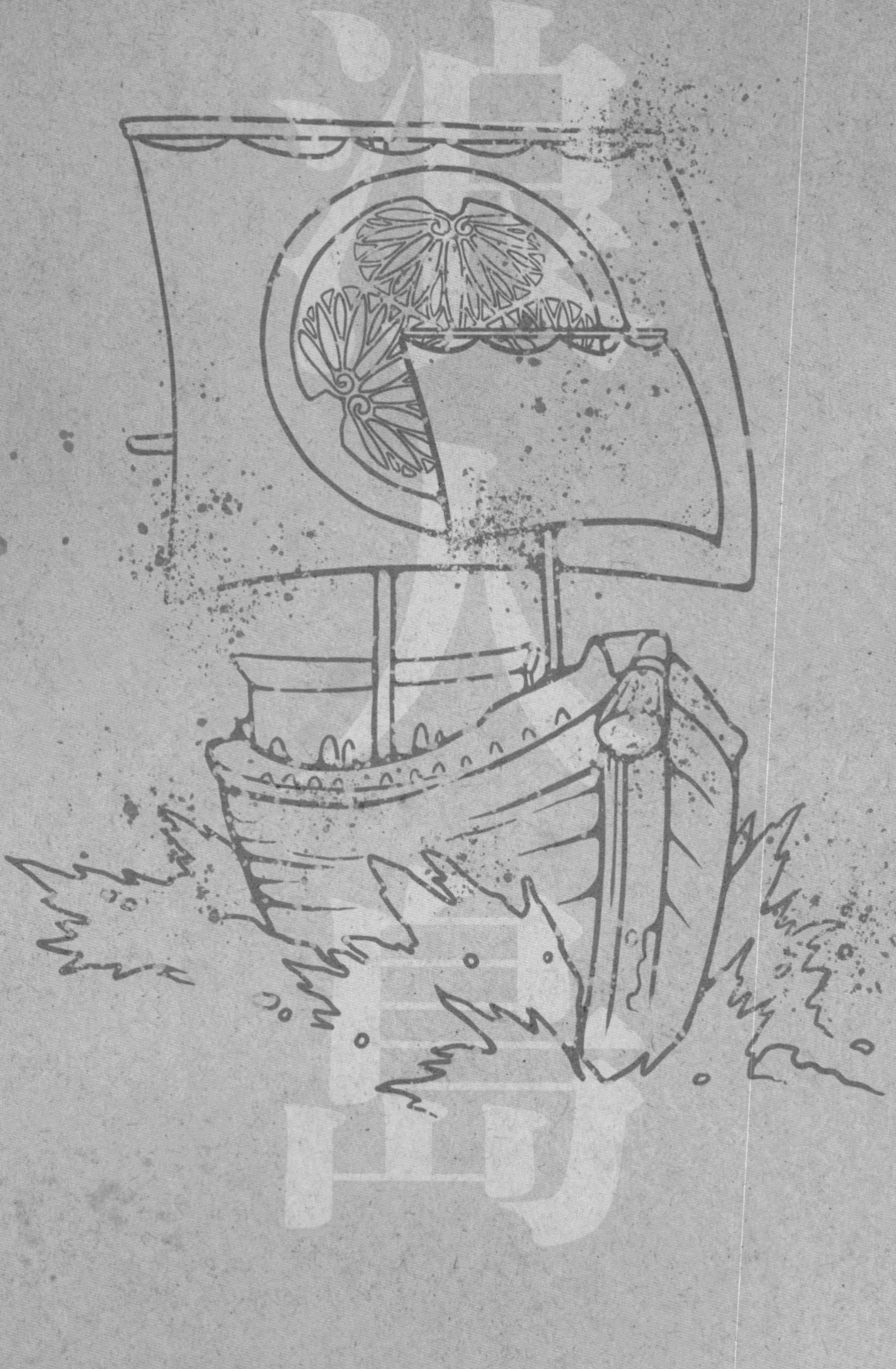

WRITTEN BY
GREG PAK

ILLUSTRATED BY
GIANNIS MILONOGIANNIS

COLORED BY
IRMA KNIIVILA

LETTERED BY
SIMON BOWLAND

COVER BY
GIANNIS MILONOGIANNIS
WITH COLORS BY **MSASSYK**

SERIES DESIGNER
MICHELLE ANKLEY

COLLECTION DESIGNER
MARIE KRUPINA

EDITOR
AMANDA LAFRANCO

SENIOR EDITOR
ERIC HARBURN

SPECIAL THANKS **CAMERON CHITTOCK**

RONIN ISLAND

CREATED BY **GREG PAK** AND
GIANNIS MILONOGIANNIS

CHAPTER NINE

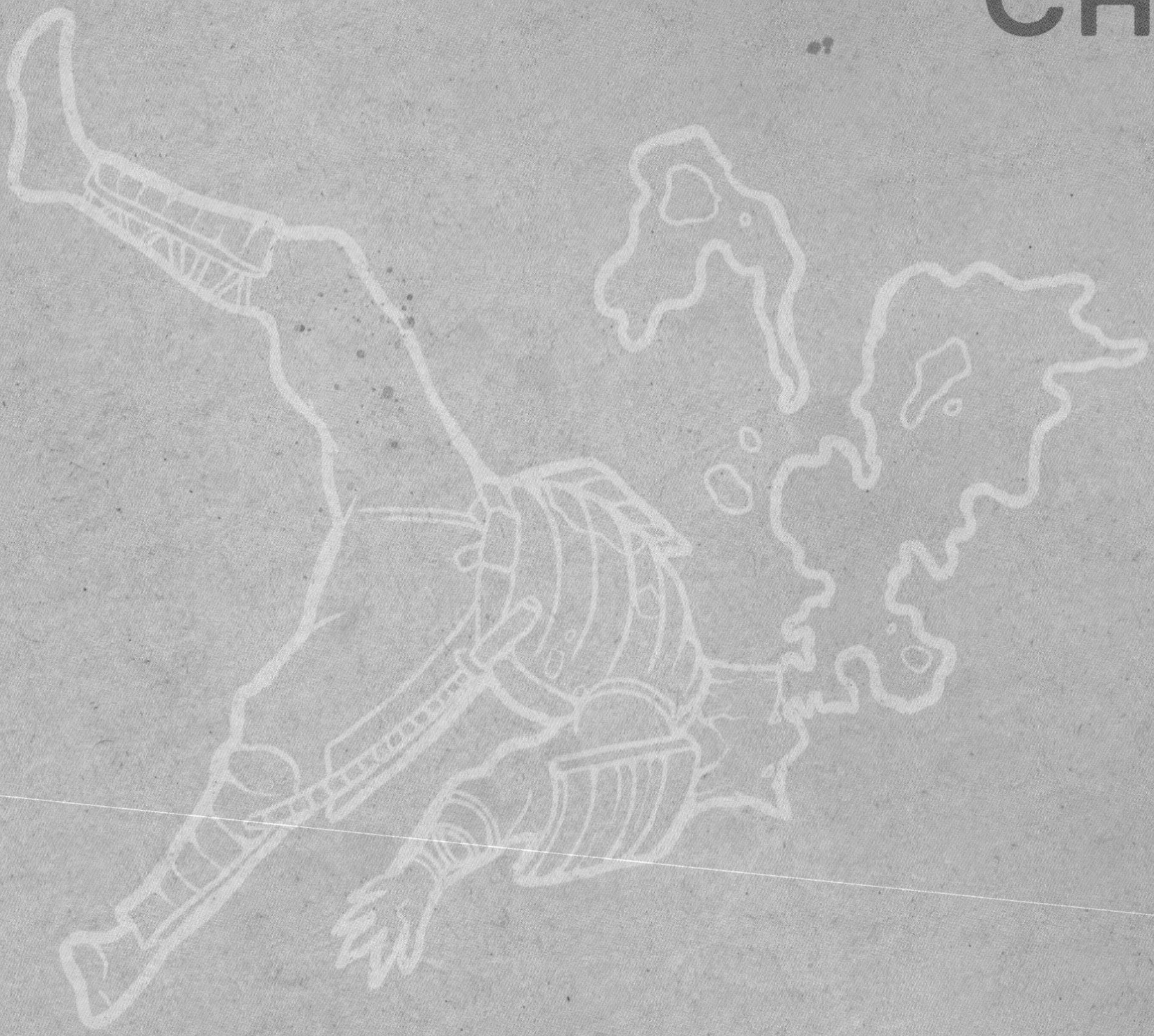

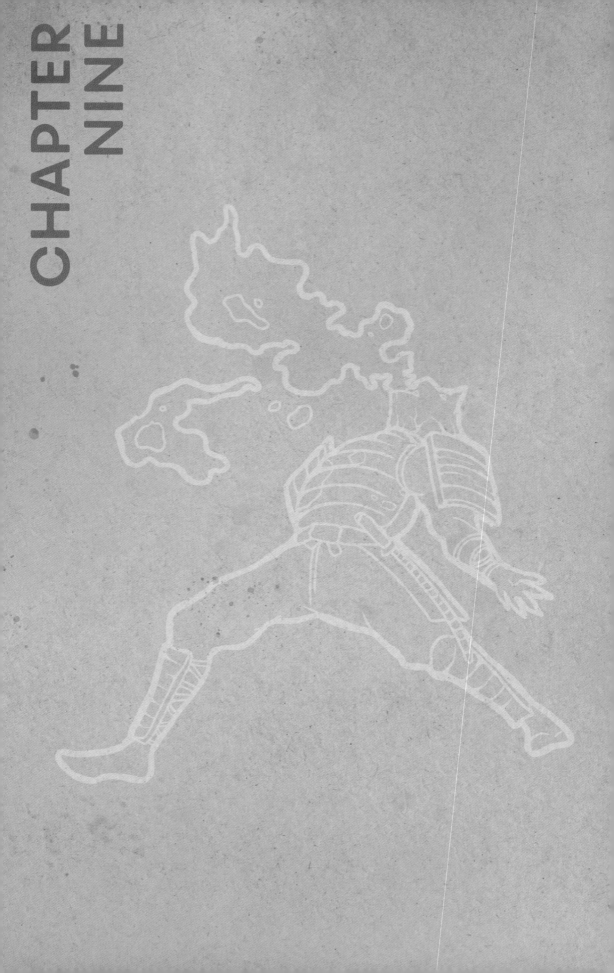

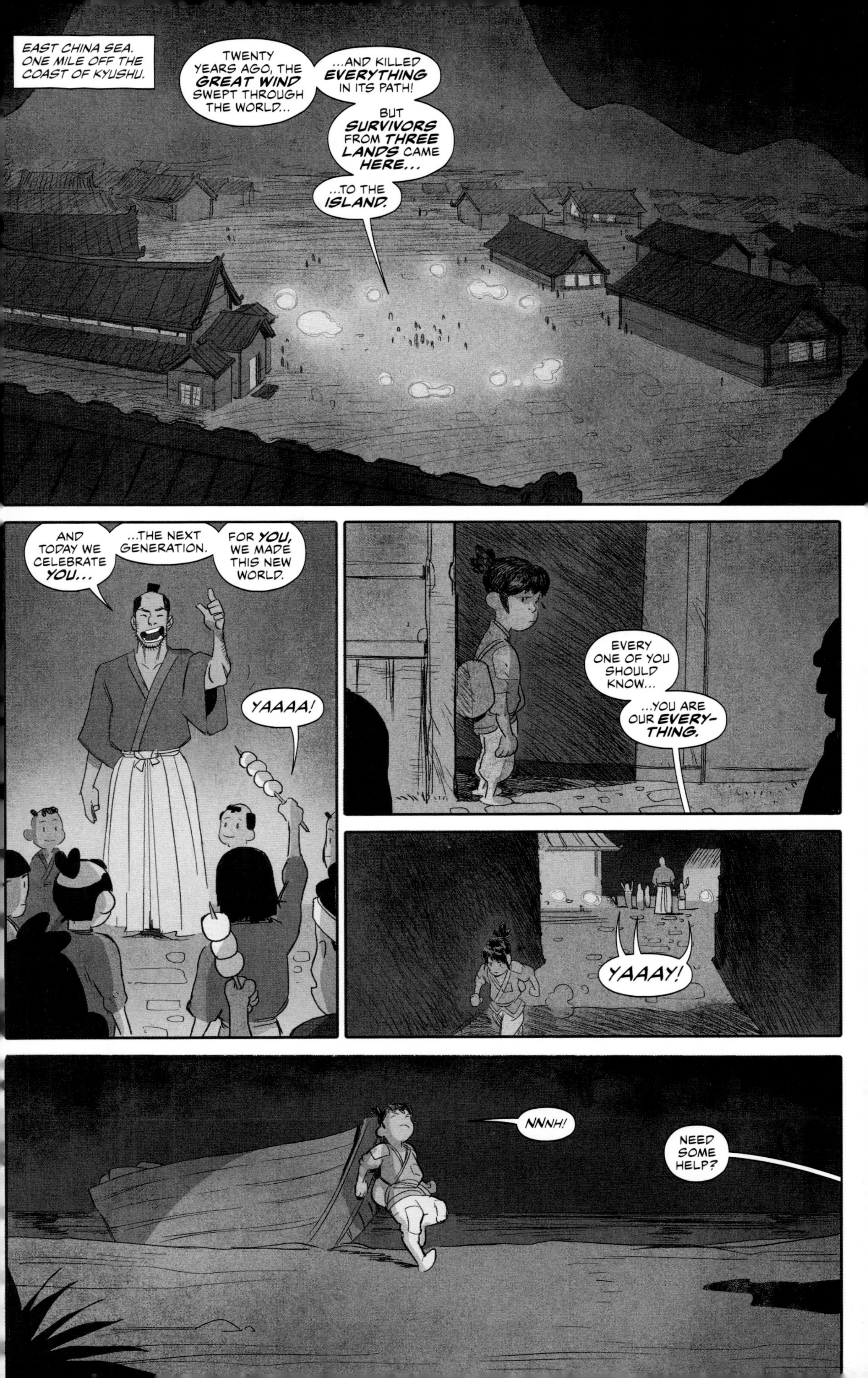
EAST CHINA SEA. ONE MILE OFF THE COAST OF KYUSHU.
TWENTY YEARS AGO, THE GREAT WIND SWEPT THROUGH THE WORLD...
...AND KILLED EVERYTHING IN ITS PATH!
BUT SURVIVORS FROM THREE LANDS CAME HERE...
...TO THE ISLAND.
AND TODAY WE CELEBRATE YOU...
...THE NEXT GENERATION.
FOR YOU, WE MADE THIS NEW WORLD.
YAAAA!
EVERY ONE OF YOU SHOULD KNOW...
...YOU ARE OUR EVERYTHING.
YAAAY!
NNNH!
NEED SOME HELP?

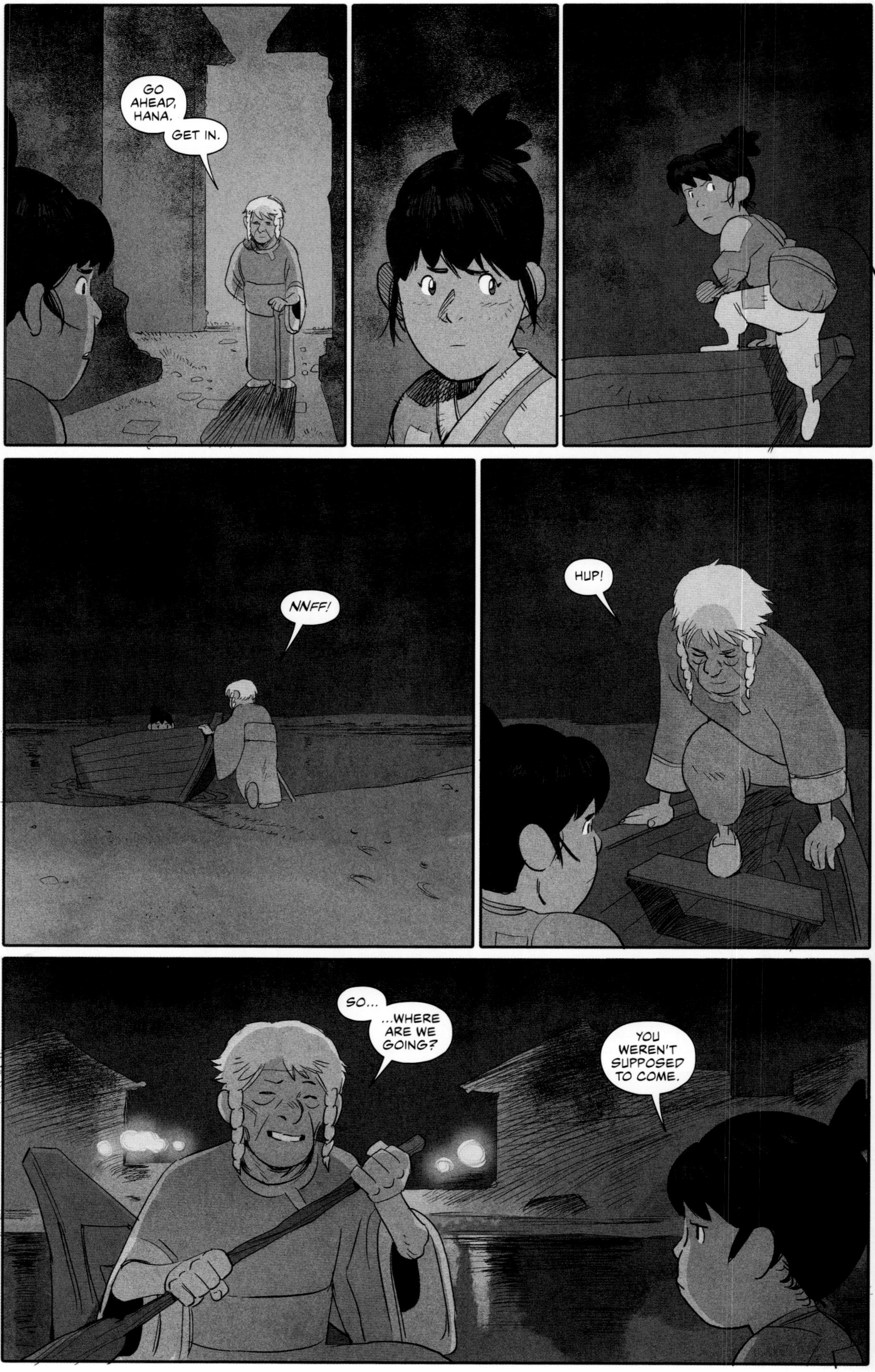
GO AHEAD, HANA.
GET IN.
NNFF!
HUP!
SO...
...WHERE ARE WE GOING?
YOU WEREN'T SUPPOSED TO COME.

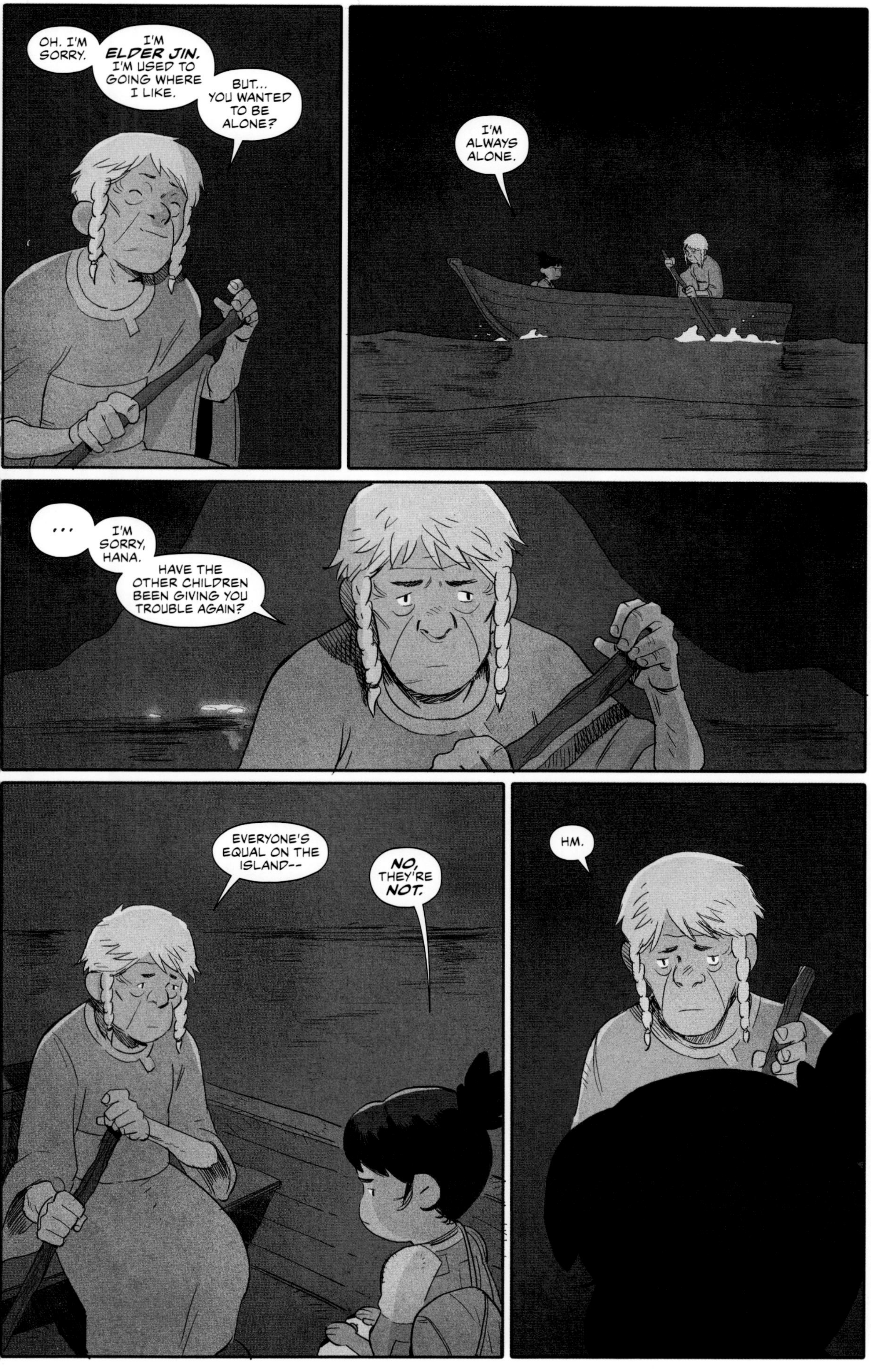
OH. I'M SORRY.
I'M ELDER JIN. I'M USED TO GOING WHERE I LIKE.
BUT... YOU WANTED TO BE ALONE?
I'M ALWAYS ALONE.
...
I'M SORRY, HANA.
HAVE THE OTHER CHILDREN BEEN GIVING YOU TROUBLE AGAIN?
EVERYONE'S EQUAL ON THE ISLAND--
NO, THEY'RE NOT.
HM.

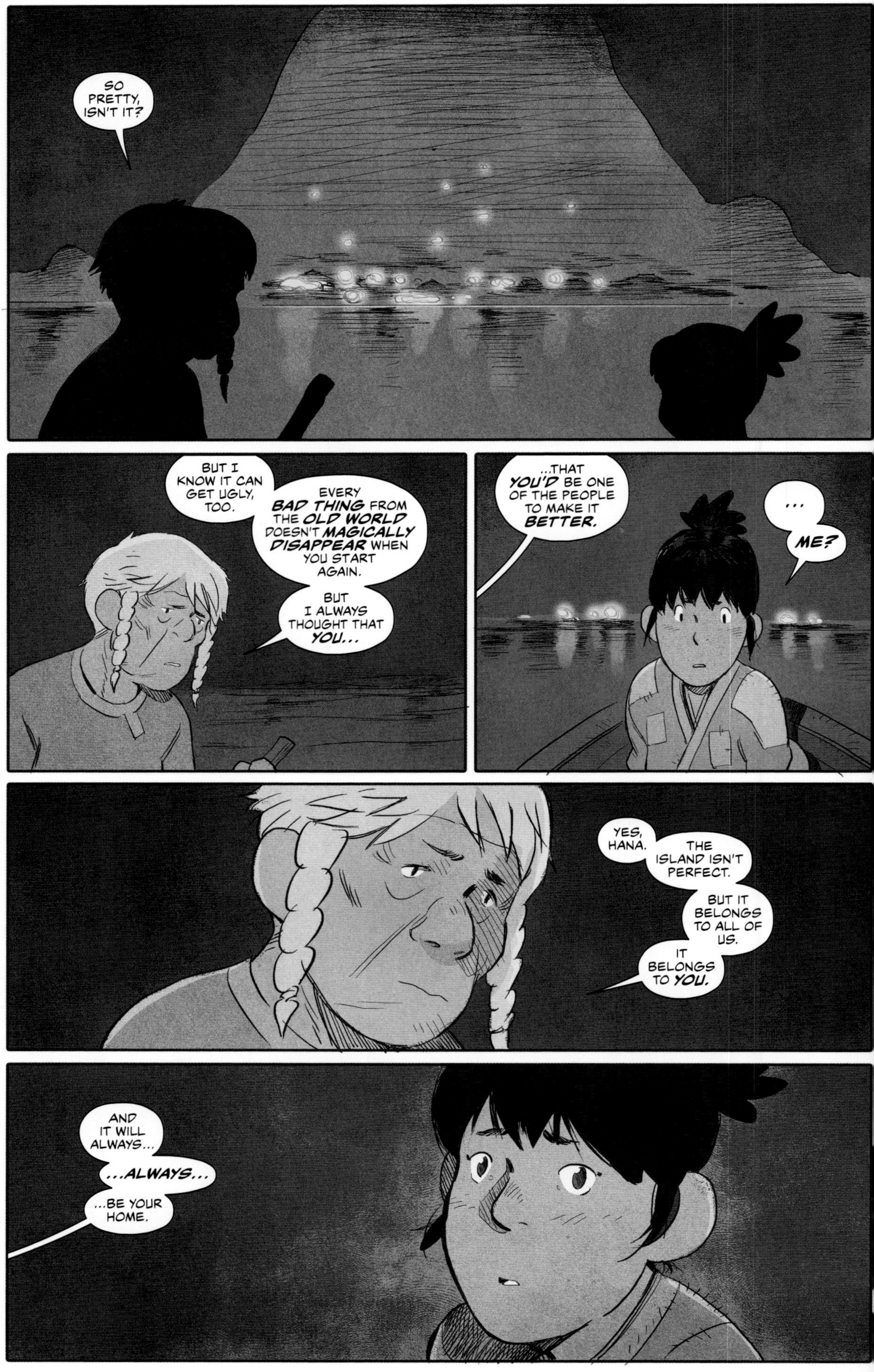
SO PRETTY, ISN'T IT?
BUT I KNOW IT CAN GET UGLY, TOO.
EVERY BAD THING FROM THE OLD WORLD DOESN'T MAGICALLY DISAPPEAR WHEN YOU START AGAIN.
BUT I ALWAYS THOUGHT THAT YOU...
...THAT YOU'D BE ONE OF THE PEOPLE TO MAKE IT BETTER.
...
ME?
YES, HANA.
THE ISLAND ISN'T PERFECT.
BUT IT BELONGS TO ALL OF US.
IT BELONGS TO YOU.
AND IT WILL ALWAYS...
...ALWAYS...
...BE YOUR HOME.

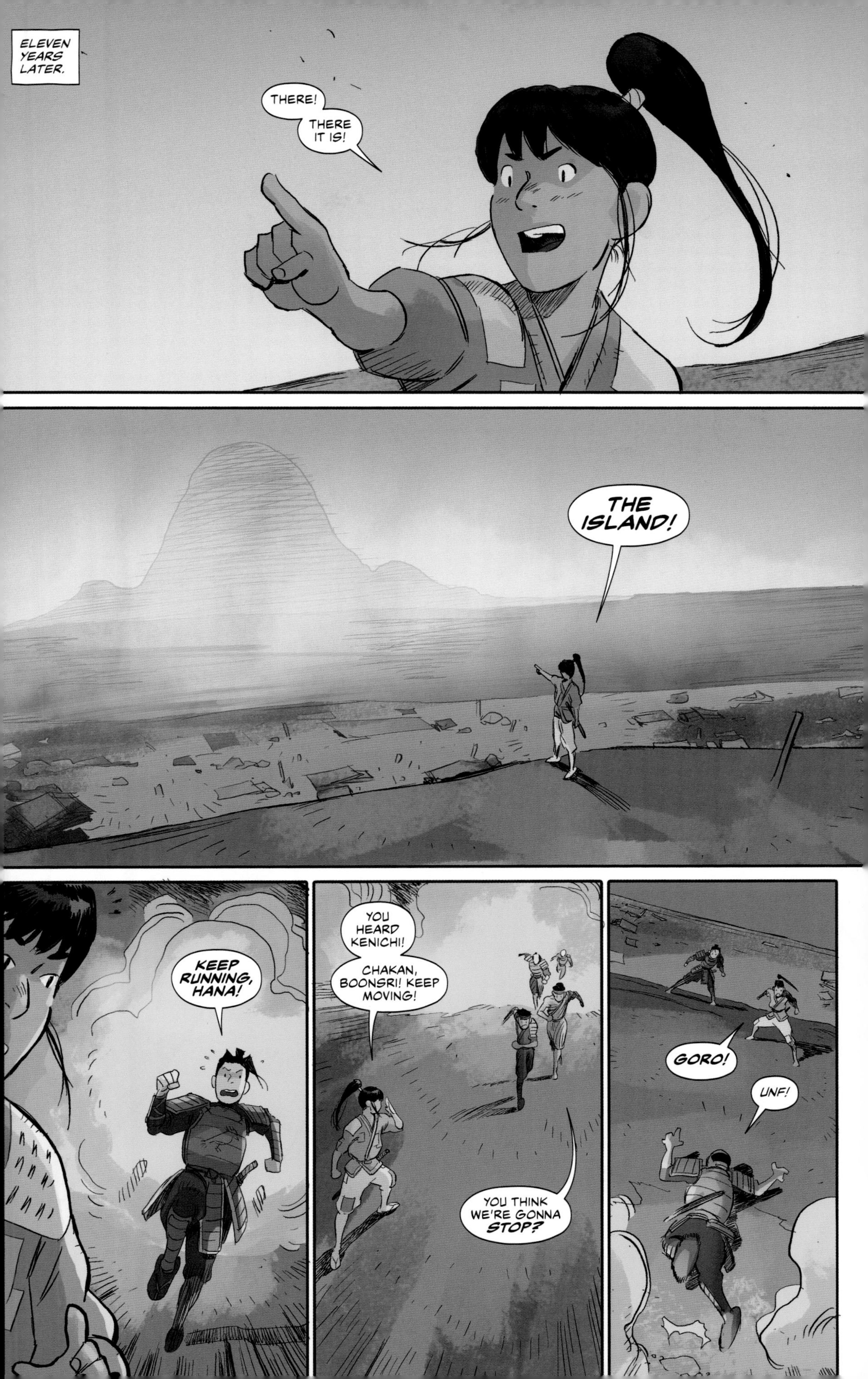
ELEVEN YEARS LATER.
THERE!
THERE IT IS!
THE ISLAND!
KEEP RUNNING, HANA!
YOU HEARD KENICHI!
CHAKAN, BOONSRI! KEEP MOVING!
YOU THINK WE'RE GONNA STOP?
GORO!
UNF!

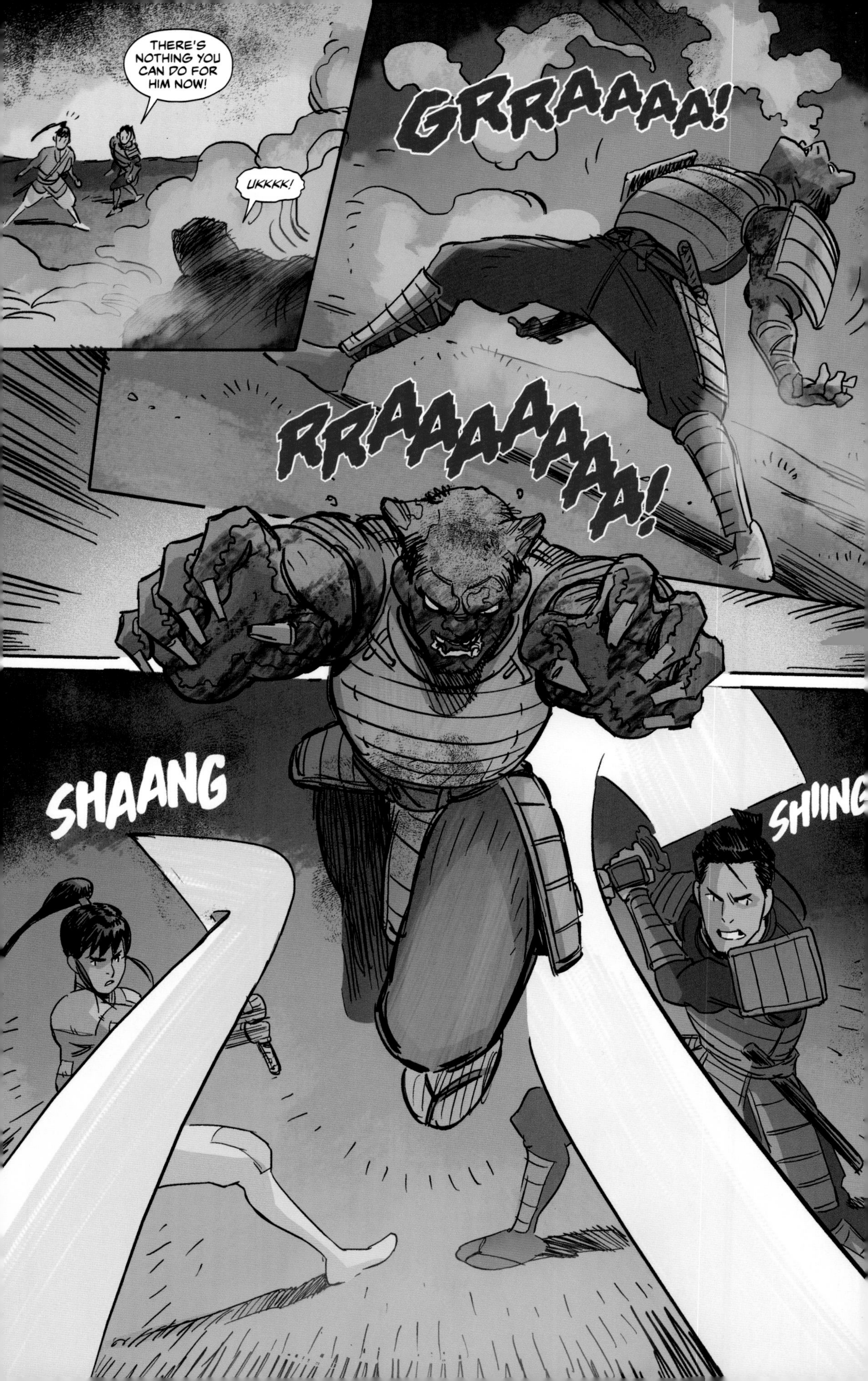
THERE'S NOTHING YOU CAN DO FOR HIM NOW!
UKKKK!
GRRAAAA!
RRAAAAAAAA!
SHAANG
SHIING

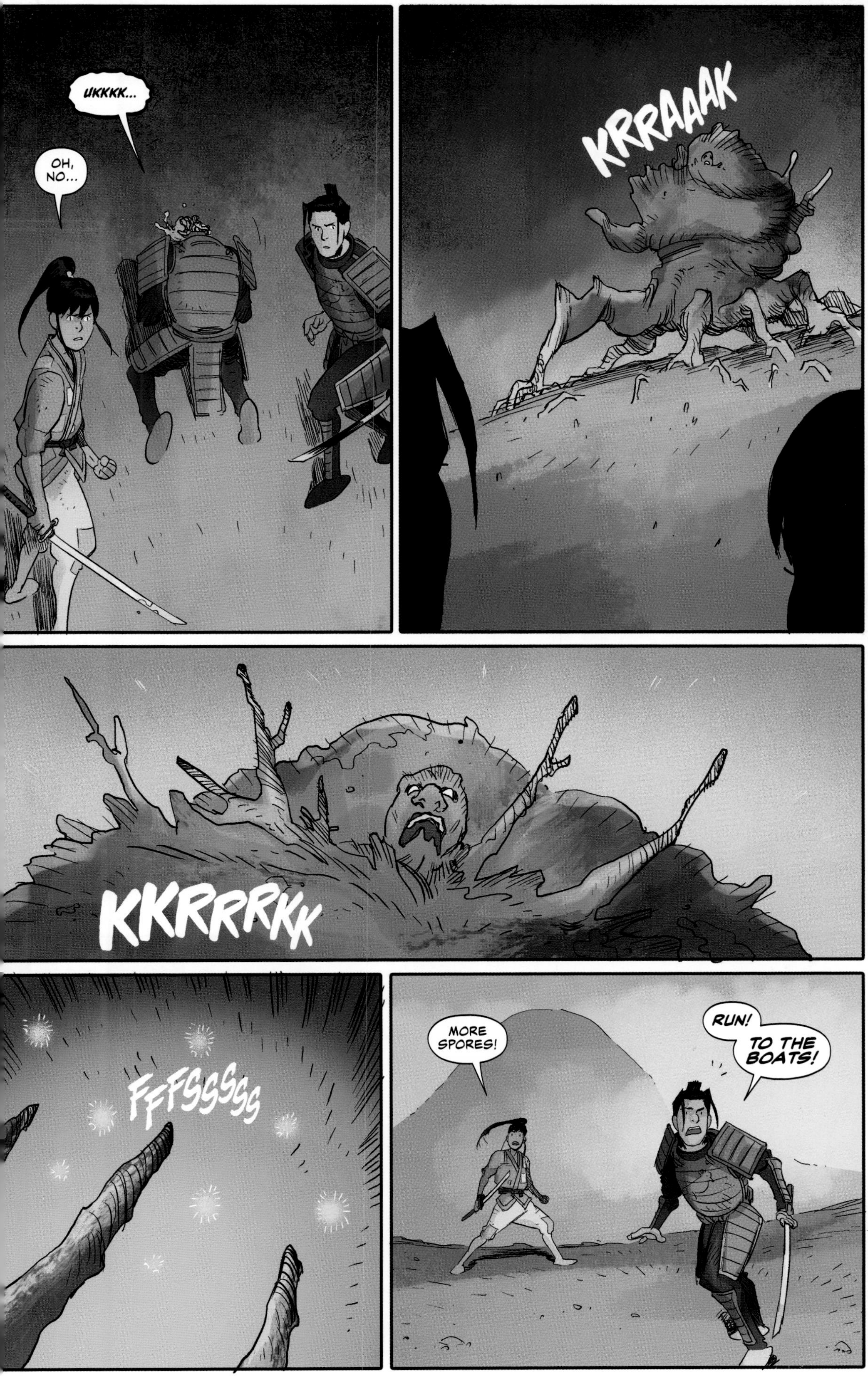
UKKKK...
OH, NO...
KRRAAAK
KKRRRKK
FFFSSSSSS
MORE SPORES!
RUN!
TO THE BOATS!

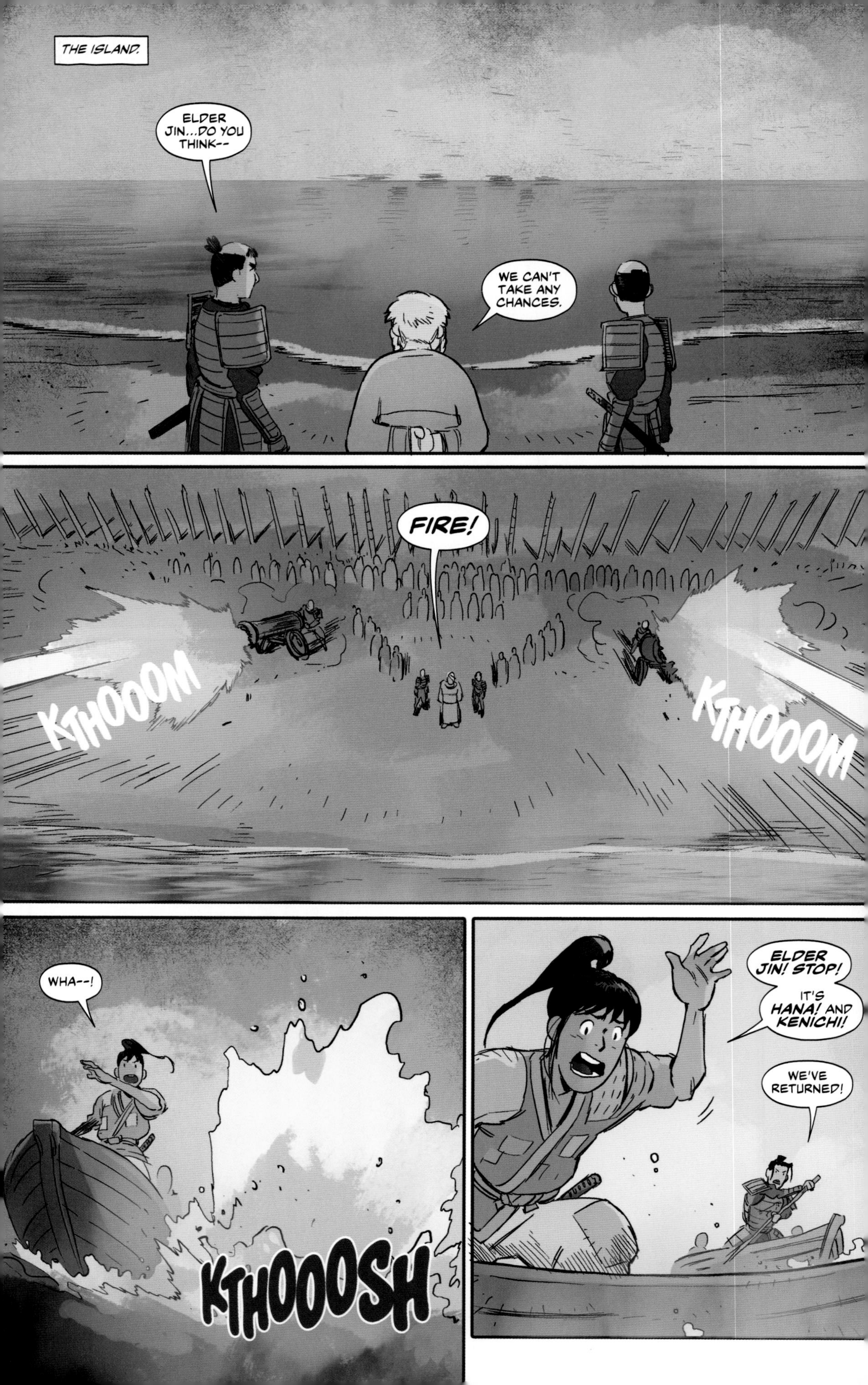
THE ISLAND.
ELDER JIN...DO YOU THINK--
WE CAN'T TAKE ANY CHANCES.
FIRE!
KTHOOOM
KTHOOOM
WHA--!
KTHOOOSH
ELDER JIN! STOP!
IT'S HANA! AND KENICHI!
WE'VE RETURNED!

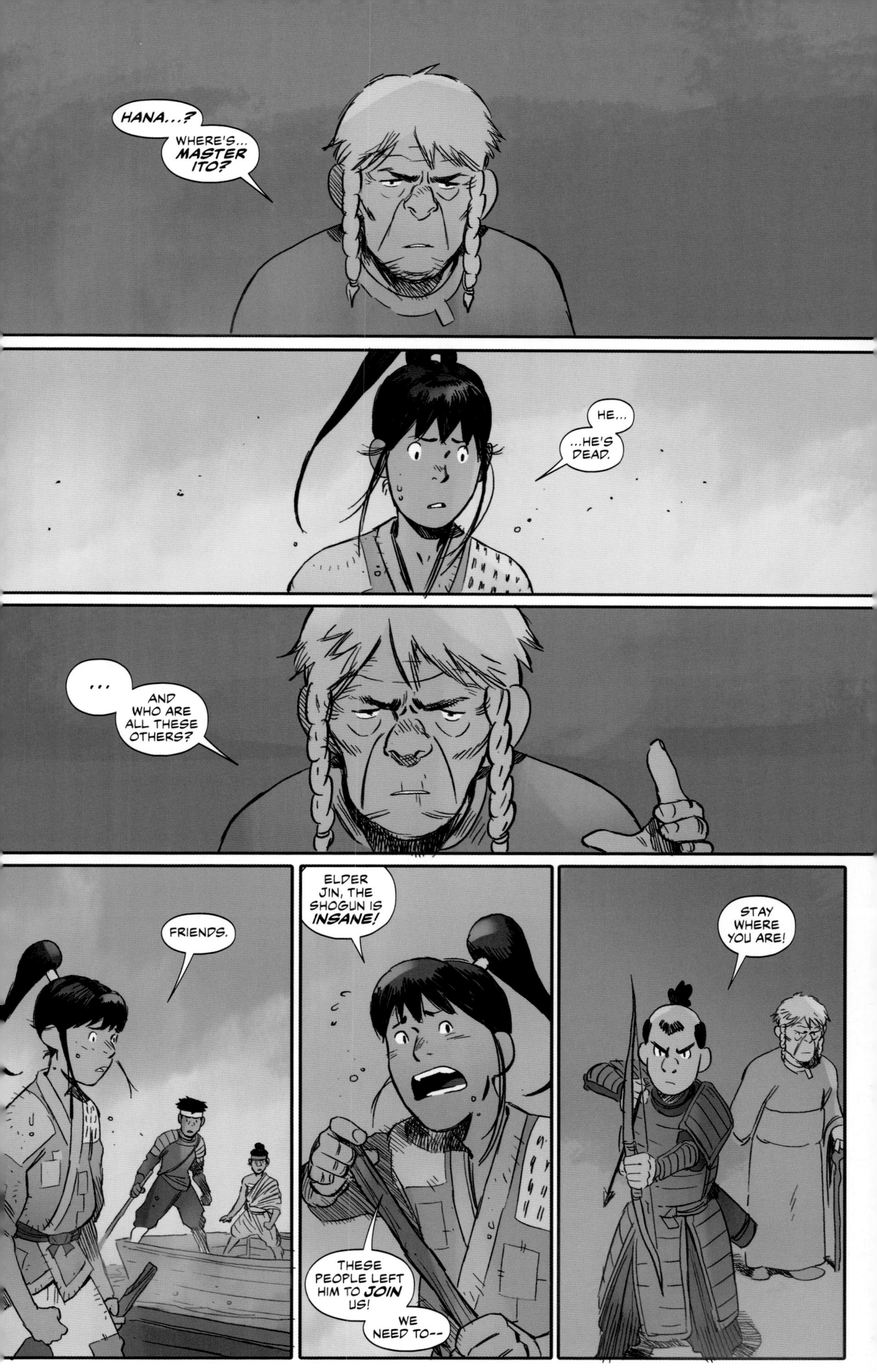
HANA...?
WHERE'S... MASTER ITO?
HE...
...HE'S DEAD.
...
AND WHO ARE ALL THESE OTHERS?
FRIENDS.
ELDER JIN, THE SHOGUN IS INSANE!
THESE PEOPLE LEFT HIM TO JOIN US!
WE NEED TO--
STAY WHERE YOU ARE!

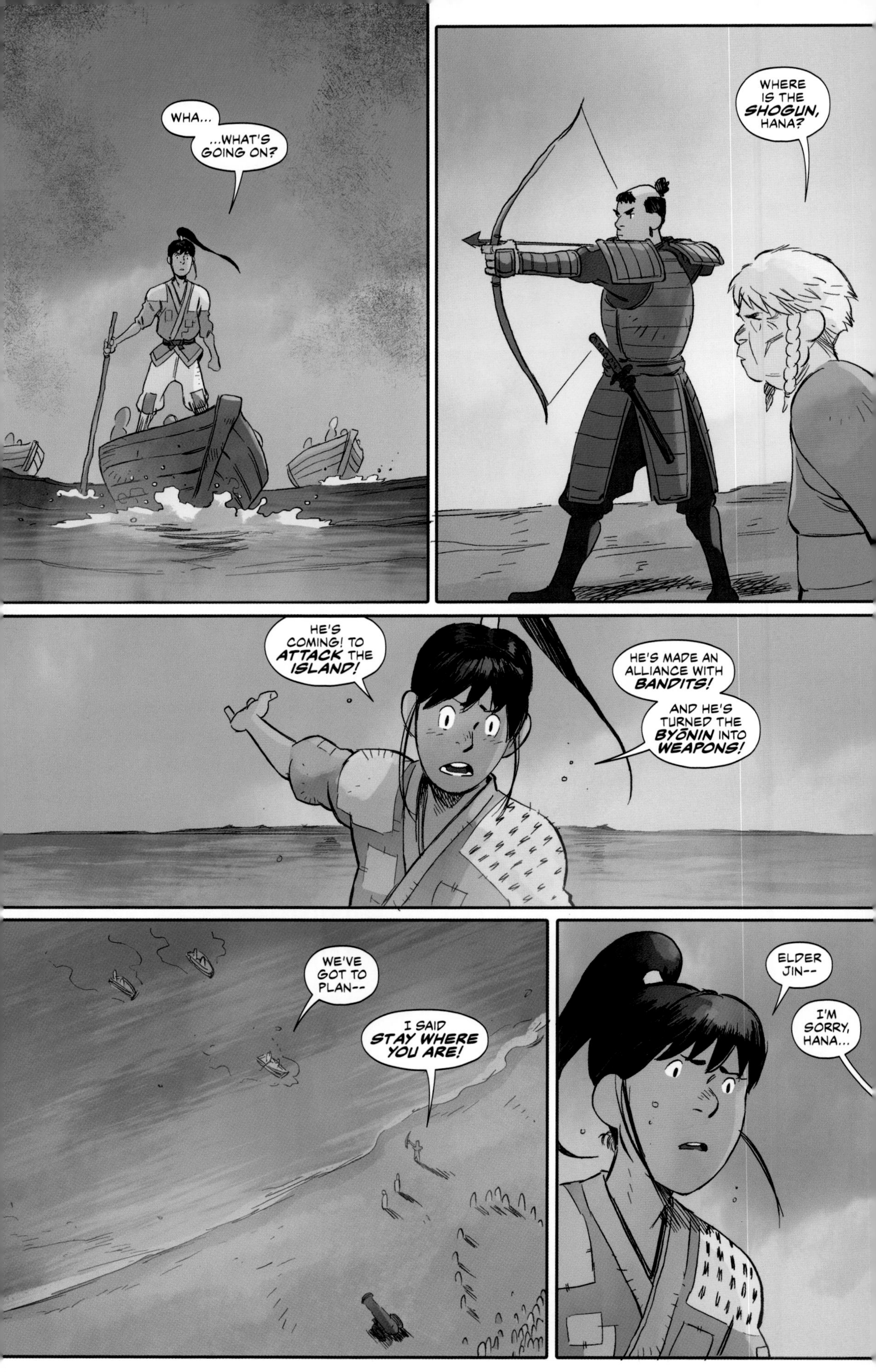
WHA...
...WHAT'S GOING ON?
WHERE IS THE SHOGUN, HANA?
HE'S COMING! TO ATTACK THE ISLAND!
HE'S MADE AN ALLIANCE WITH BANDITS!
AND HE'S TURNED THE BYŌNIN INTO WEAPONS!
WE'VE GOT TO PLAN--
I SAID STAY WHERE YOU ARE!
ELDER JIN--
I'M SORRY, HANA...

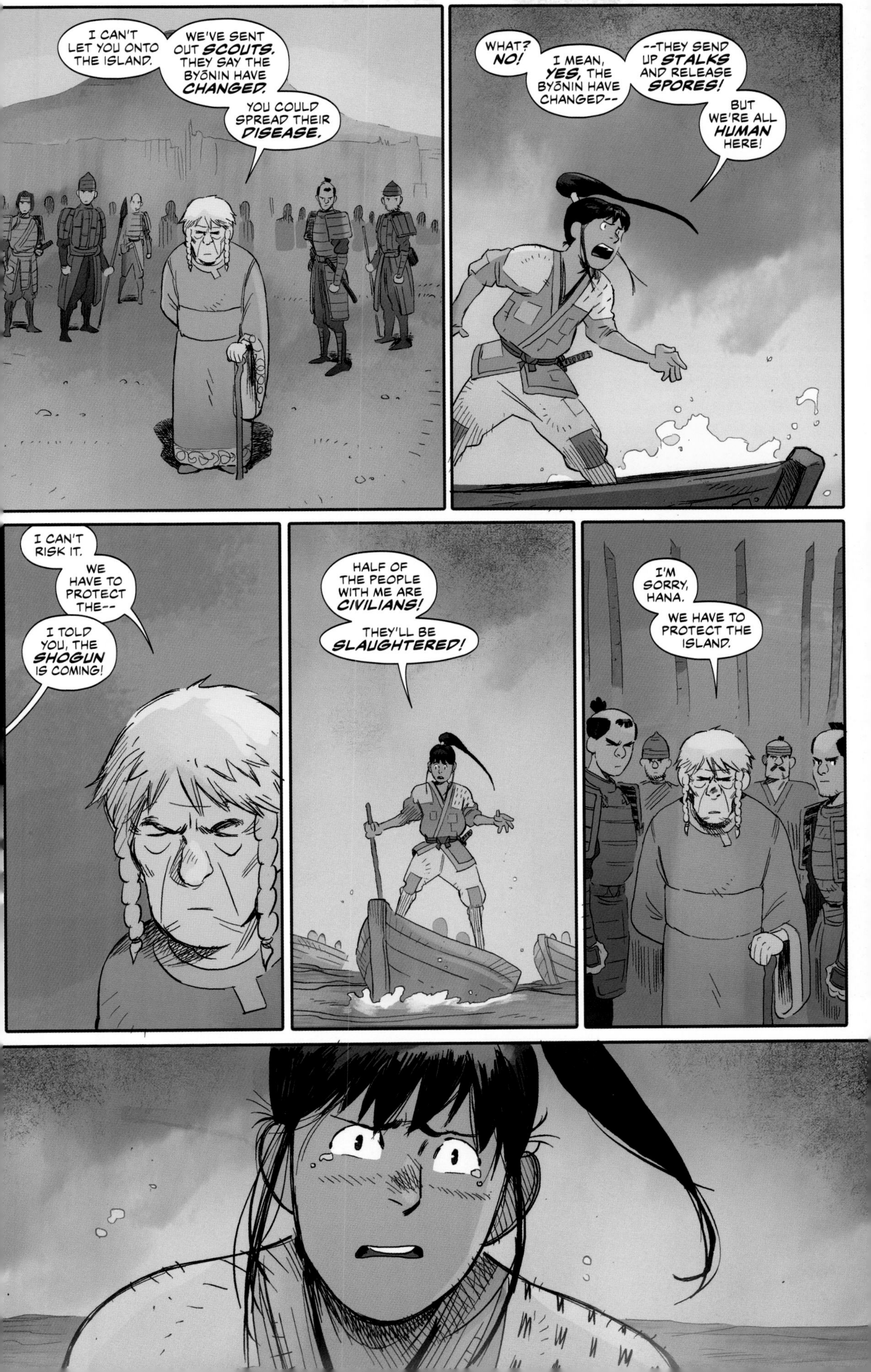

I CAN'T LET YOU ONTO THE ISLAND.
WE'VE SENT OUT SCOUTS. THEY SAY THE BYŌNIN HAVE CHANGED.
YOU COULD SPREAD THEIR DISEASE.
WHAT? NO!
I MEAN, YES, THE BYŌNIN HAVE CHANGED--
--THEY SEND UP STALKS AND RELEASE SPORES!
BUT WE'RE ALL HUMAN HERE!
I CAN'T RISK IT.
WE HAVE TO PROTECT THE--
I TOLD YOU, THE SHOGUN IS COMING!
HALF OF THE PEOPLE WITH ME ARE CIVILIANS!
THEY'LL BE SLAUGHTERED!
I'M SORRY, HANA.
WE HAVE TO PROTECT THE ISLAND.

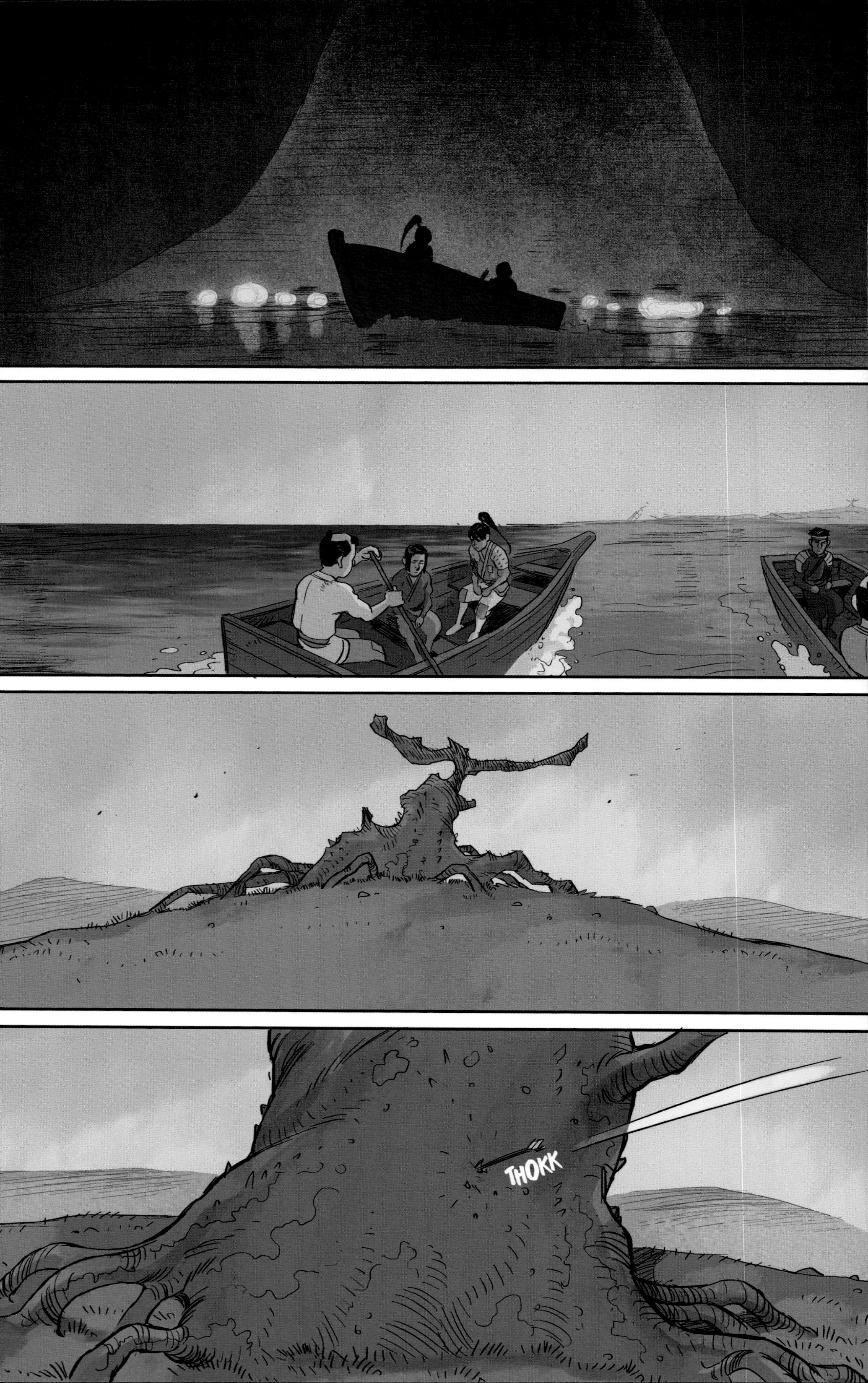
THOKK

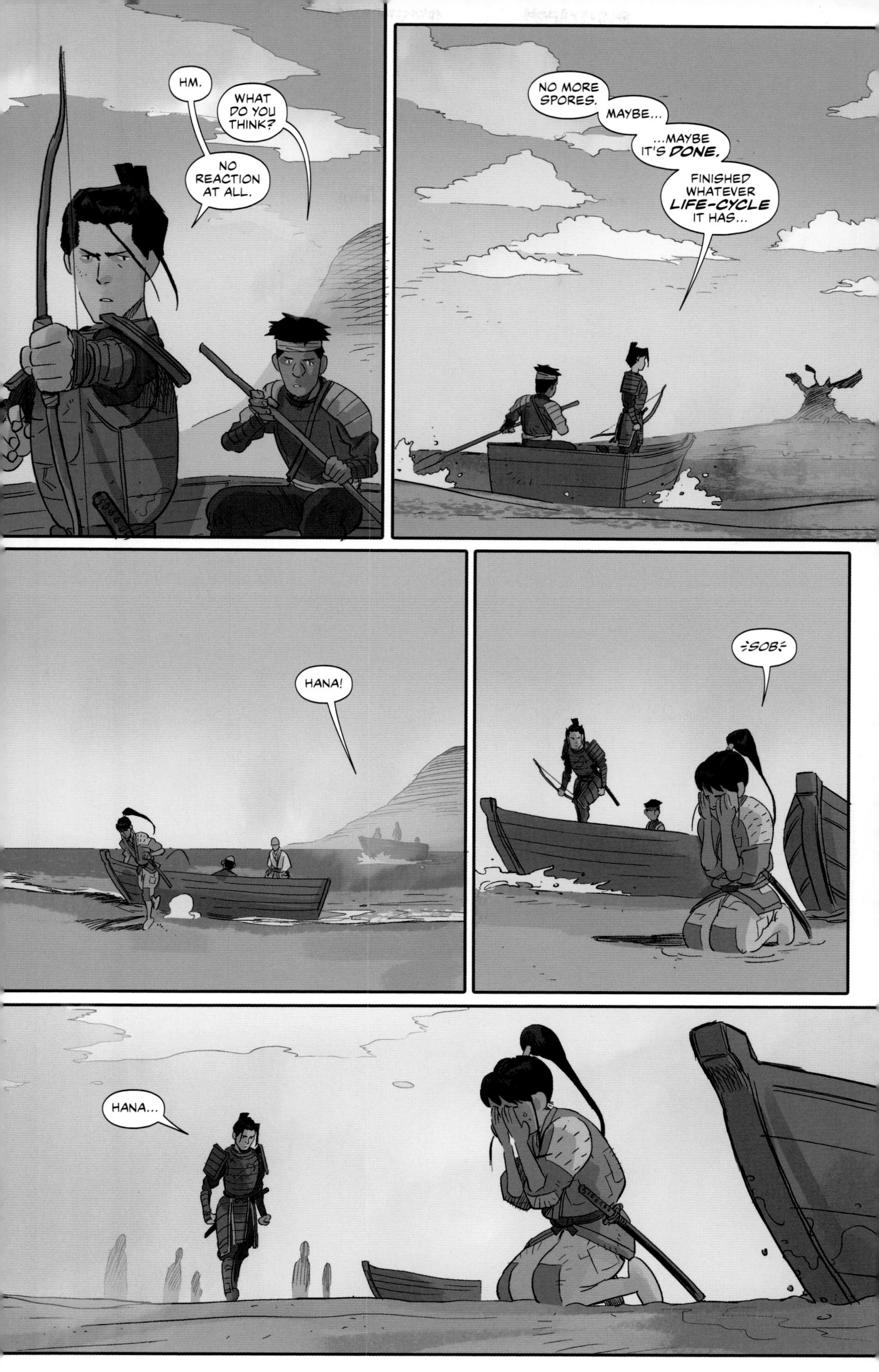
HM.
WHAT DO YOU THINK?
NO REACTION AT ALL.
NO MORE SPORES.
MAYBE...
...MAYBE IT'S DONE.
FINISHED WHATEVER LIFE-CYCLE IT HAS...
HANA!
SOB
HANA...

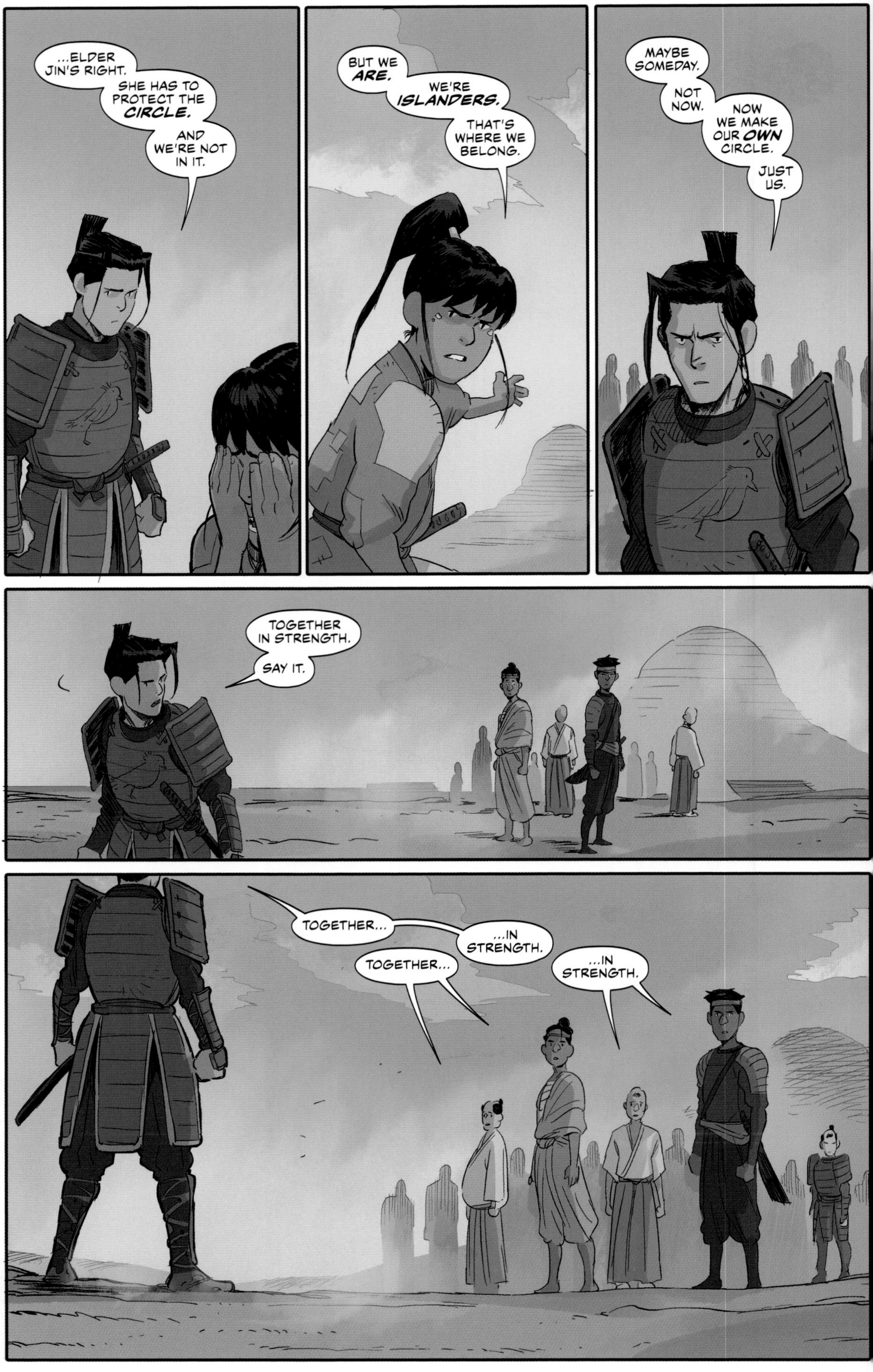
...ELDER JIN'S RIGHT.
SHE HAS TO PROTECT THE ***CIRCLE.***
AND WE'RE NOT IN IT.
BUT WE ***ARE.***
WE'RE ***ISLANDERS.***
THAT'S WHERE WE BELONG.
MAYBE SOMEDAY.
NOT NOW.
NOW WE MAKE OUR ***OWN*** CIRCLE.
JUST US.
TOGETHER IN STRENGTH.
SAY IT.
TOGETHER...
...IN STRENGTH.
TOGETHER...
...IN STRENGTH.

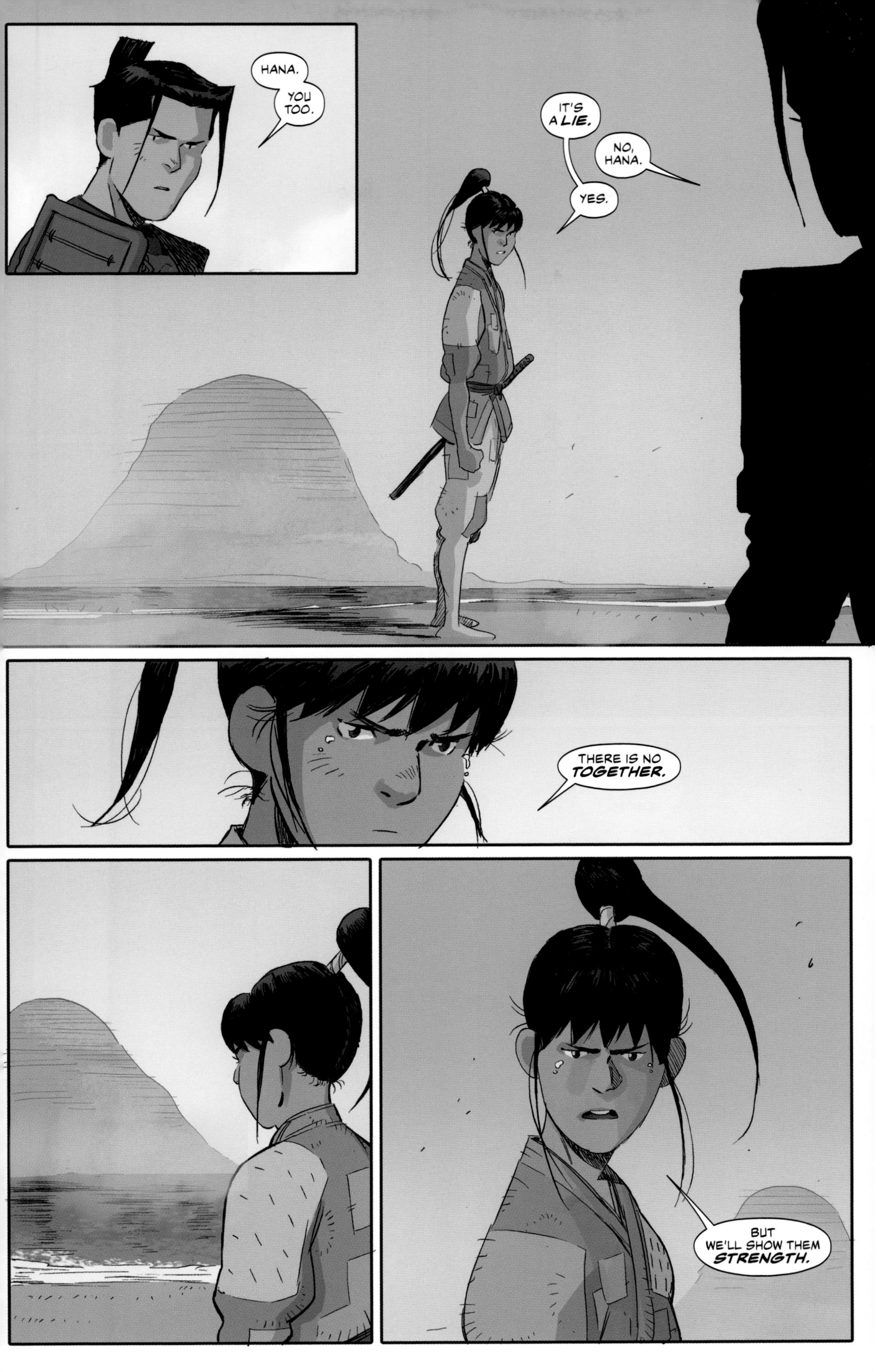
HANA.
YOU TOO.
IT'S A LIE.
NO, HANA.
YES.
THERE IS NO TOGETHER.
BUT WE'LL SHOW THEM STRENGTH.

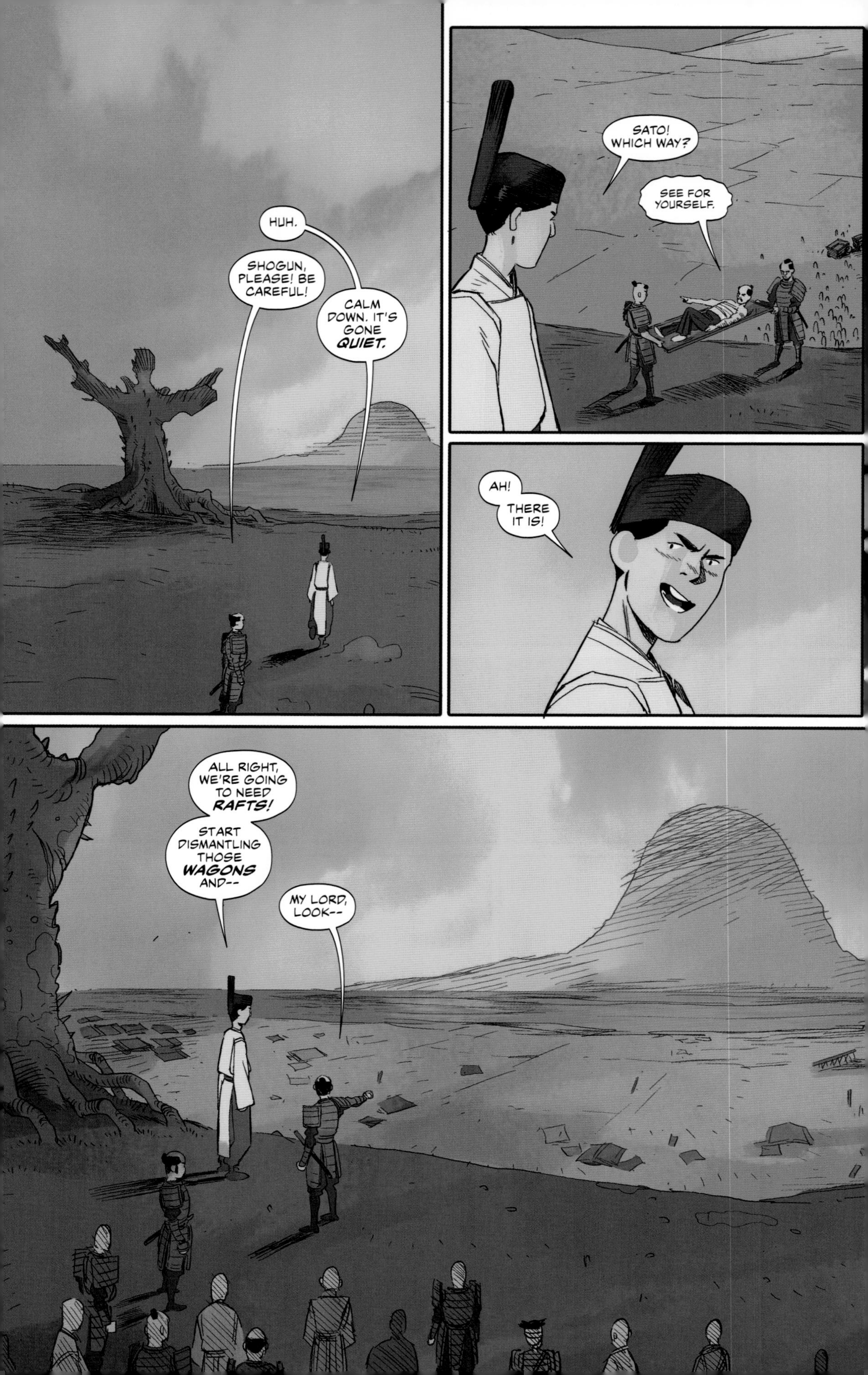
HUH.
SHOGUN, PLEASE! BE CAREFUL!
CALM DOWN. IT'S GONE QUIET.
SATO! WHICH WAY?
SEE FOR YOURSELF.
AH!
THERE IT IS!
ALL RIGHT, WE'RE GOING TO NEED RAFTS!
START DISMANTLING THOSE WAGONS AND--
MY LORD, LOOK--

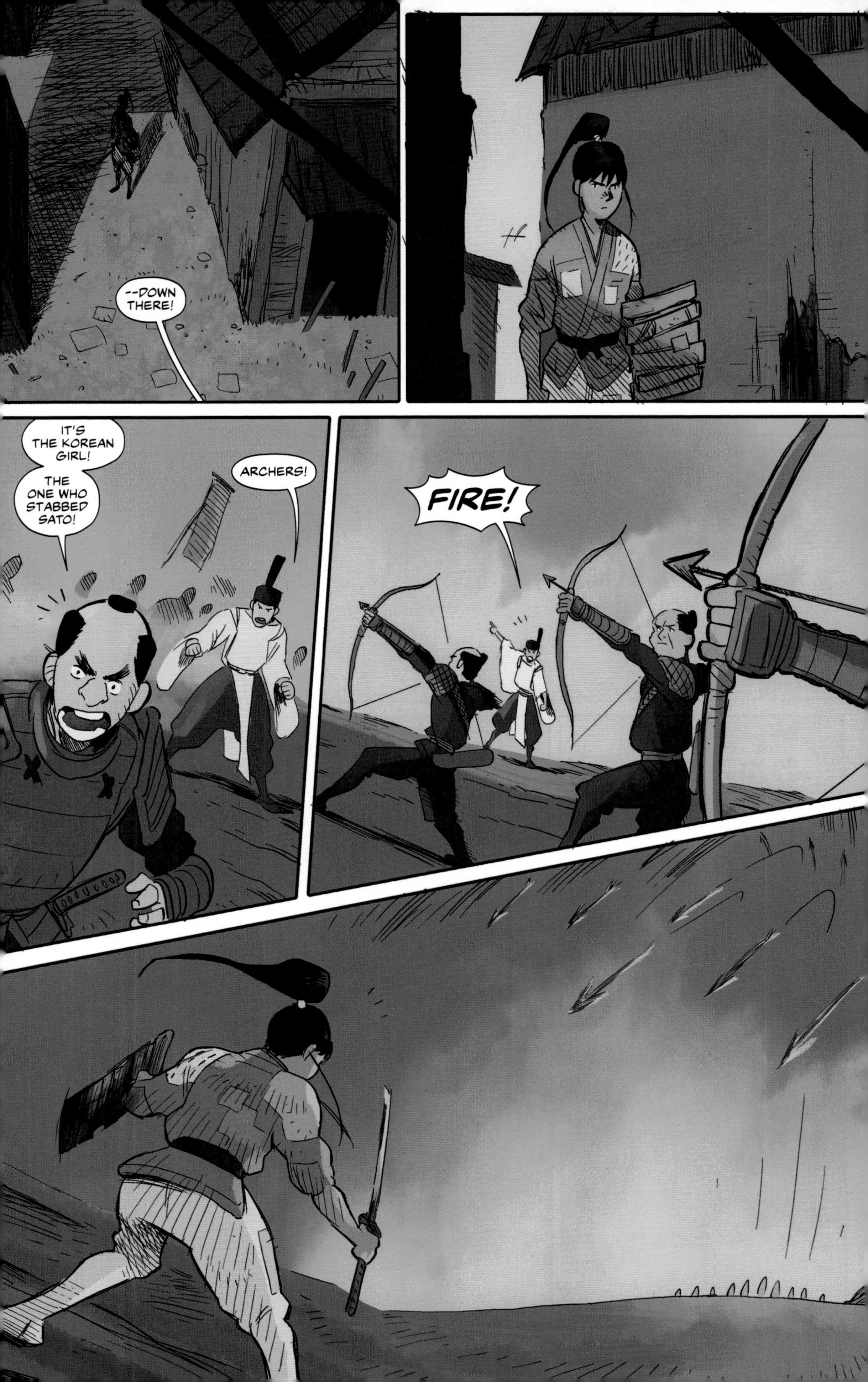
--DOWN THERE!
IT'S THE KOREAN GIRL!
THE ONE WHO STABBED SATO!
ARCHERS!
FIRE!

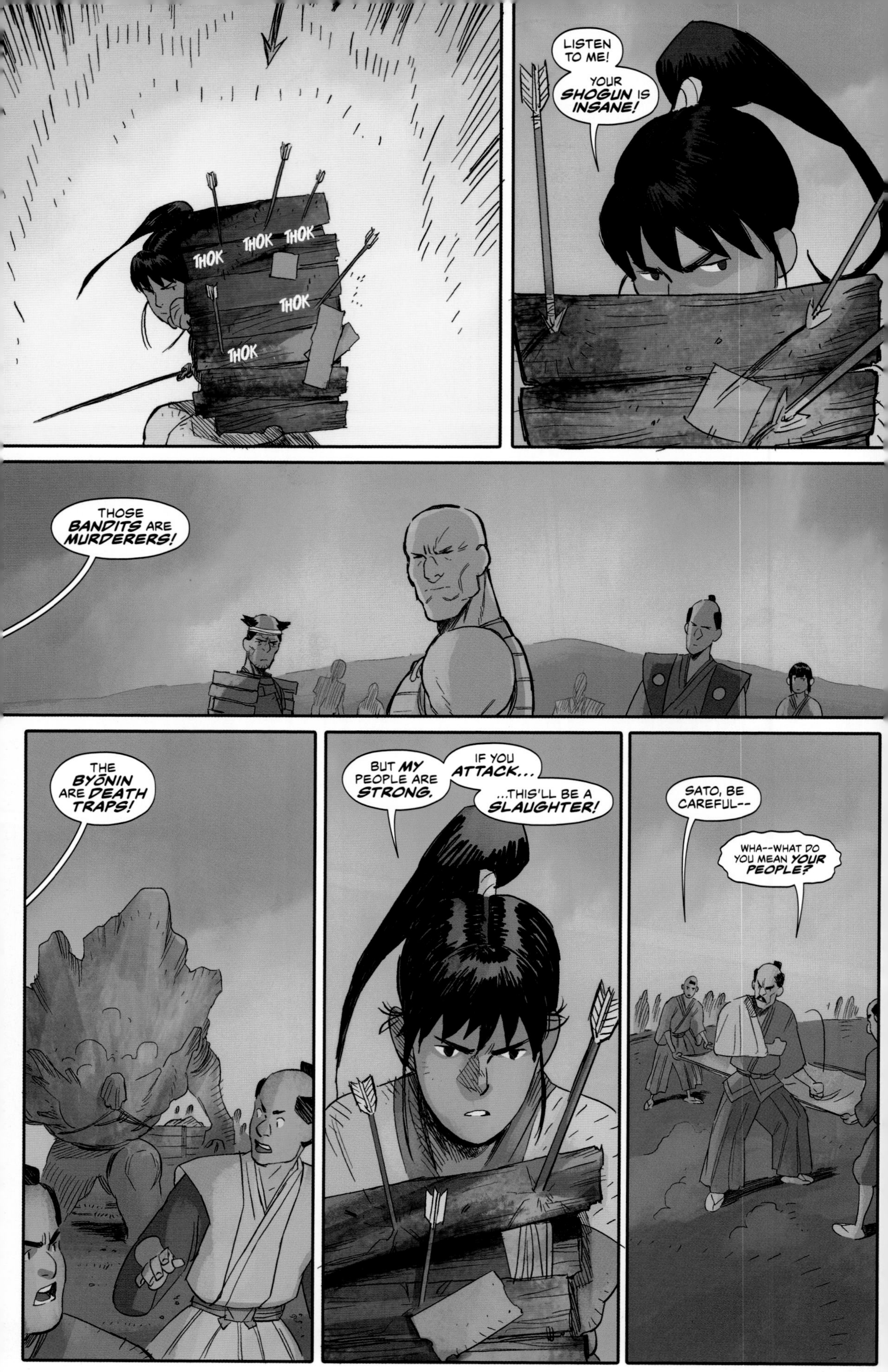
THOK
THOK
THOK
THOK
THOK
LISTEN TO ME!
YOUR SHOGUN IS INSANE!
THOSE BANDITS ARE MURDERERS!
THE BYŌNIN ARE DEATH TRAPS!
BUT MY PEOPLE ARE STRONG.
IF YOU ATTACK...
...THIS'LL BE A SLAUGHTER!
SATO, BE CAREFUL--
WHA--WHAT DO YOU MEAN YOUR PEOPLE?

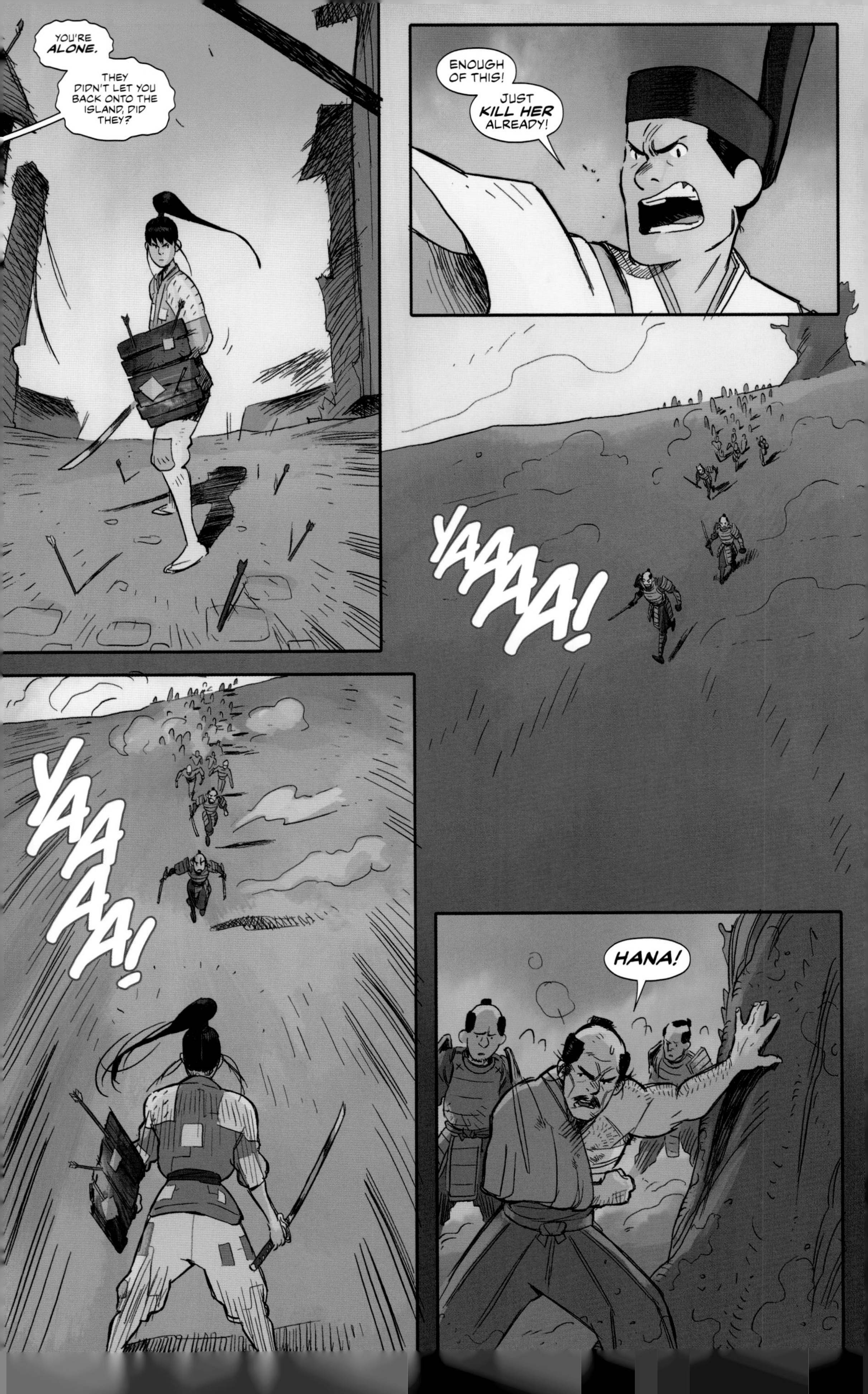
YOU'RE ALONE.
THEY DIDN'T LET YOU BACK ONTO THE ISLAND, DID THEY?
ENOUGH OF THIS!
JUST KILL HER ALREADY!
YAAAAA!
YAAAAA!
HANA!

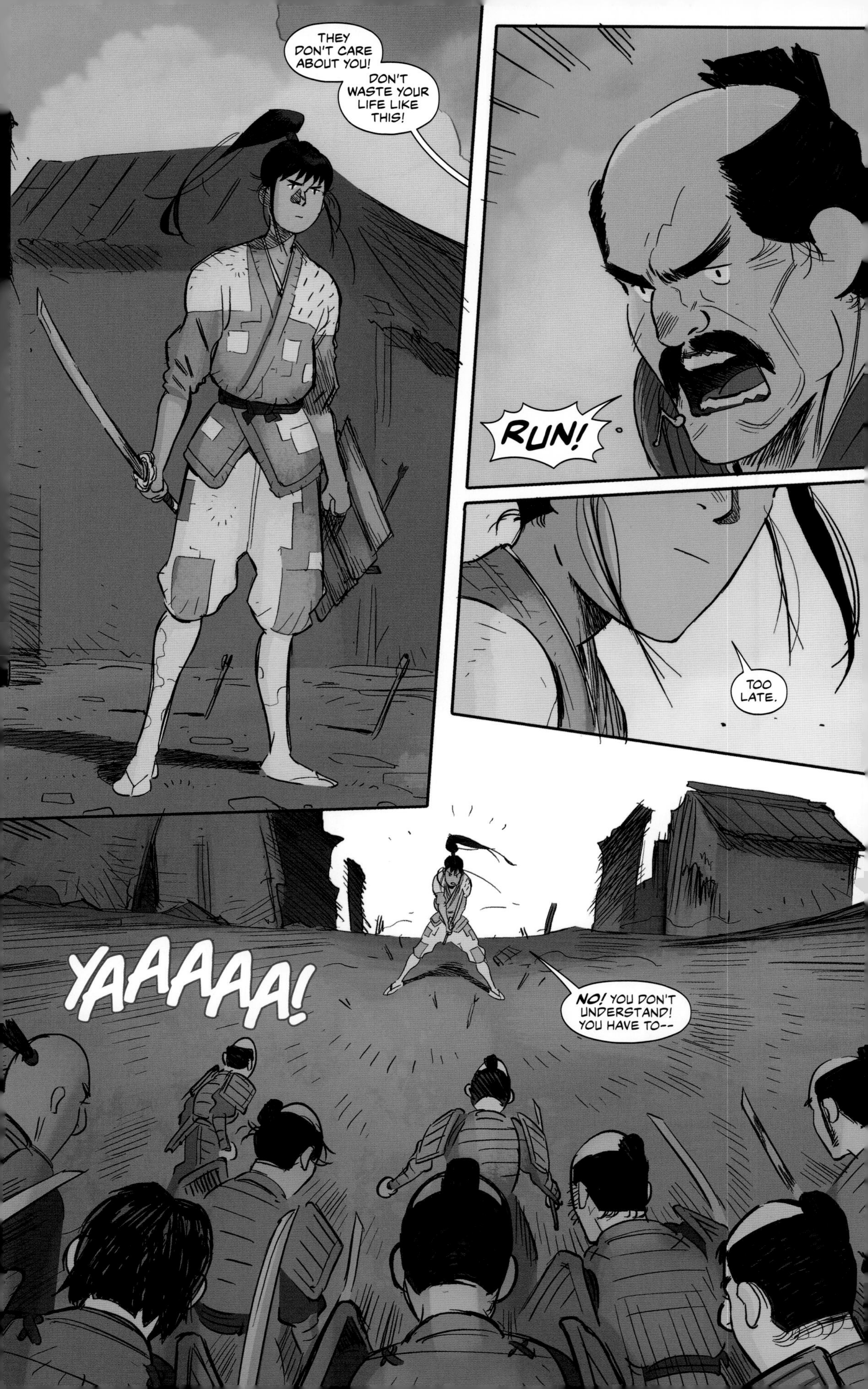
THEY DON'T CARE ABOUT YOU!
DON'T WASTE YOUR LIFE LIKE THIS!
RUN!
TOO LATE.
YAAAAA!
NO! YOU DON'T UNDERSTAND! YOU HAVE TO--

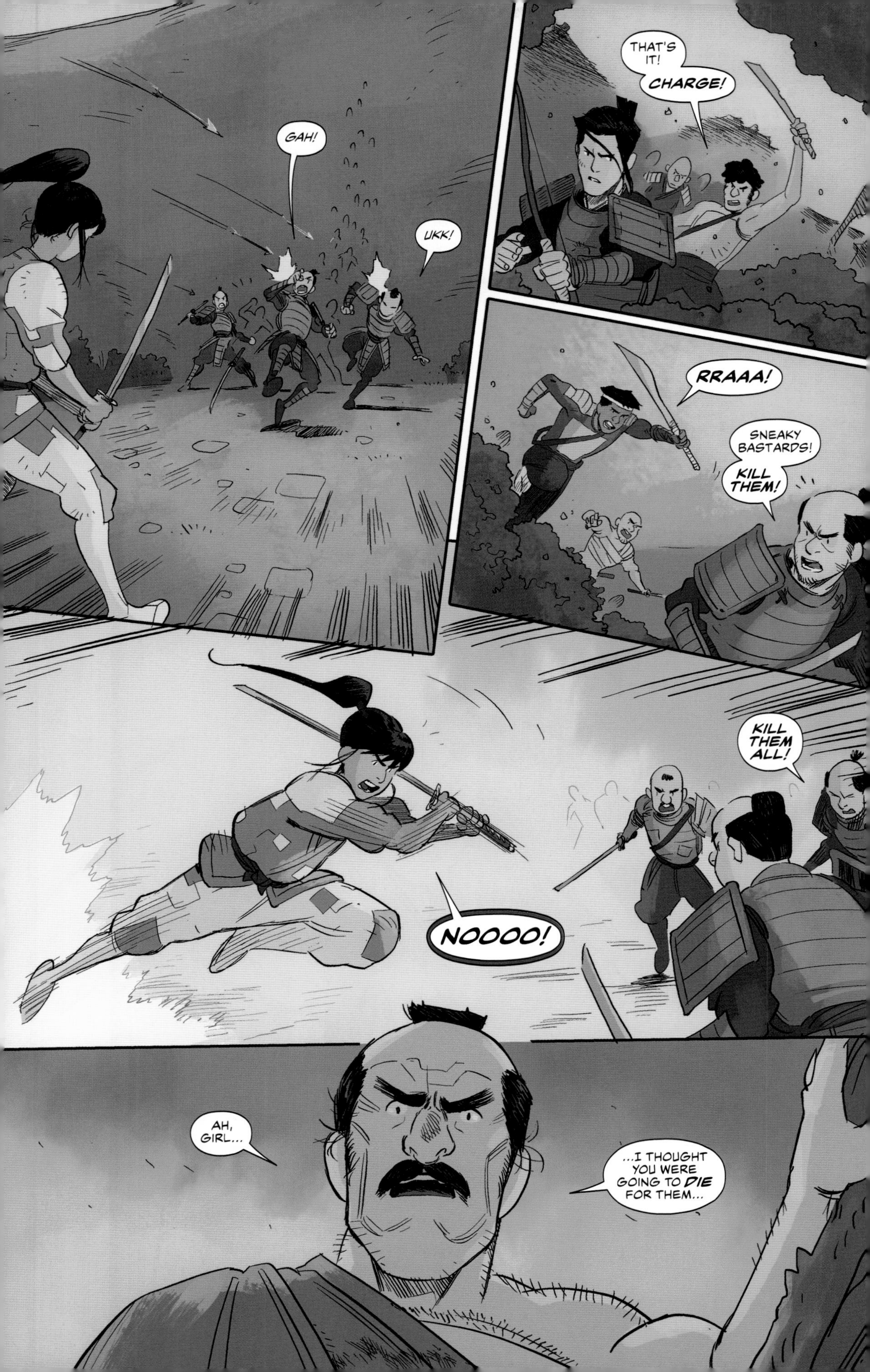
GAH!
UKK!
THAT'S IT!
CHARGE!
RRAAA!
SNEAKY BASTARDS!
KILL THEM!
KILL THEM ALL!
NOOOO!
AH, GIRL...
...I THOUGHT YOU WERE GOING TO DIE FOR THEM...

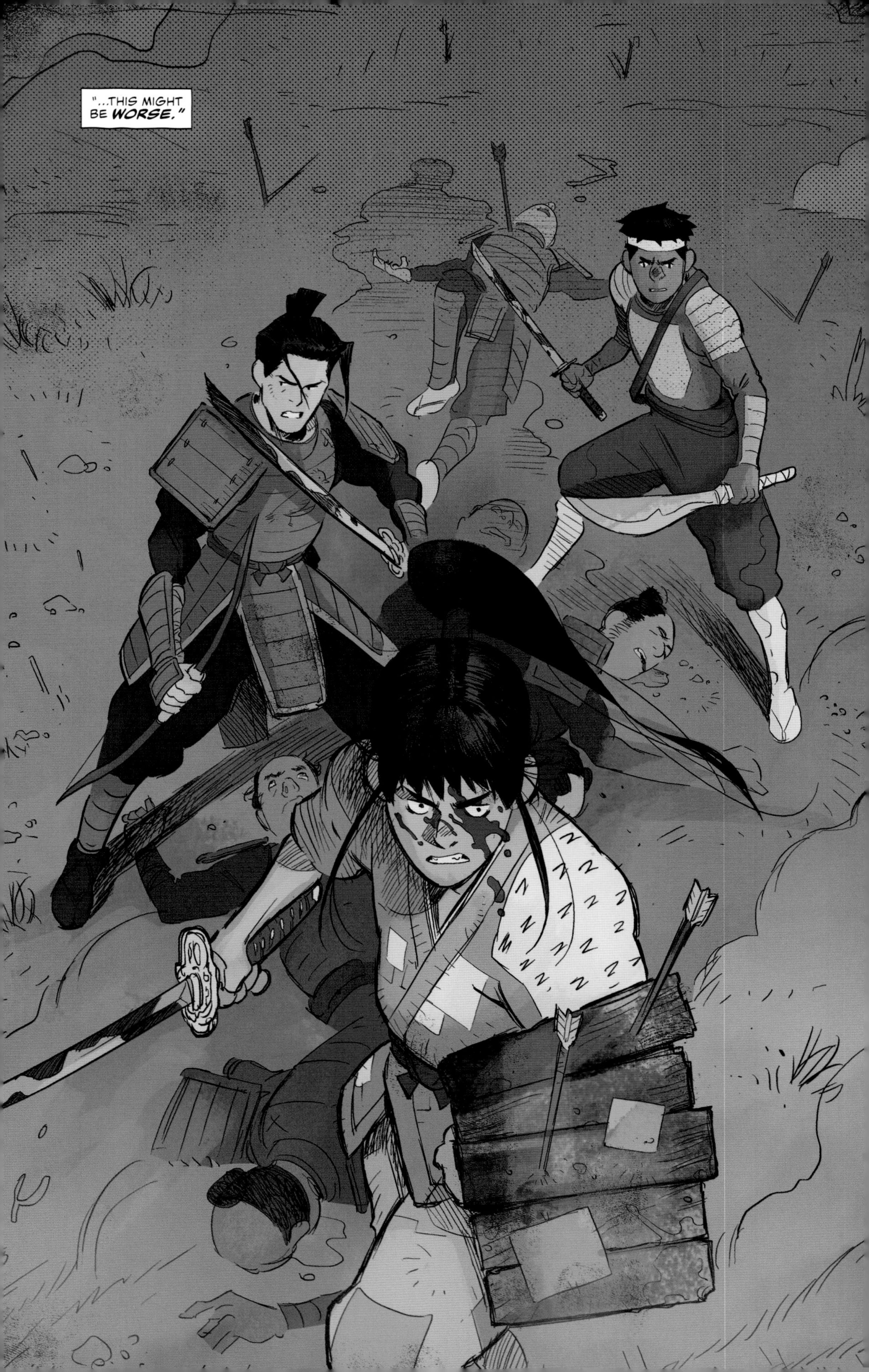
"...THIS MIGHT BE WORSE."

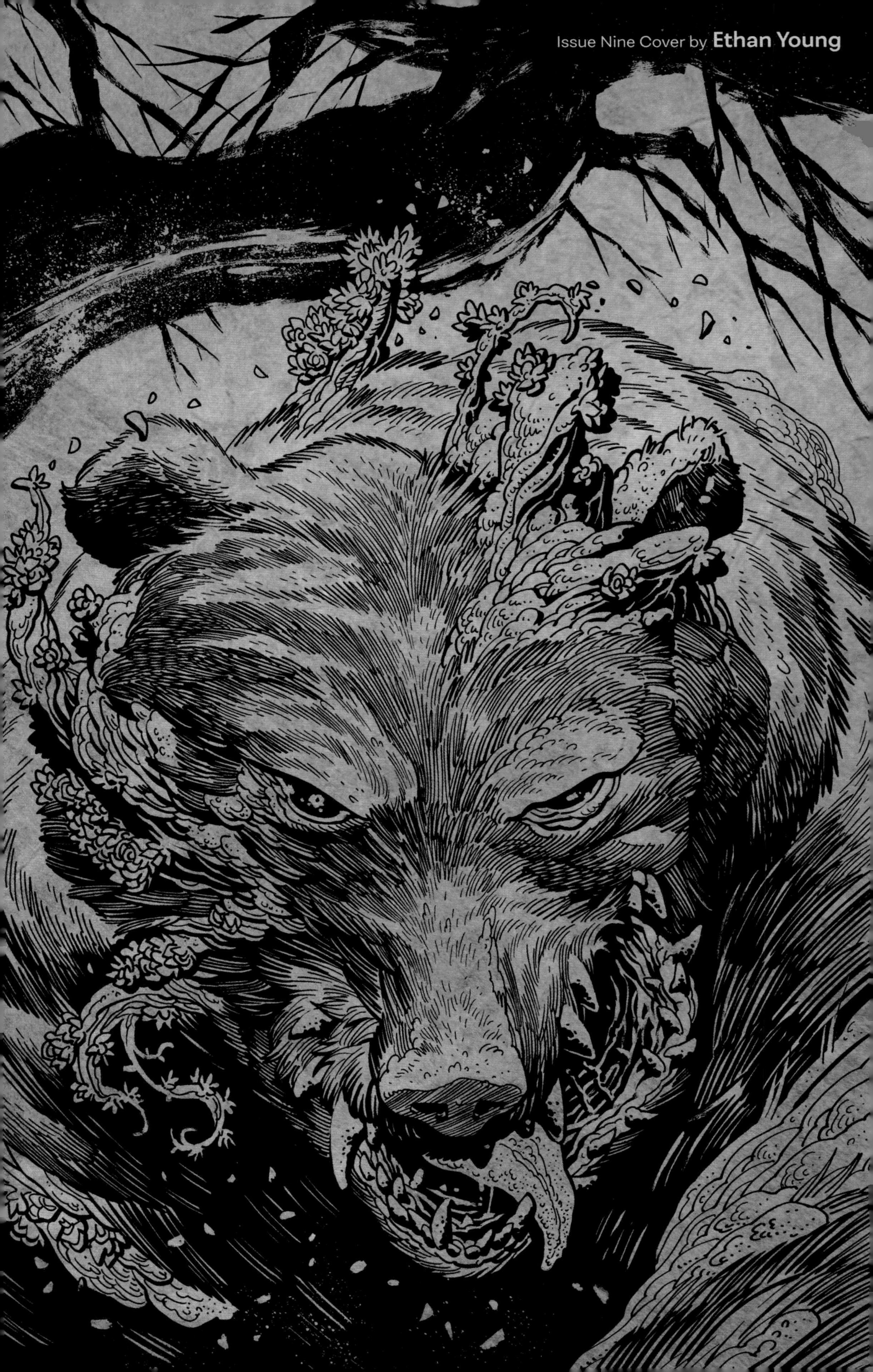

Issue Nine Cover by **Ethan Young**

CHAPTER TEN

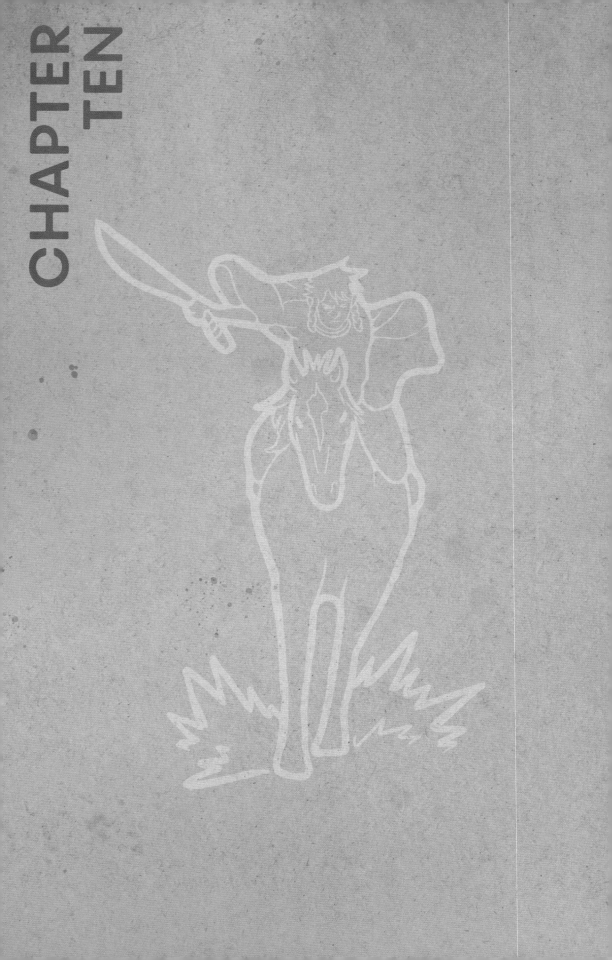

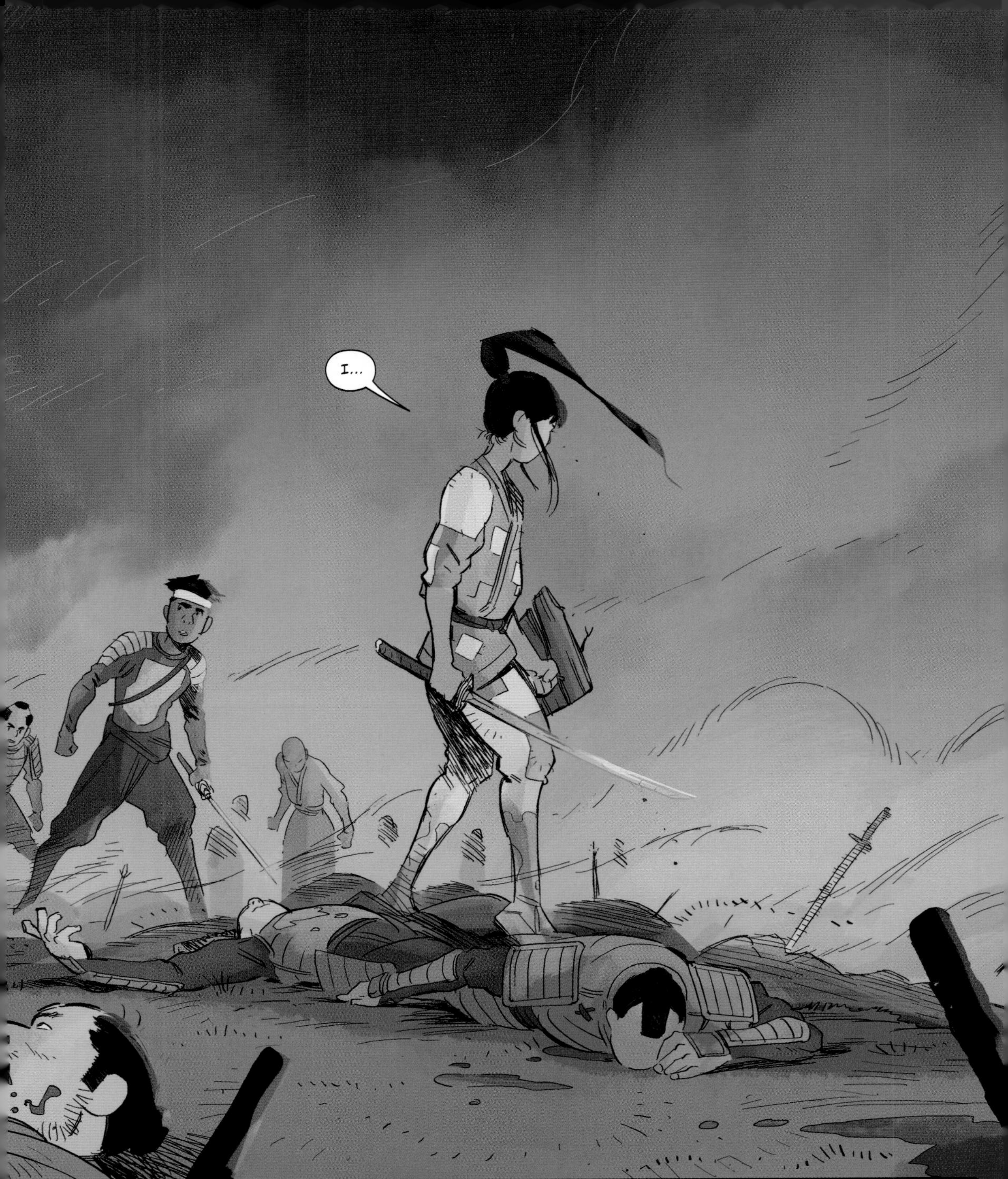
I...
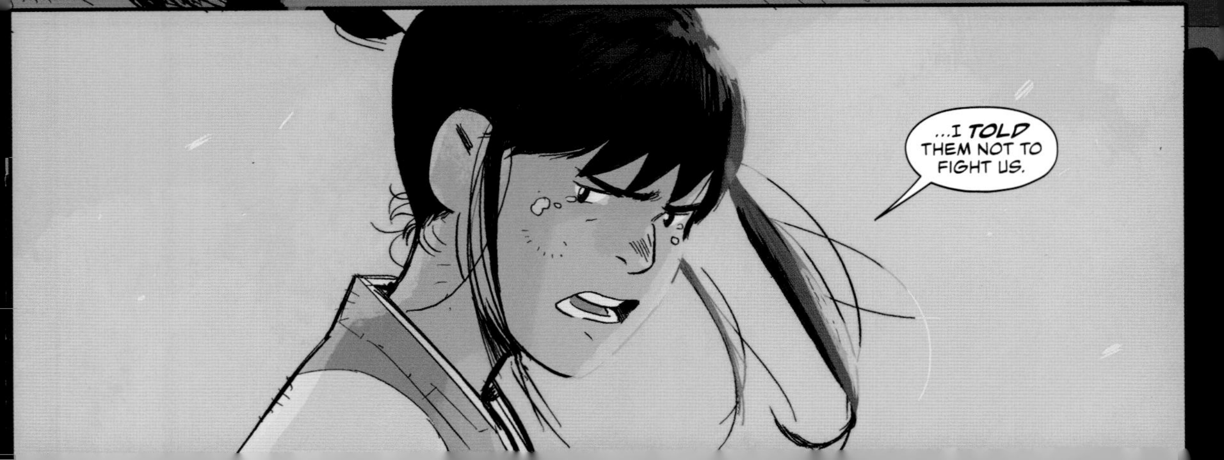
...I *TOLD* THEM NOT TO FIGHT US.

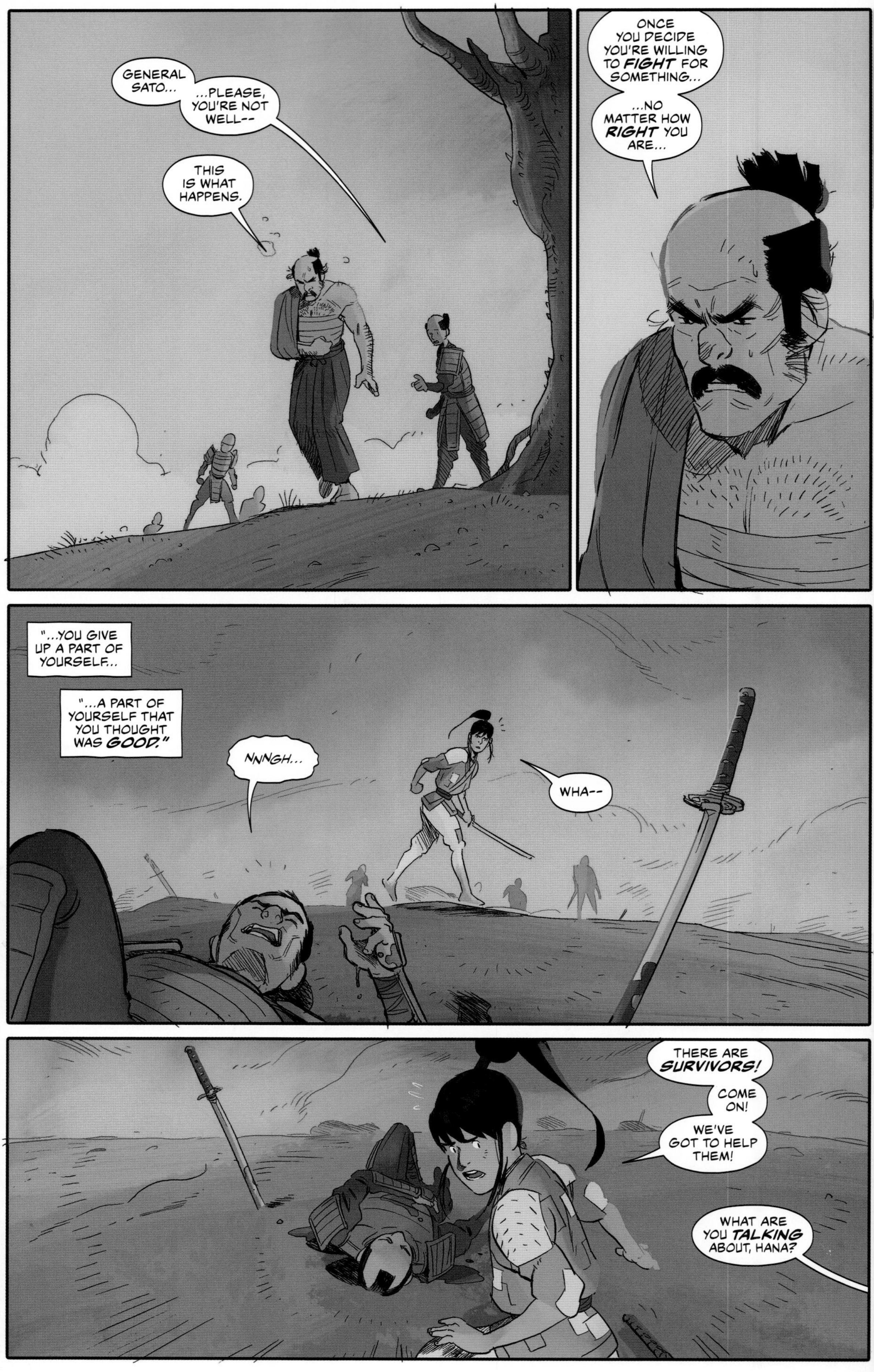
GENERAL SATO...
...PLEASE, YOU'RE NOT WELL--
THIS IS WHAT HAPPENS.
ONCE YOU DECIDE YOU'RE WILLING TO FIGHT FOR SOMETHING...
...NO MATTER HOW RIGHT YOU ARE...
"...YOU GIVE UP A PART OF YOURSELF...
"...A PART OF YOURSELF THAT YOU THOUGHT WAS GOOD."
NNNGH...
WHA--
THERE ARE SURVIVORS!
COME ON!
WE'VE GOT TO HELP THEM!
WHAT ARE YOU TALKING ABOUT, HANA?

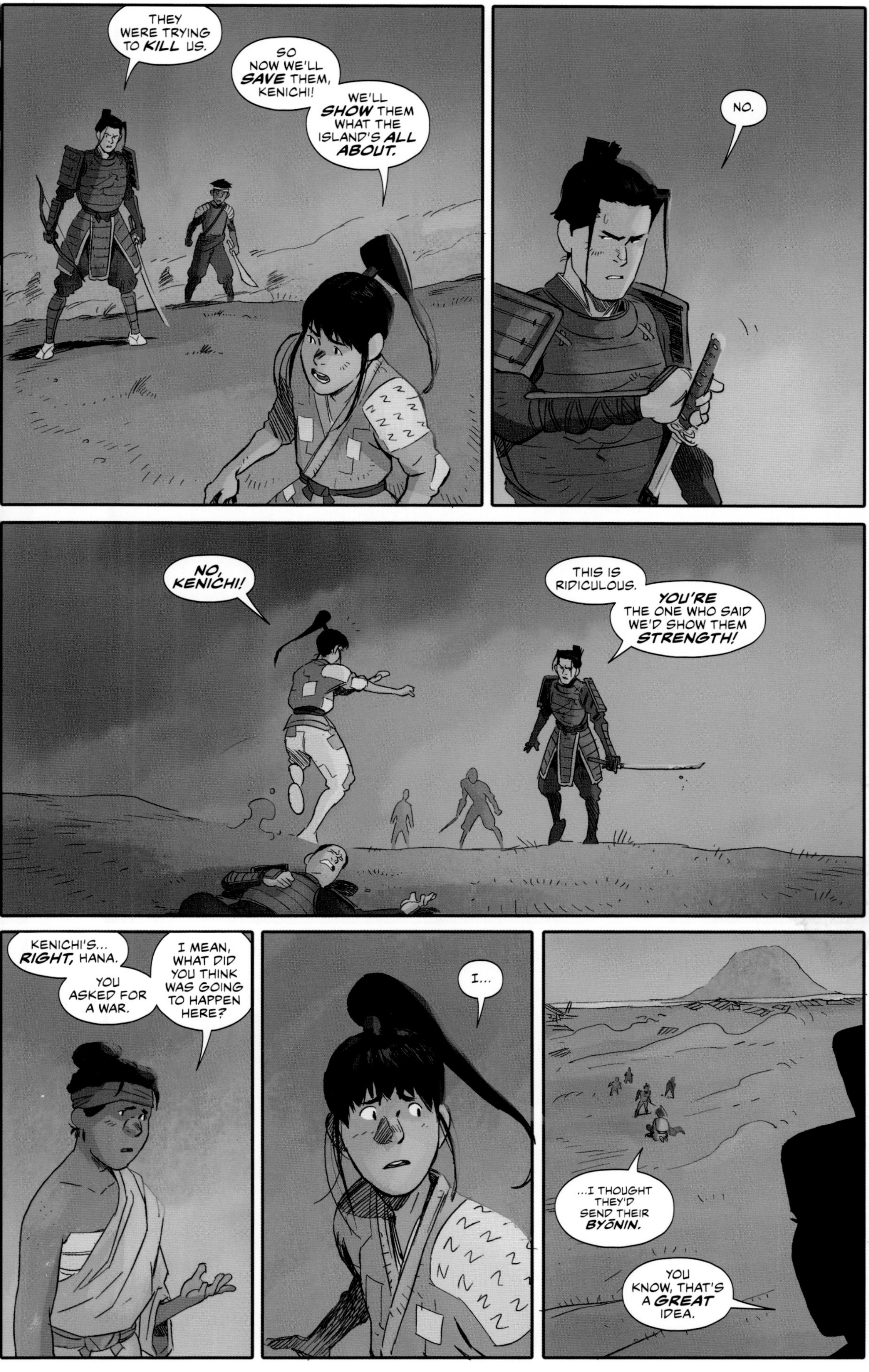
THEY WERE TRYING TO KILL US.
SO NOW WE'LL SAVE THEM, KENICHI!
WE'LL SHOW THEM WHAT THE ISLAND'S ALL ABOUT.
NO.
NO, KENICHI!
THIS IS RIDICULOUS.
YOU'RE THE ONE WHO SAID WE'D SHOW THEM STRENGTH!
KENICHI'S... RIGHT, HANA.
YOU ASKED FOR A WAR.
I MEAN, WHAT DID YOU THINK WAS GOING TO HAPPEN HERE?
I...
...I THOUGHT THEY'D SEND THEIR BYŌNIN.
YOU KNOW, THAT'S A GREAT IDEA.

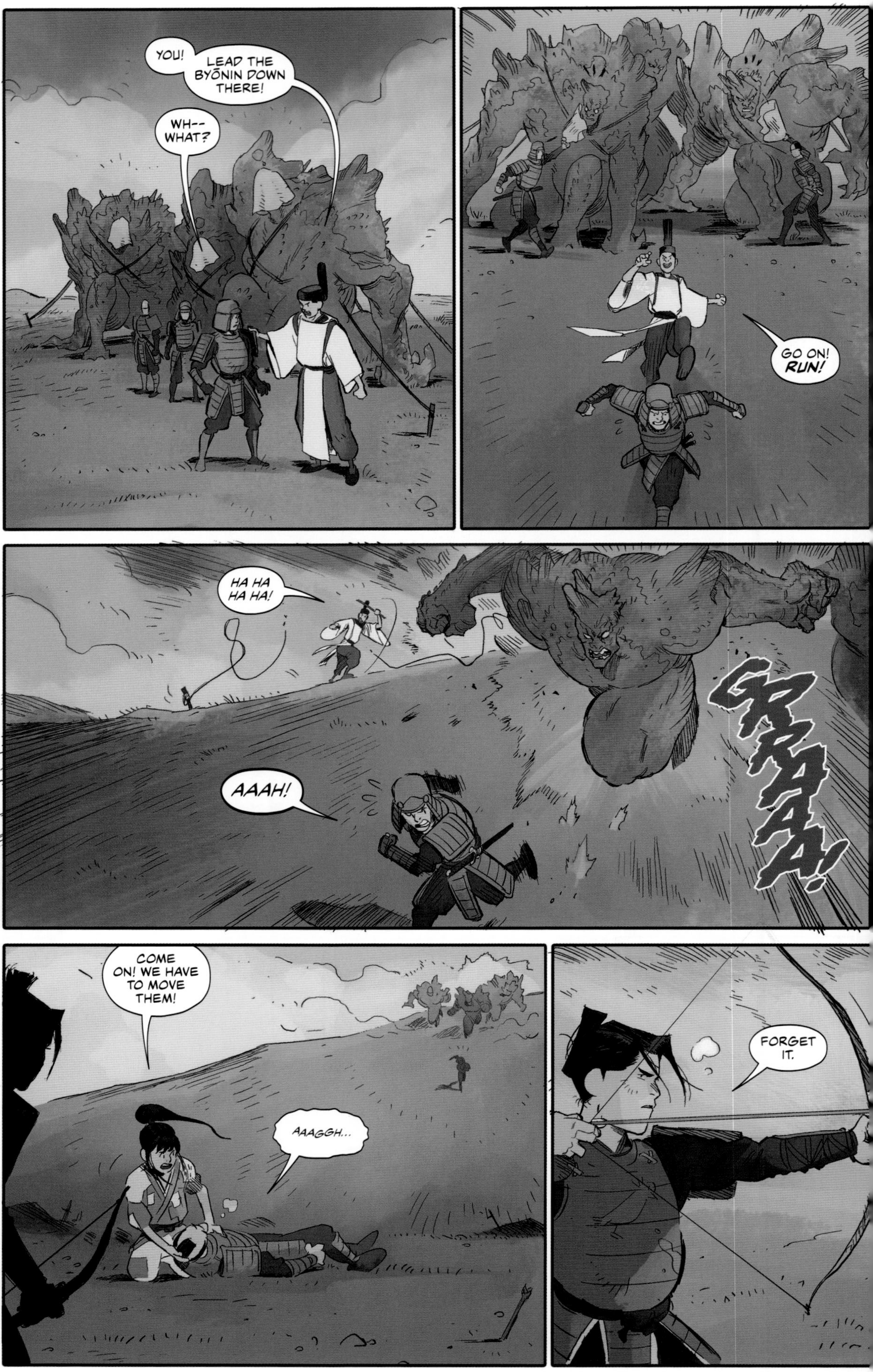
YOU!
LEAD THE BYŌNIN DOWN THERE!
WH-- WHAT?
GO ON! RUN!
HA HA HA HA!
AAAH!
GRAAA!
COME ON! WE HAVE TO MOVE THEM!
AAAGGH...
FORGET IT.

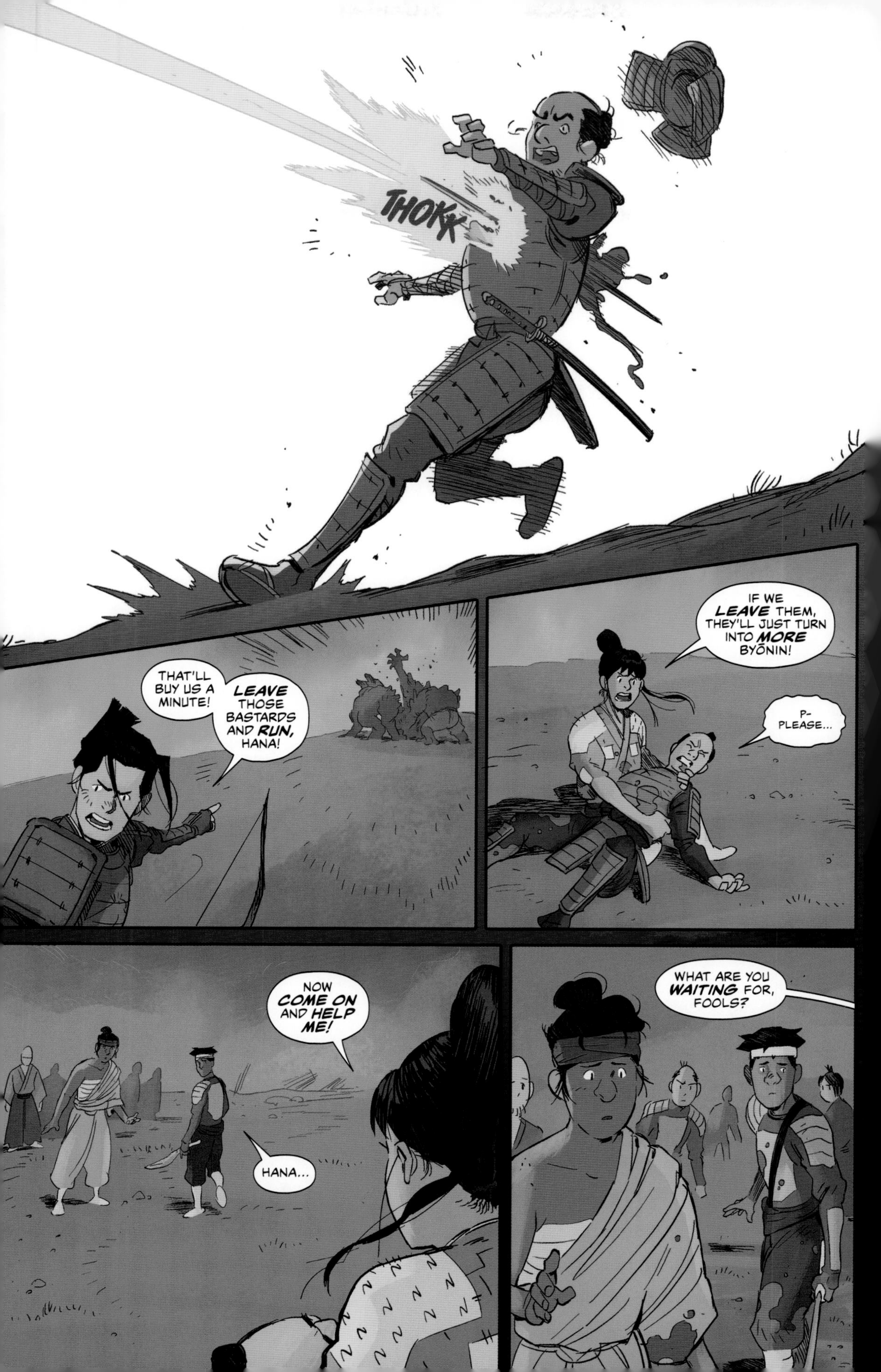
THOKK
THAT'LL BUY US A MINUTE!
LEAVE THOSE BASTARDS AND RUN, HANA!
IF WE LEAVE THEM, THEY'LL JUST TURN INTO MORE BYŌNIN!
P- PLEASE...
NOW COME ON AND HELP ME!
HANA...
WHAT ARE YOU WAITING FOR, FOOLS?

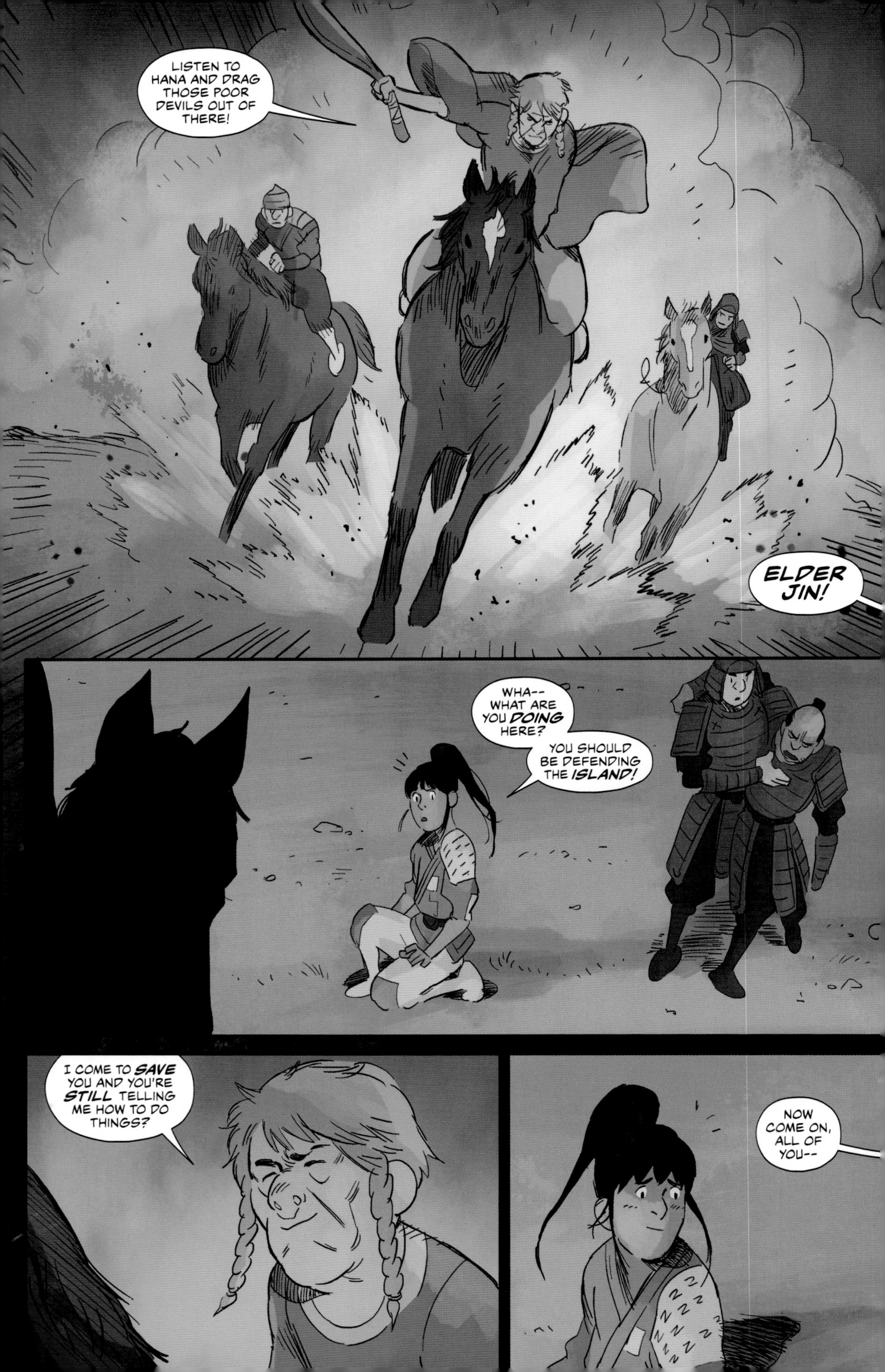
LISTEN TO HANA AND DRAG THOSE POOR DEVILS OUT OF THERE!
ELDER JIN!
WHA-- WHAT ARE YOU DOING HERE?
YOU SHOULD BE DEFENDING THE ISLAND!
I COME TO SAVE YOU AND YOU'RE STILL TELLING ME HOW TO DO THINGS?
NOW COME ON, ALL OF YOU--

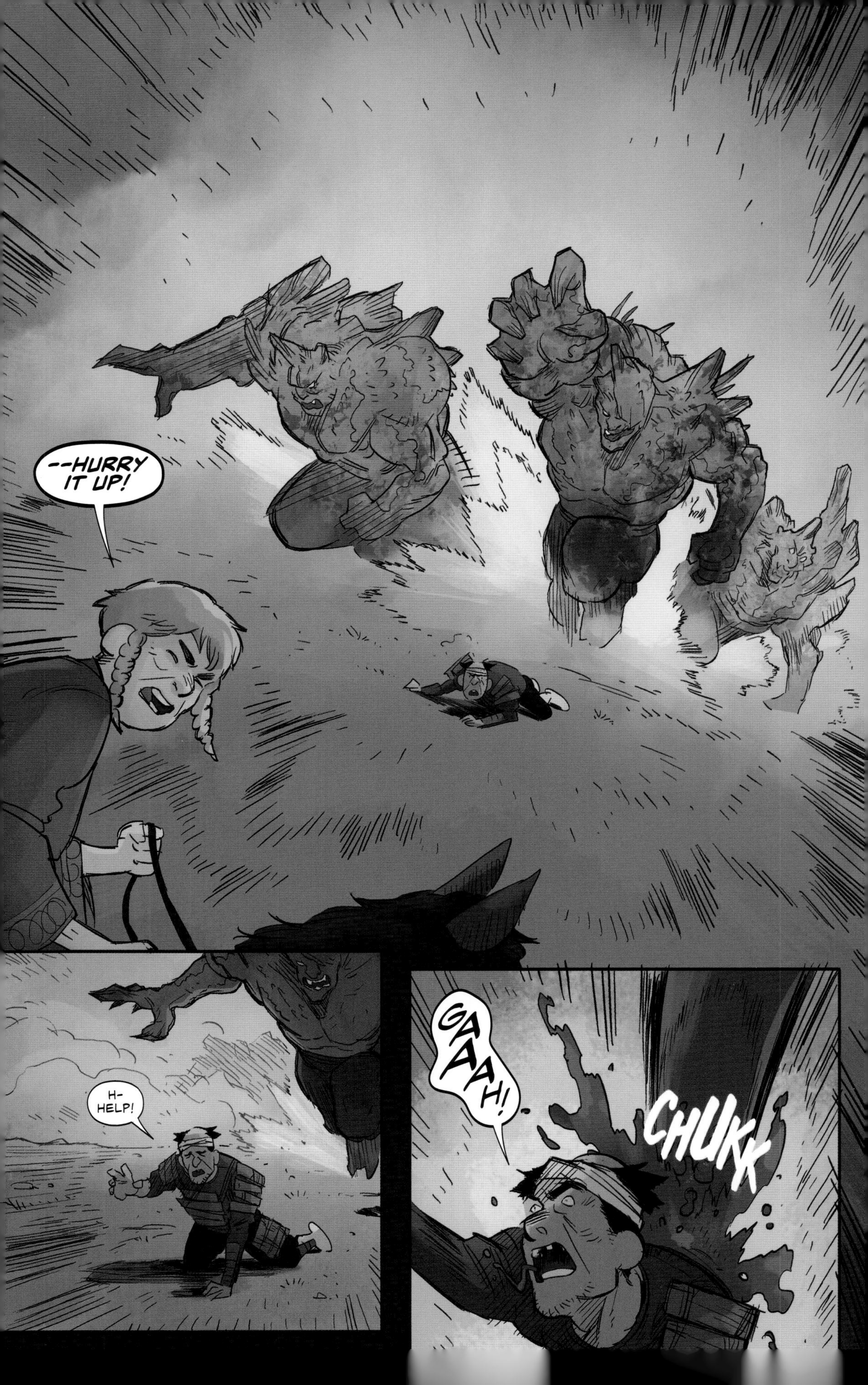
--HURRY IT UP!
H-HELP!
GAAAH!
CHUKK

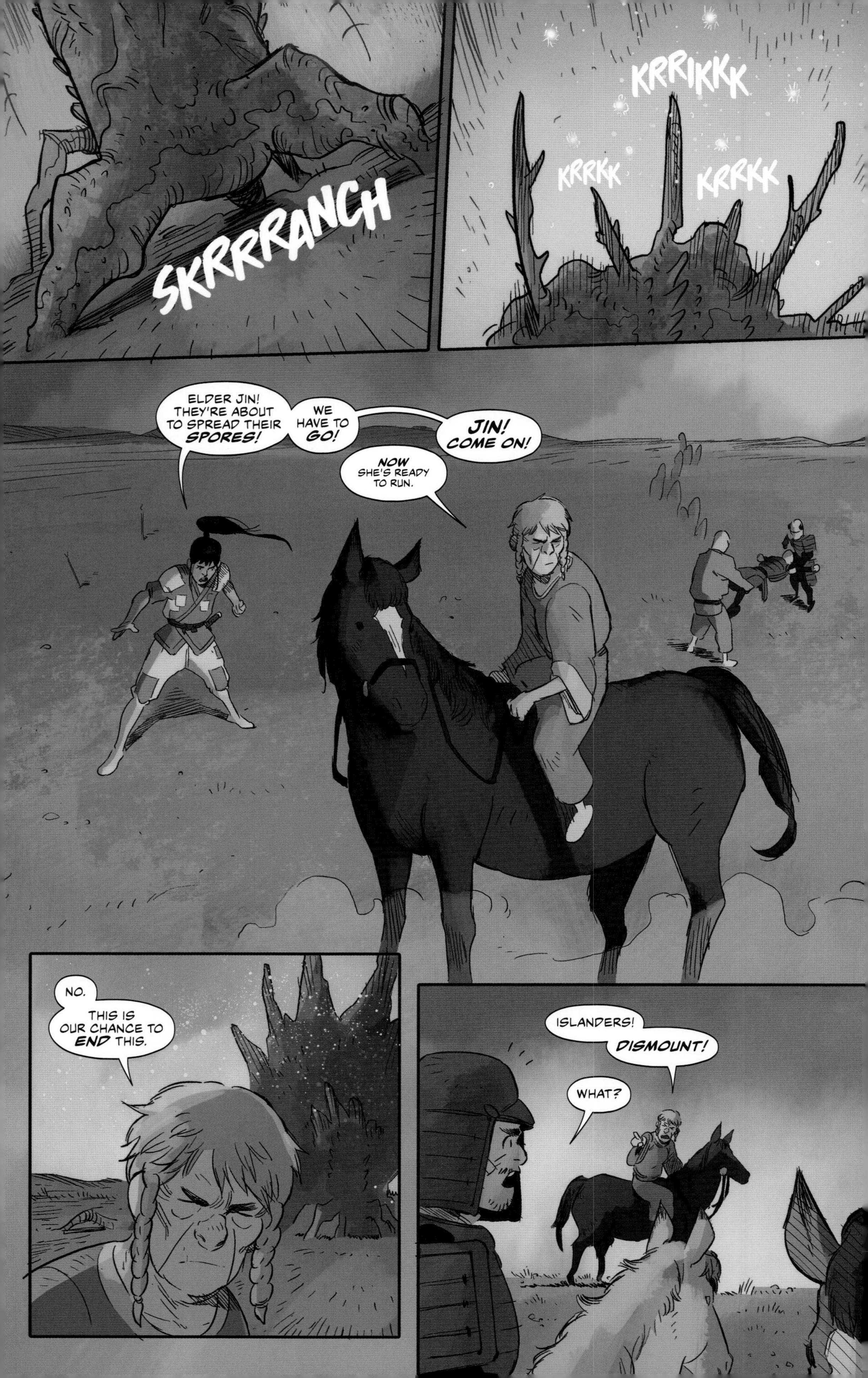
SKRRRANCH
KRRIKKK
KRRKK
KRRKK
ELDER JIN! THEY'RE ABOUT TO SPREAD THEIR SPORES!
WE HAVE TO GO!
JIN! COME ON!
NOW SHE'S READY TO RUN.
NO.
THIS IS OUR CHANCE TO END THIS.
ISLANDERS!
DISMOUNT!
WHAT?

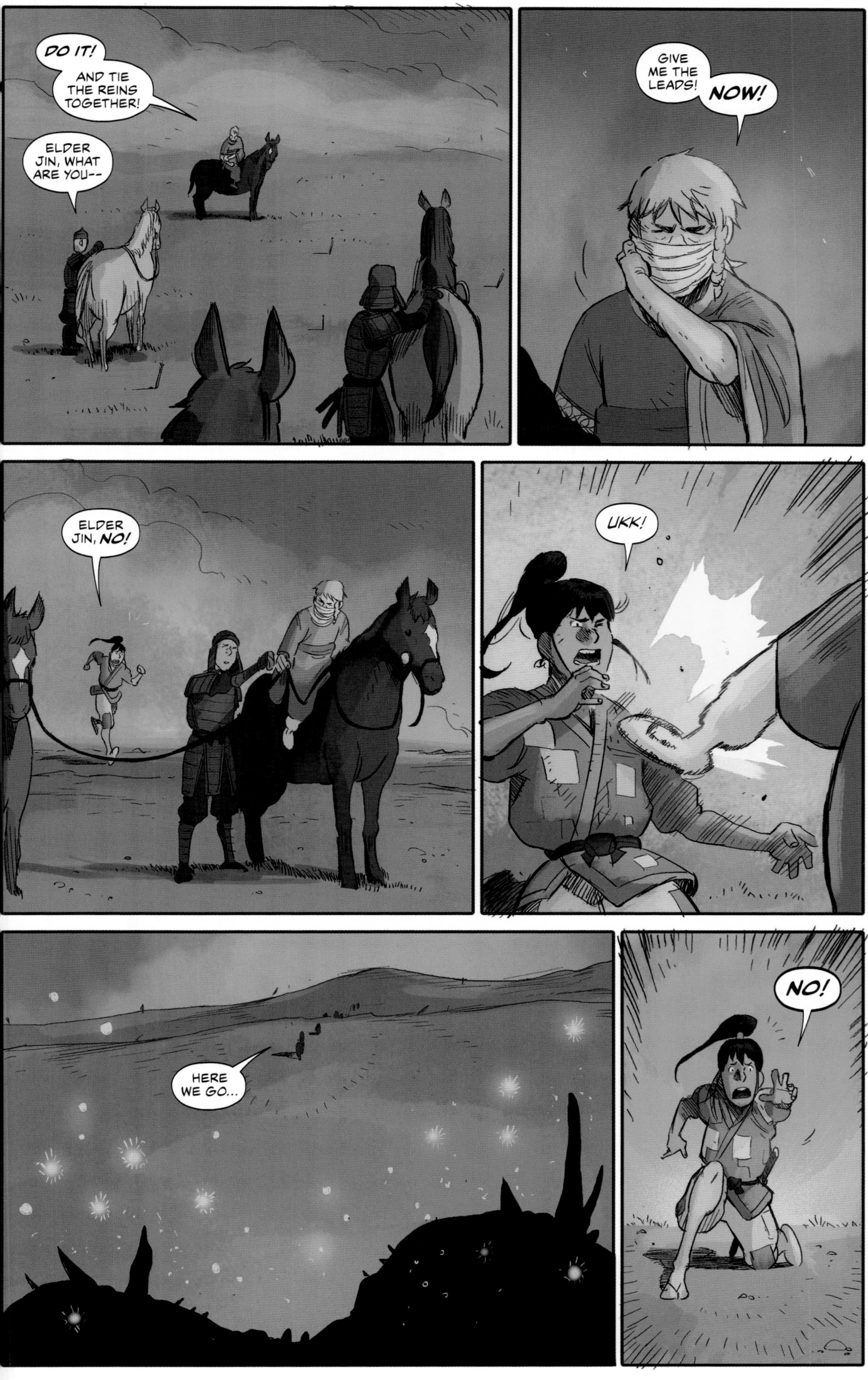
DO IT!
AND TIE THE REINS TOGETHER!
ELDER JIN, WHAT ARE YOU--
GIVE ME THE LEADS!
NOW!
ELDER JIN, NO!
UKK!
HERE WE GO...
NO!

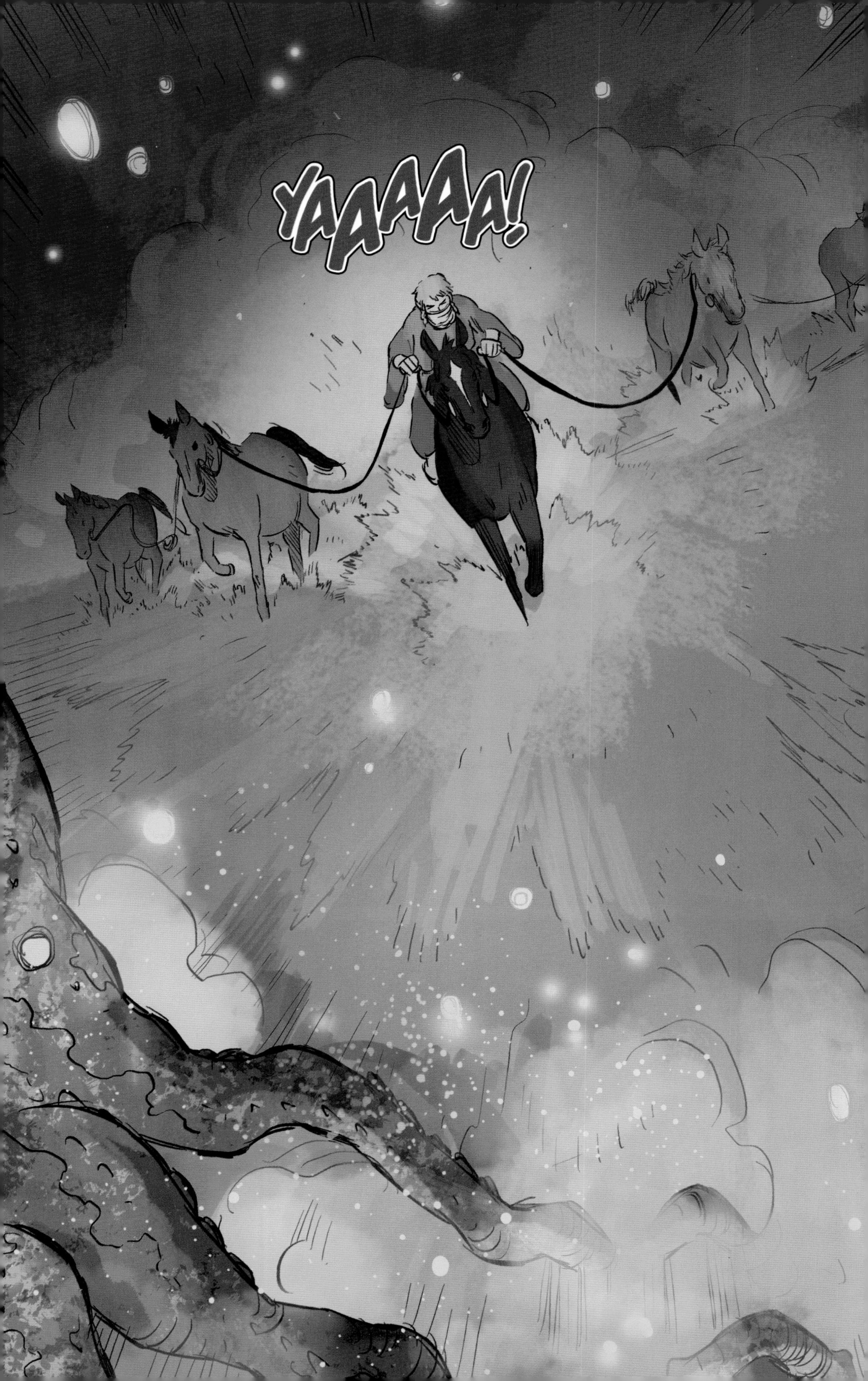
YAAAAA!

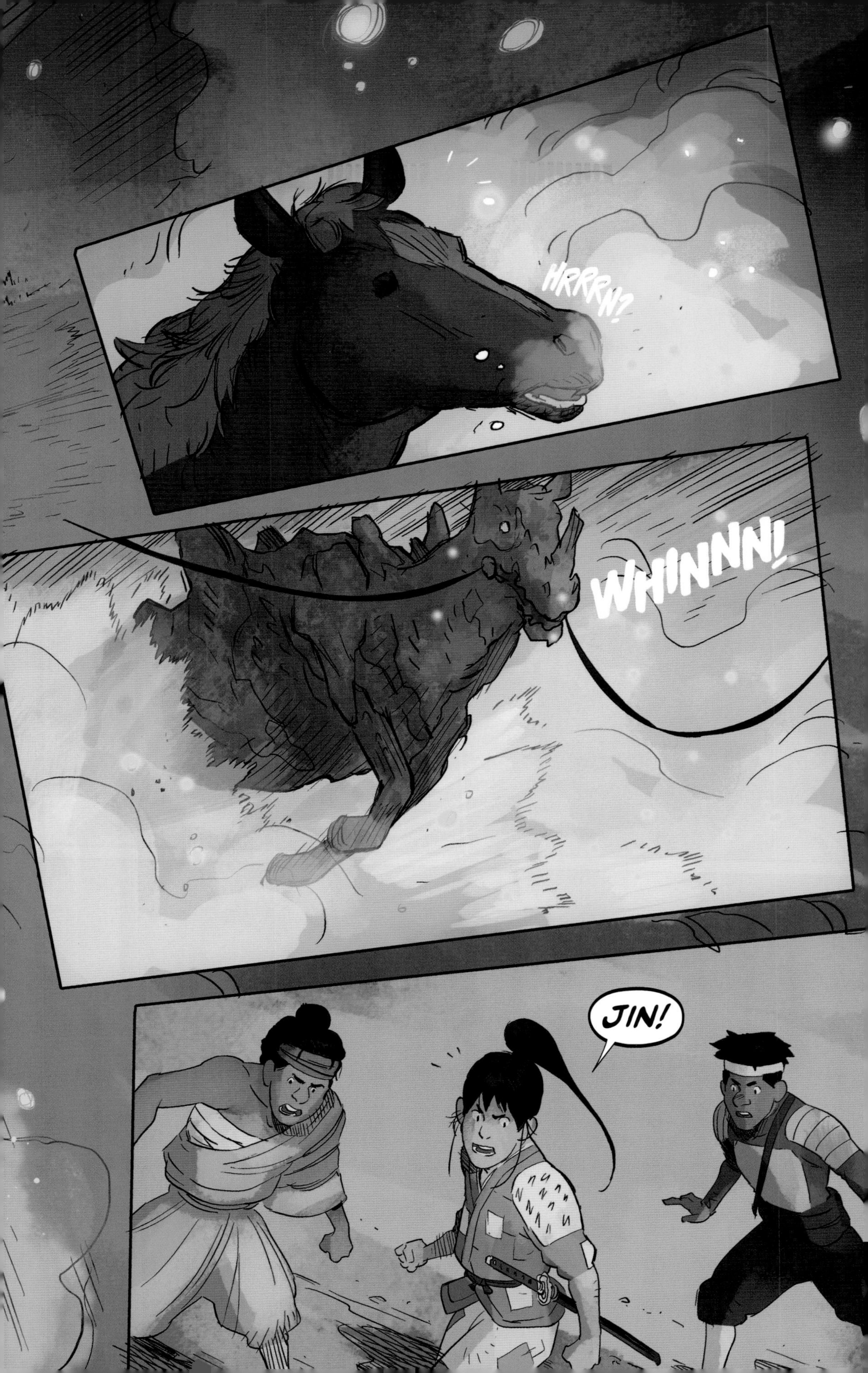
HRRRN?
WHINNN!
JIN!

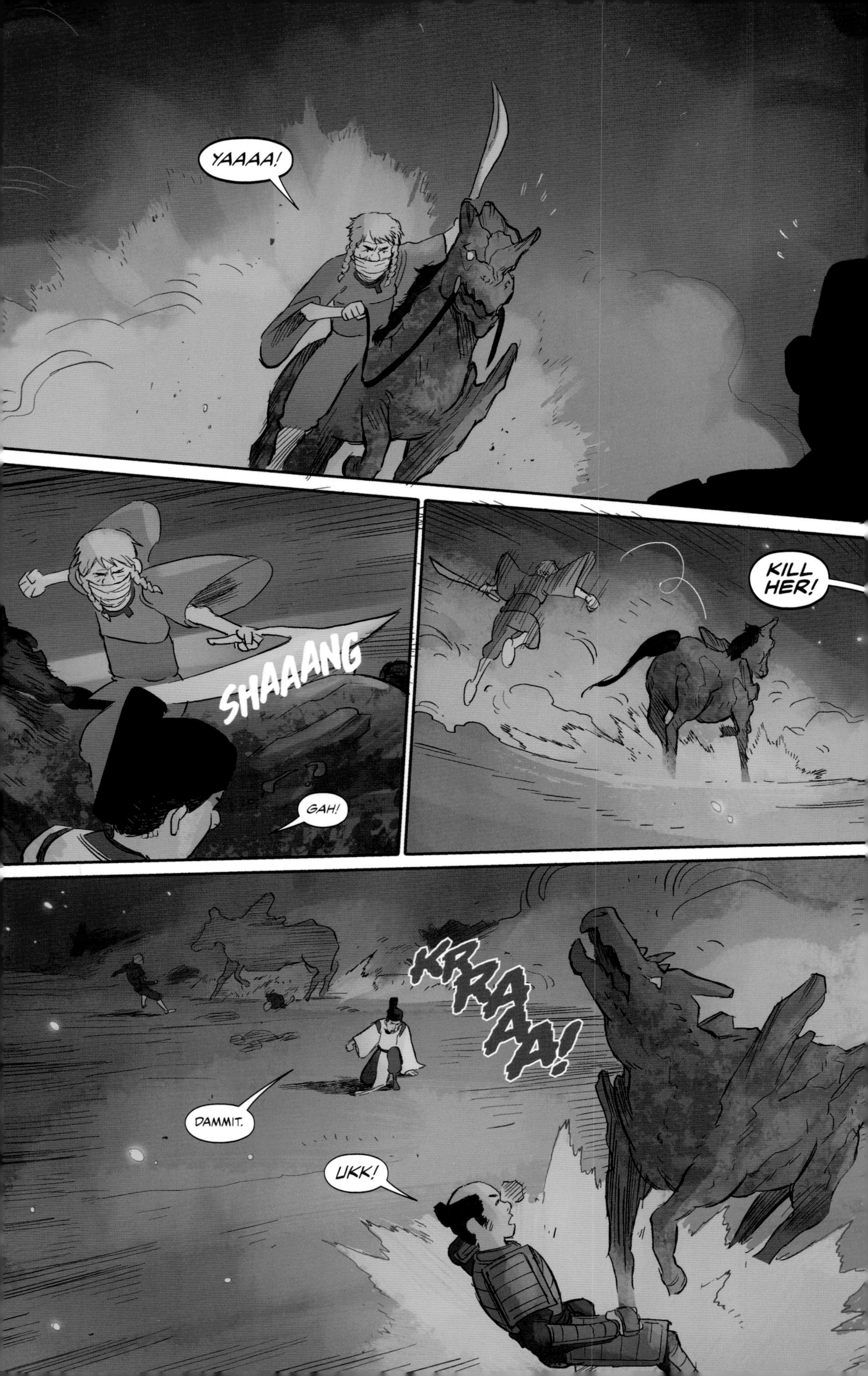
YAAAA!
SHAAANG
GAH!
KILL HER!
KRRAAA!
DAMMIT.
UKK!

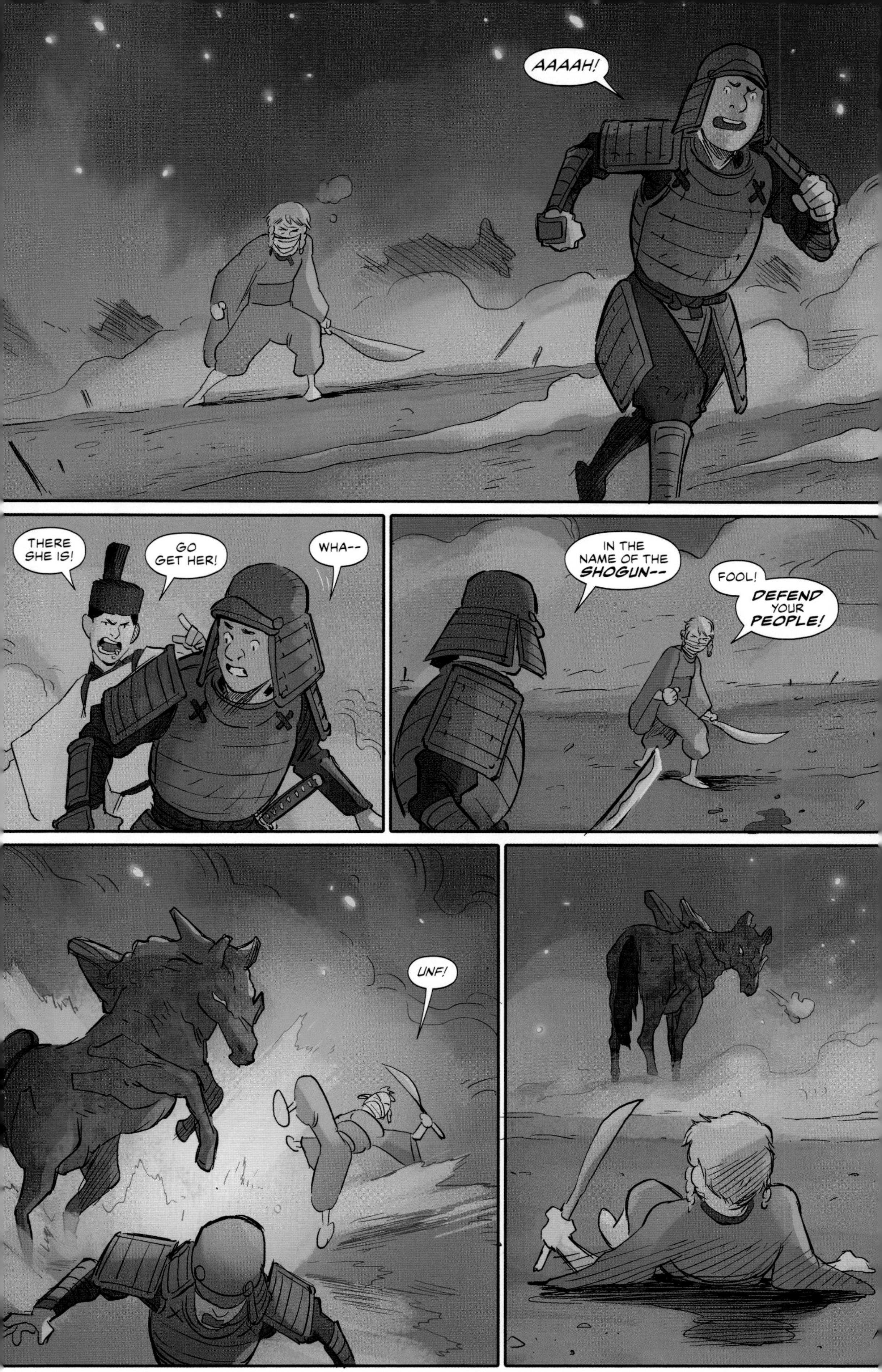
AAAAH!
THERE SHE IS!
GO GET HER!
WHA--
IN THE NAME OF THE SHOGUN--
FOOL! DEFEND YOUR PEOPLE!
UNF!

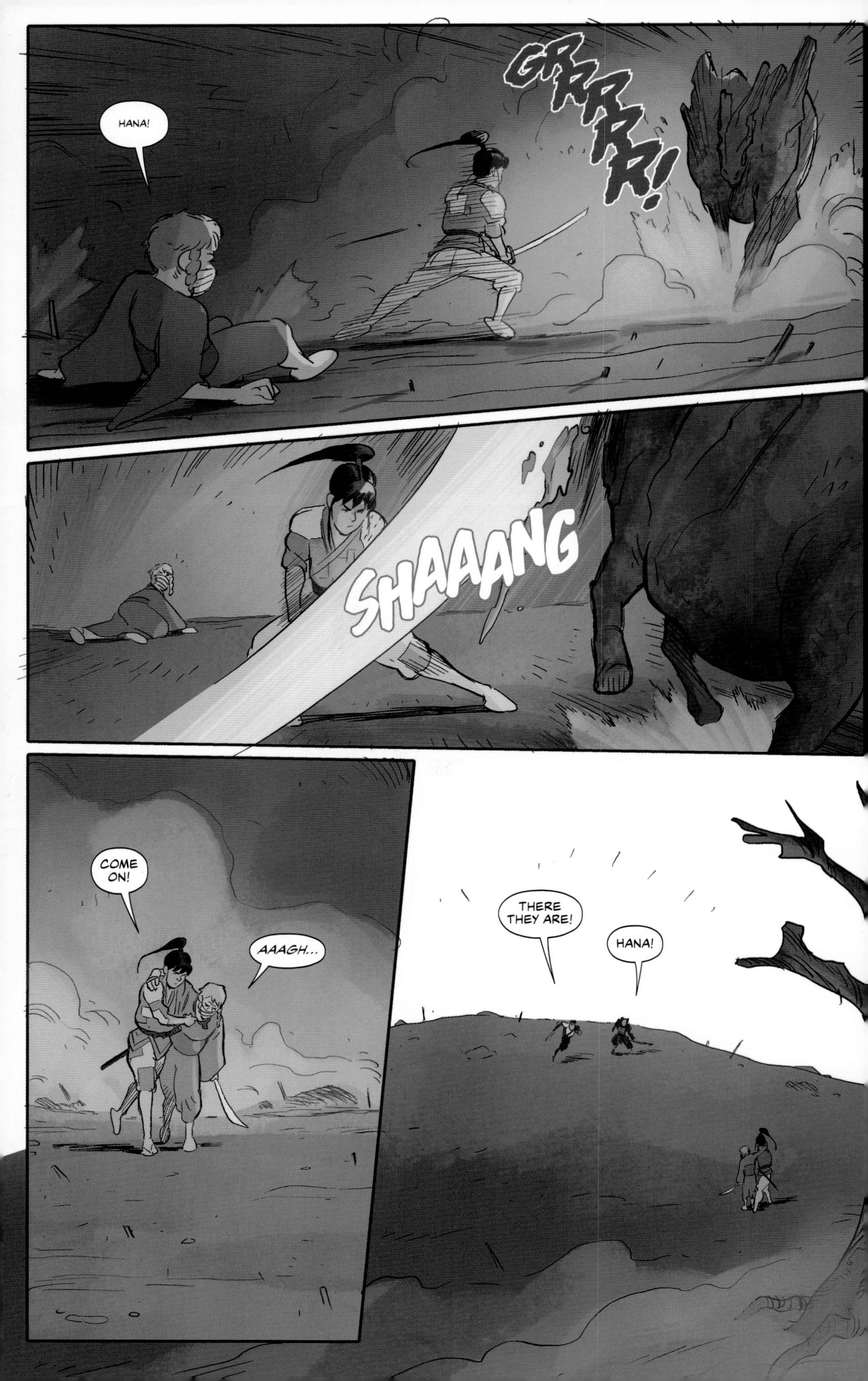
HANA!
GRRRR!
SHAAANG
COME ON!
AAAGH...
THERE THEY ARE!
HANA!

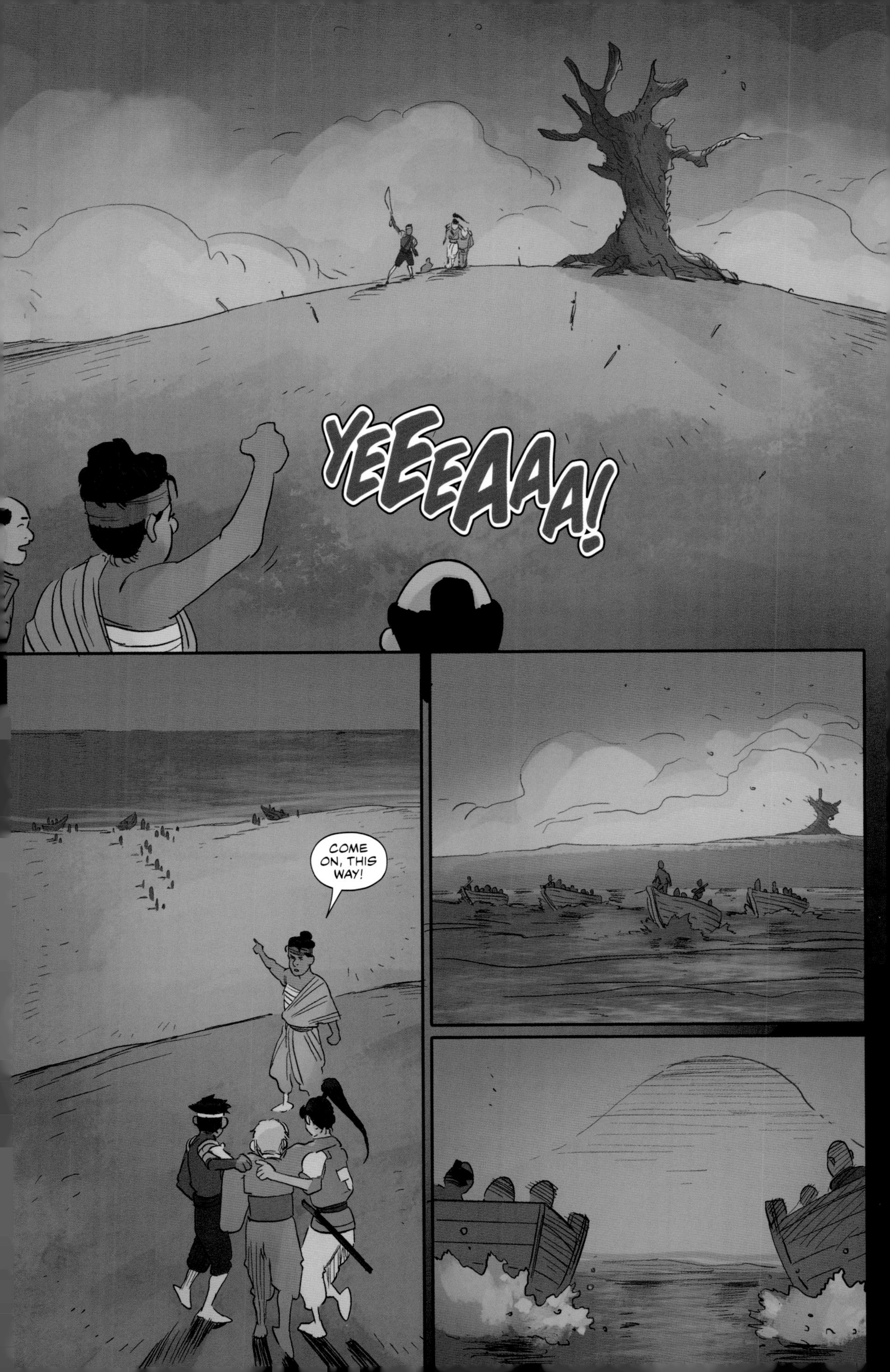
YEEEAAAA!
COME ON, THIS WAY!

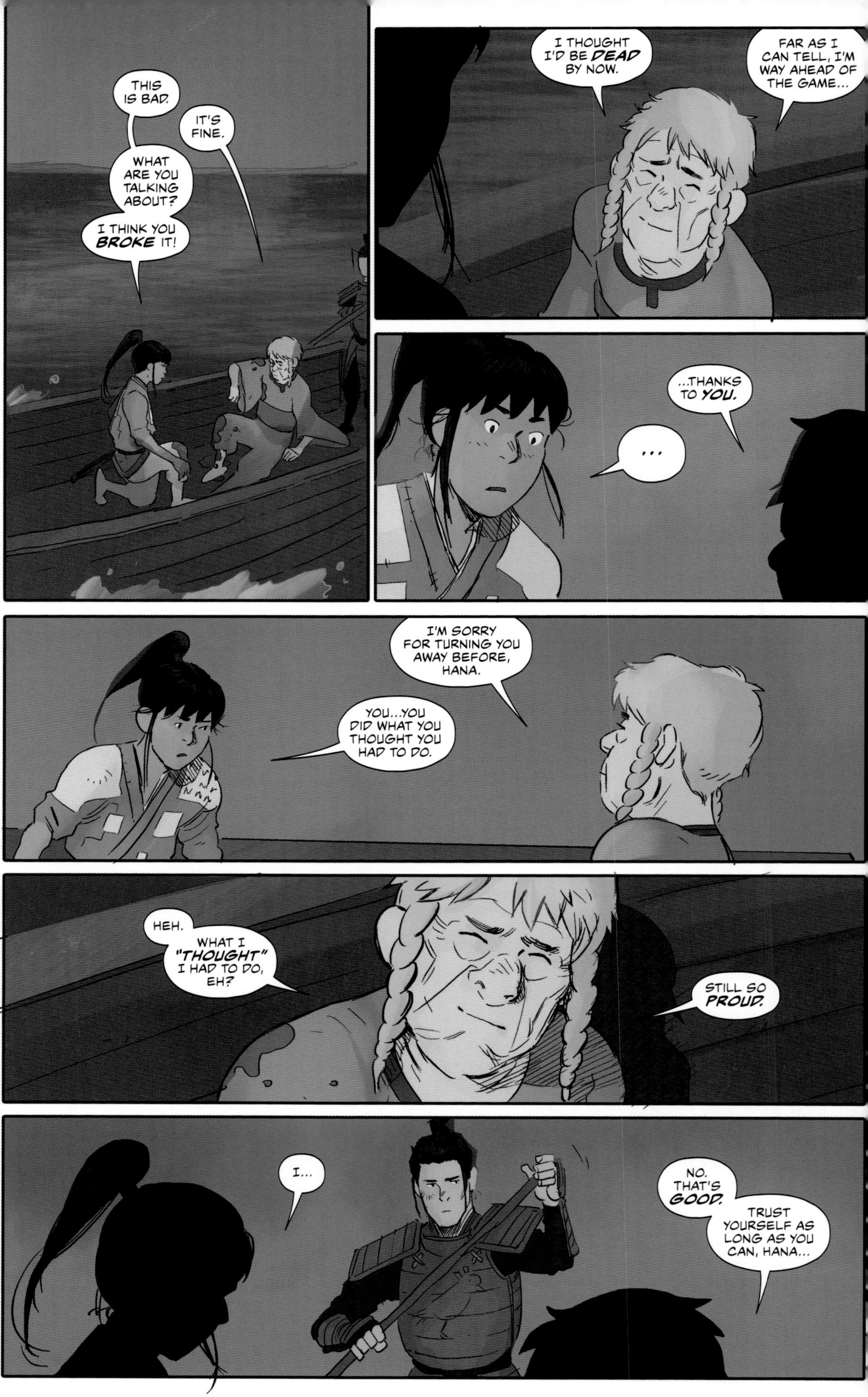
THIS IS BAD.
IT'S FINE.
WHAT ARE YOU TALKING ABOUT?
I THINK YOU BROKE IT!
I THOUGHT I'D BE DEAD BY NOW.
FAR AS I CAN TELL, I'M WAY AHEAD OF THE GAME...
...THANKS TO YOU.
...
I'M SORRY FOR TURNING YOU AWAY BEFORE, HANA.
YOU...YOU DID WHAT YOU THOUGHT YOU HAD TO DO.
HEH.
WHAT I "THOUGHT" I HAD TO DO, EH?
STILL SO PROUD.
I...
NO. THAT'S GOOD.
TRUST YOURSELF AS LONG AS YOU CAN, HANA...

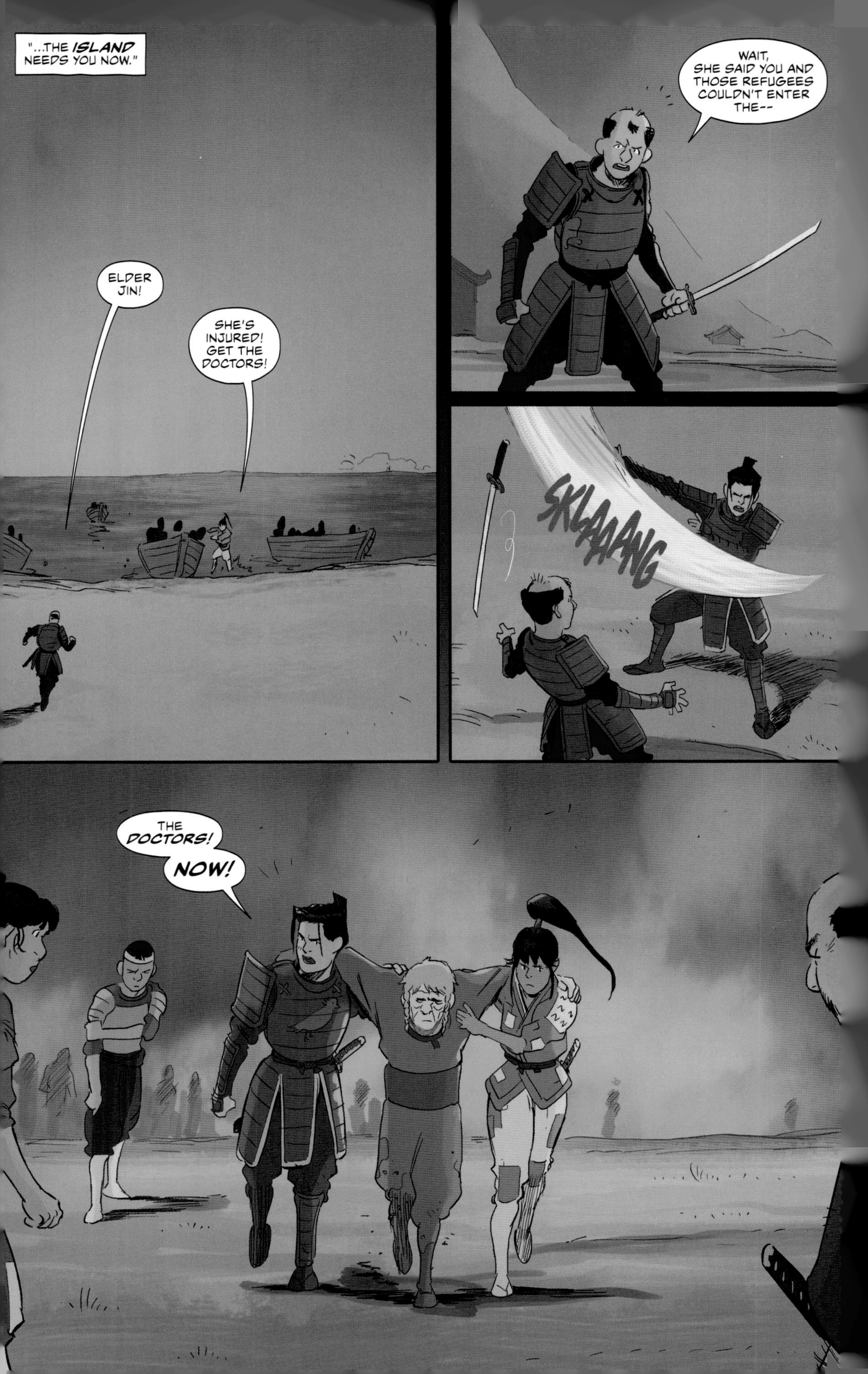
"...THE *ISLAND* NEEDS YOU NOW."
ELDER JIN!
SHE'S INJURED! GET THE DOCTORS!
WAIT, SHE SAID YOU AND THOSE REFUGEES COULDN'T ENTER THE--
SKLAAAANG
THE *DOCTORS!*
NOW!

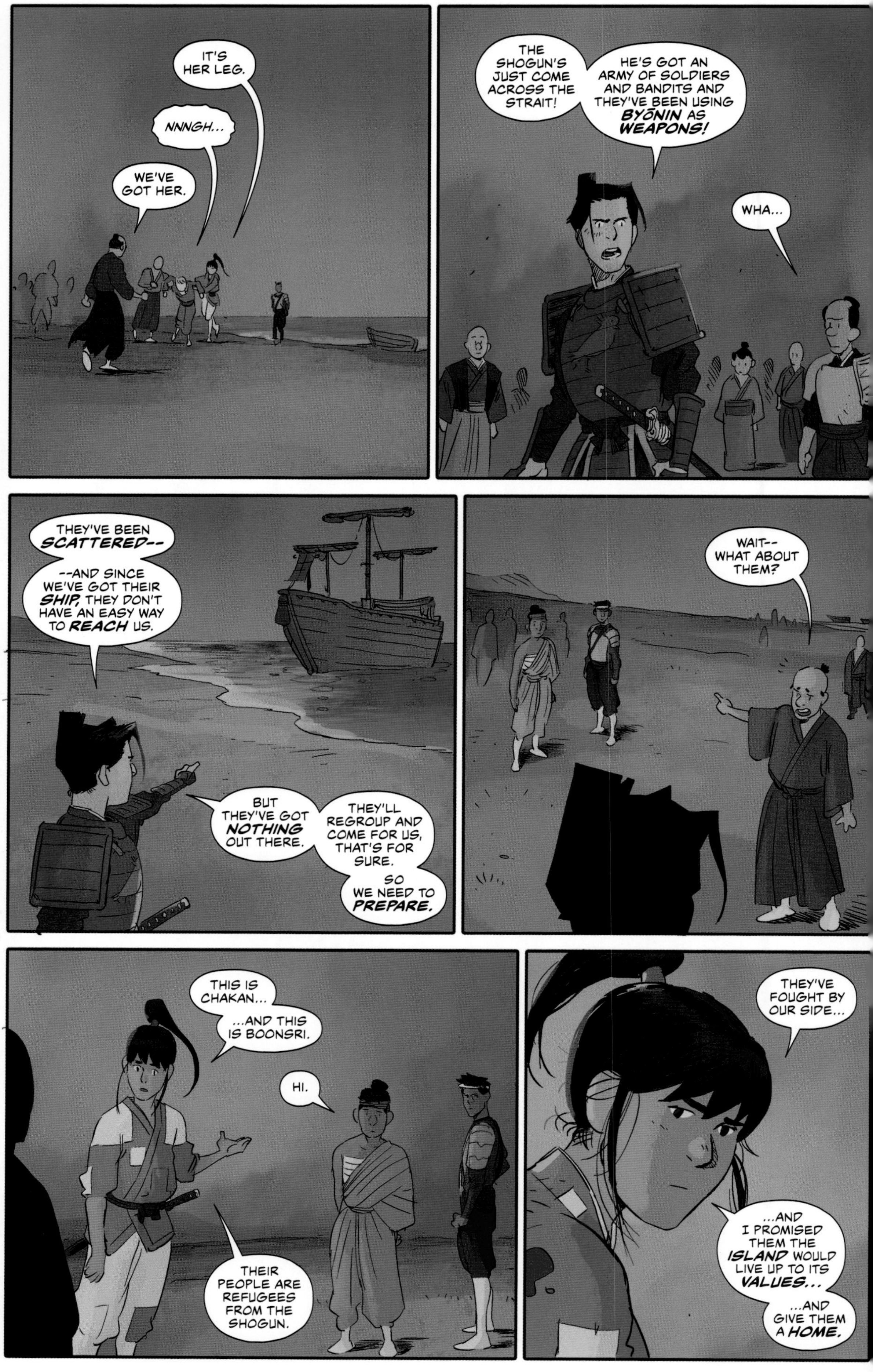
IT'S HER LEG.
NNNGH...
WE'VE GOT HER.
THE SHOGUN'S JUST COME ACROSS THE STRAIT!
HE'S GOT AN ARMY OF SOLDIERS AND BANDITS AND THEY'VE BEEN USING BYŌNIN AS WEAPONS!
WHA...
THEY'VE BEEN SCATTERED--
--AND SINCE WE'VE GOT THEIR SHIP, THEY DON'T HAVE AN EASY WAY TO REACH US.
BUT THEY'VE GOT NOTHING OUT THERE.
THEY'LL REGROUP AND COME FOR US, THAT'S FOR SURE.
SO WE NEED TO PREPARE.
WAIT--WHAT ABOUT THEM?
THIS IS CHAKAN...
...AND THIS IS BOONSRI.
HI.
THEIR PEOPLE ARE REFUGEES FROM THE SHOGUN.
THEY'VE FOUGHT BY OUR SIDE...
...AND I PROMISED THEM THE ISLAND WOULD LIVE UP TO ITS VALUES...
...AND GIVE THEM A HOME.

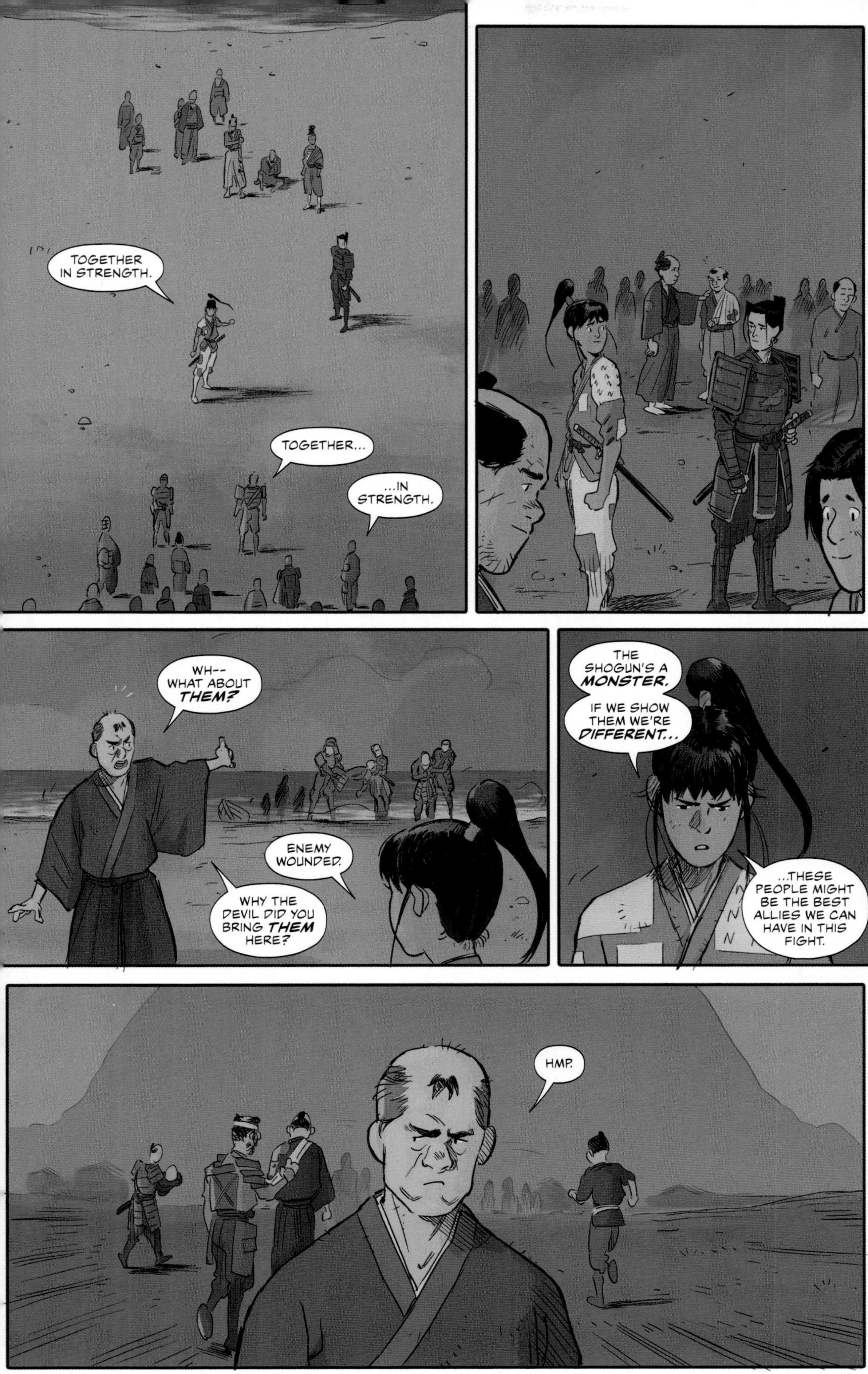

TOGETHER IN STRENGTH.
TOGETHER...
...IN STRENGTH.
WH-- WHAT ABOUT *THEM?*
ENEMY WOUNDED.
WHY THE DEVIL DID YOU BRING *THEM* HERE?
THE SHOGUN'S A *MONSTER.*
IF WE SHOW THEM WE'RE *DIFFERENT...*
...THESE PEOPLE MIGHT BE THE BEST ALLIES WE CAN HAVE IN THIS FIGHT.
HMP.

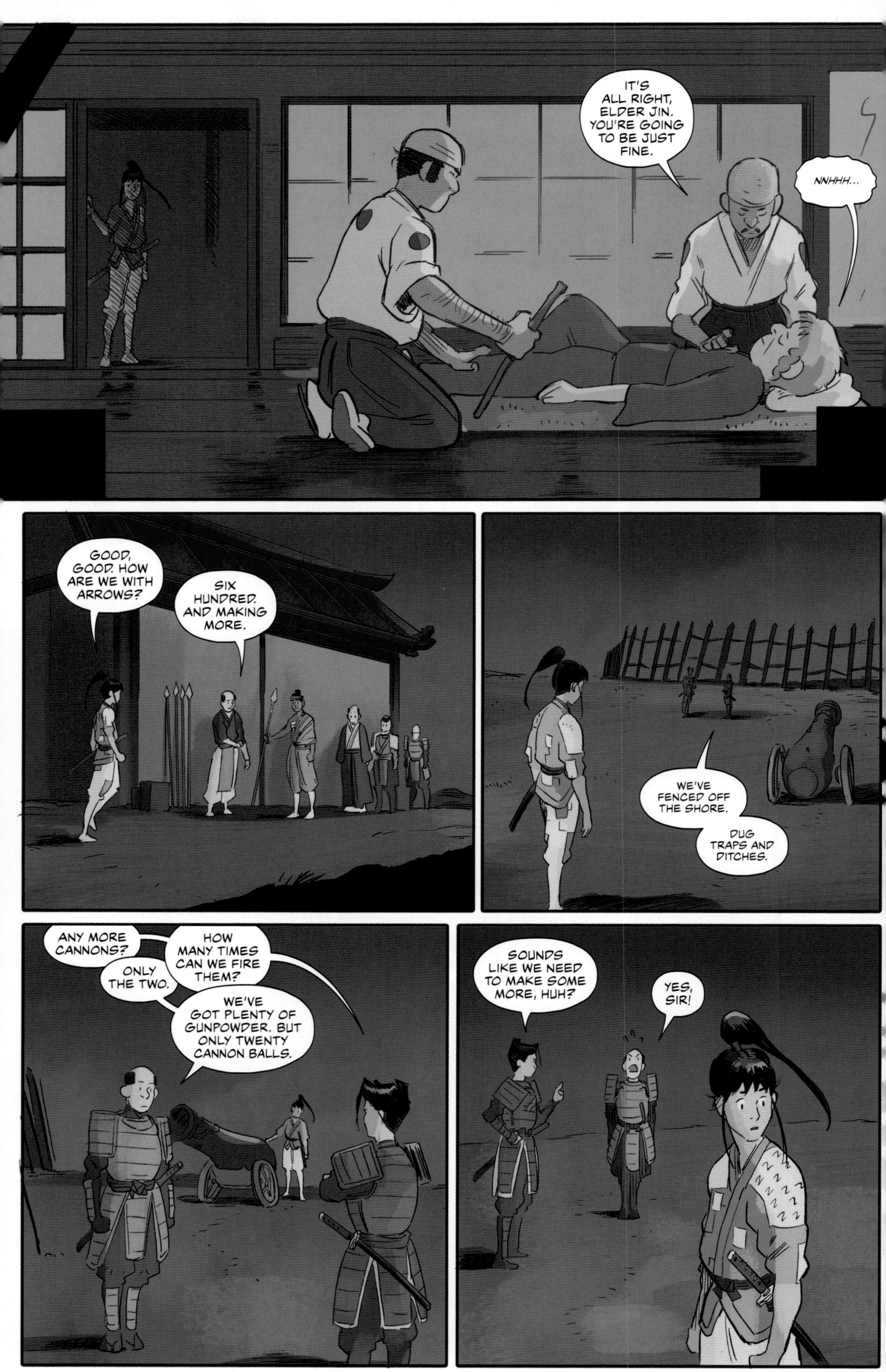
IT'S ALL RIGHT, ELDER JIN. YOU'RE GOING TO BE JUST FINE.
NNHHH...
GOOD, GOOD. HOW ARE WE WITH ARROWS?
SIX HUNDRED. AND MAKING MORE.
WE'VE FENCED OFF THE SHORE.
DUG TRAPS AND DITCHES.
ANY MORE CANNONS?
ONLY THE TWO.
HOW MANY TIMES CAN WE FIRE THEM?
WE'VE GOT PLENTY OF GUNPOWDER. BUT ONLY TWENTY CANNON BALLS.
SOUNDS LIKE WE NEED TO MAKE SOME MORE, HUH?
YES, SIR!

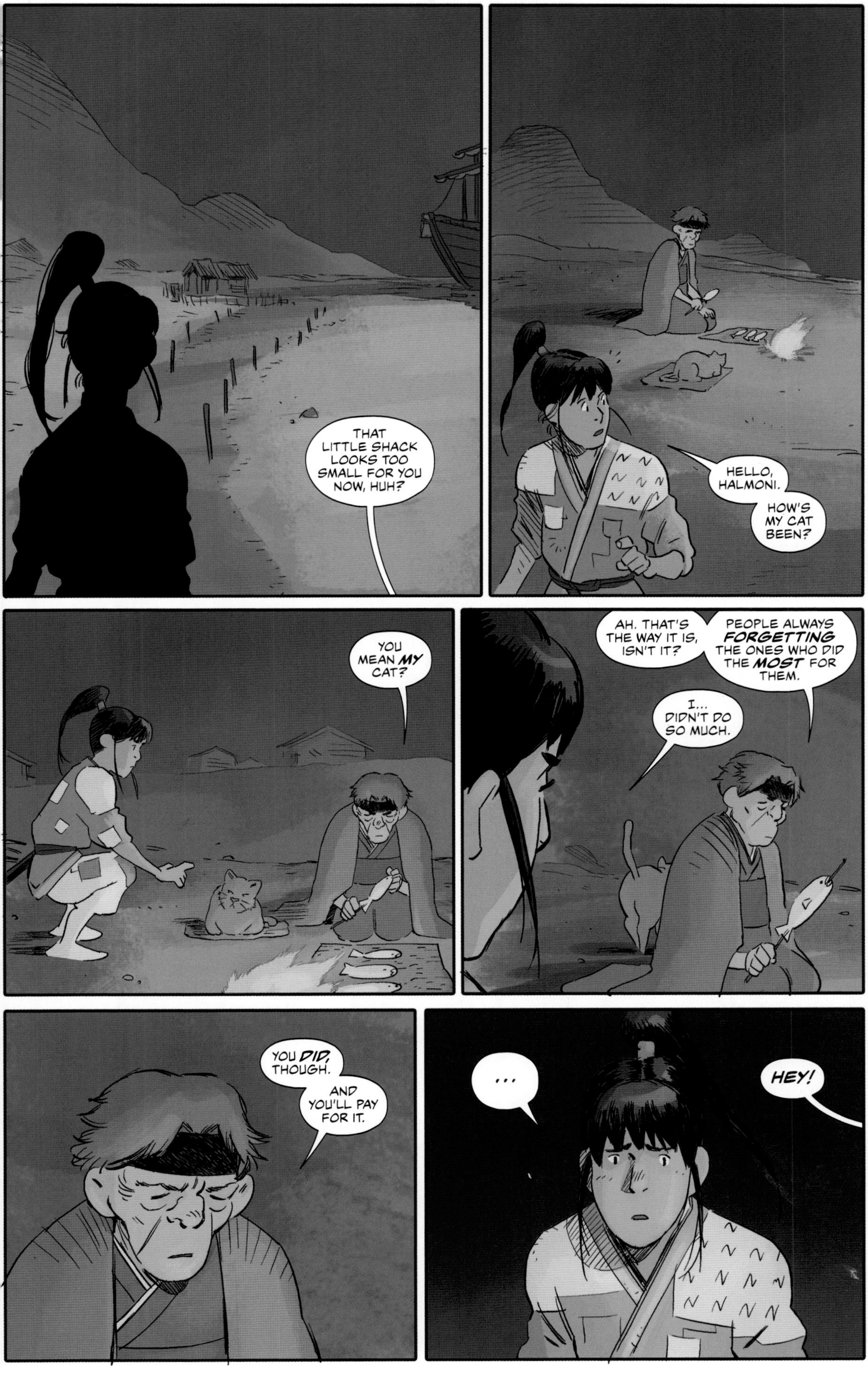
THAT LITTLE SHACK LOOKS TOO SMALL FOR YOU NOW, HUH?
HELLO, HALMONI.
HOW'S MY CAT BEEN?
YOU MEAN *MY* CAT?
AH. THAT'S THE WAY IT IS, ISN'T IT?
PEOPLE ALWAYS *FORGETTING* THE ONES WHO DID THE *MOST* FOR THEM.
I... DIDN'T DO SO MUCH.
YOU *DID*, THOUGH.
AND YOU'LL PAY FOR IT.
...
HEY!

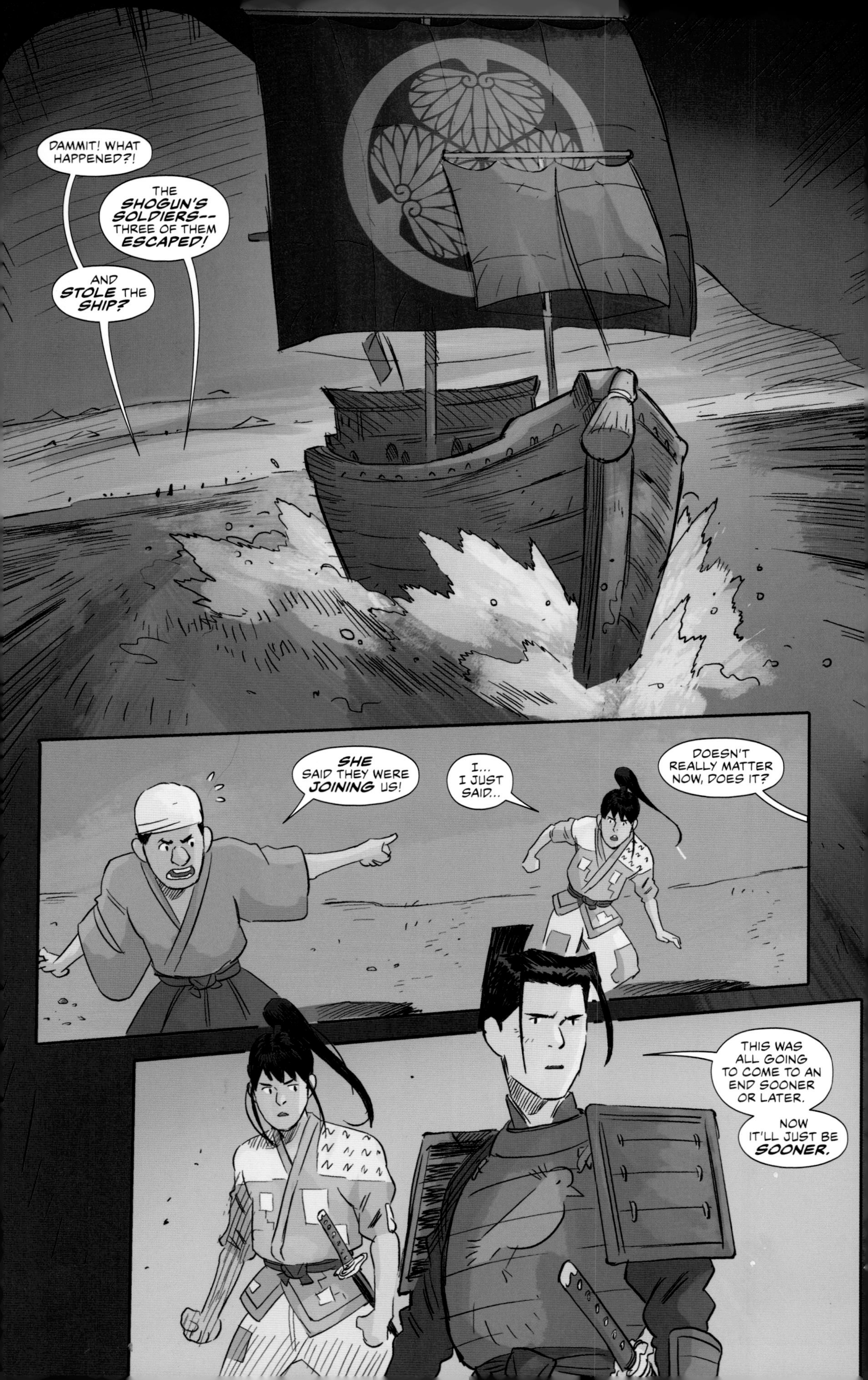
DAMMIT! WHAT HAPPENED?!
THE SHOGUN'S SOLDIERS-- THREE OF THEM ESCAPED!
AND STOLE THE SHIP?
SHE SAID THEY WERE JOINING US!
I... I JUST SAID...
DOESN'T REALLY MATTER NOW, DOES IT?
THIS WAS ALL GOING TO COME TO AN END SOONER OR LATER.
NOW IT'LL JUST BE SOONER.

Issue Ten Cover by
Ethan Young

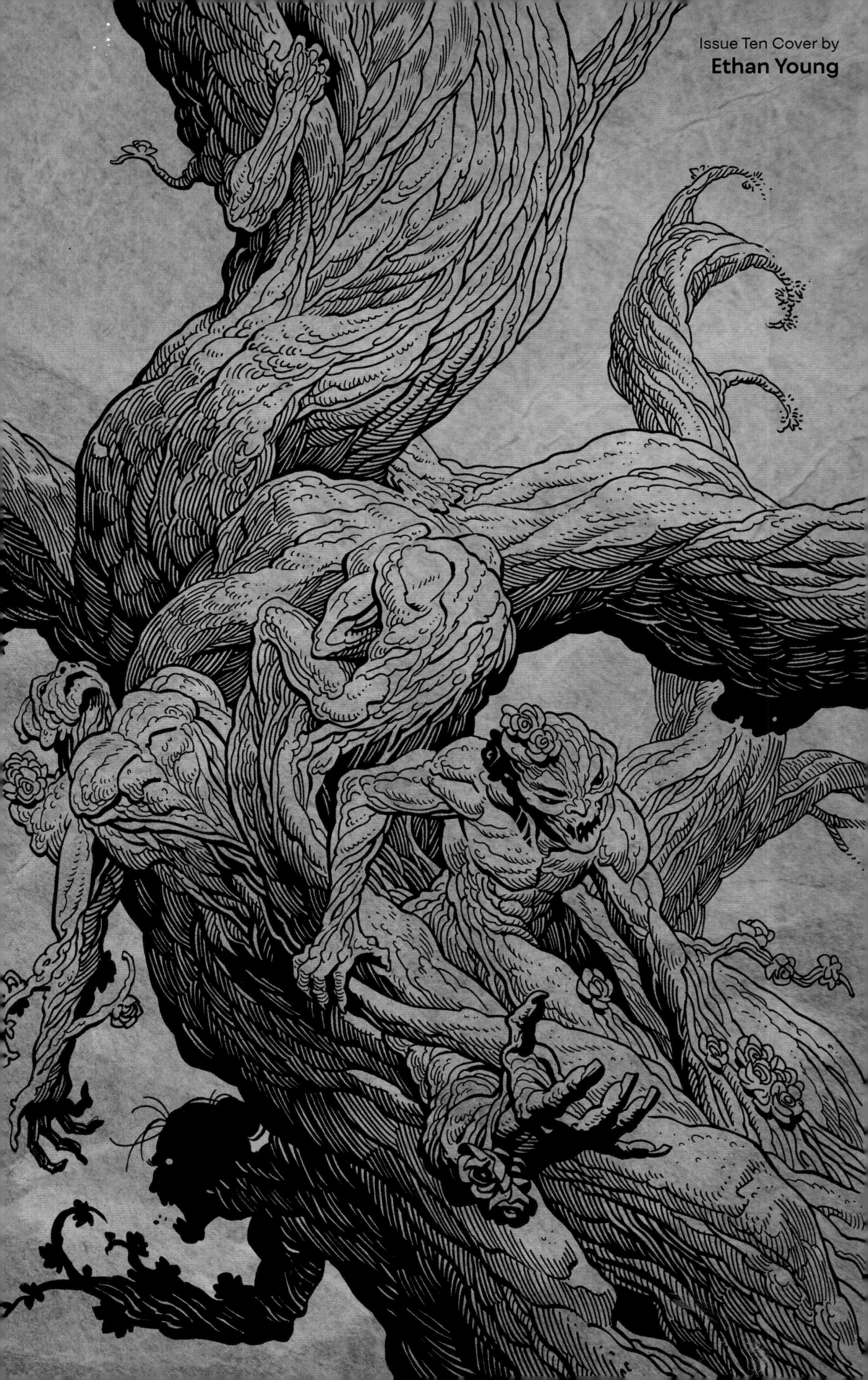

CHAPTER ELEVEN

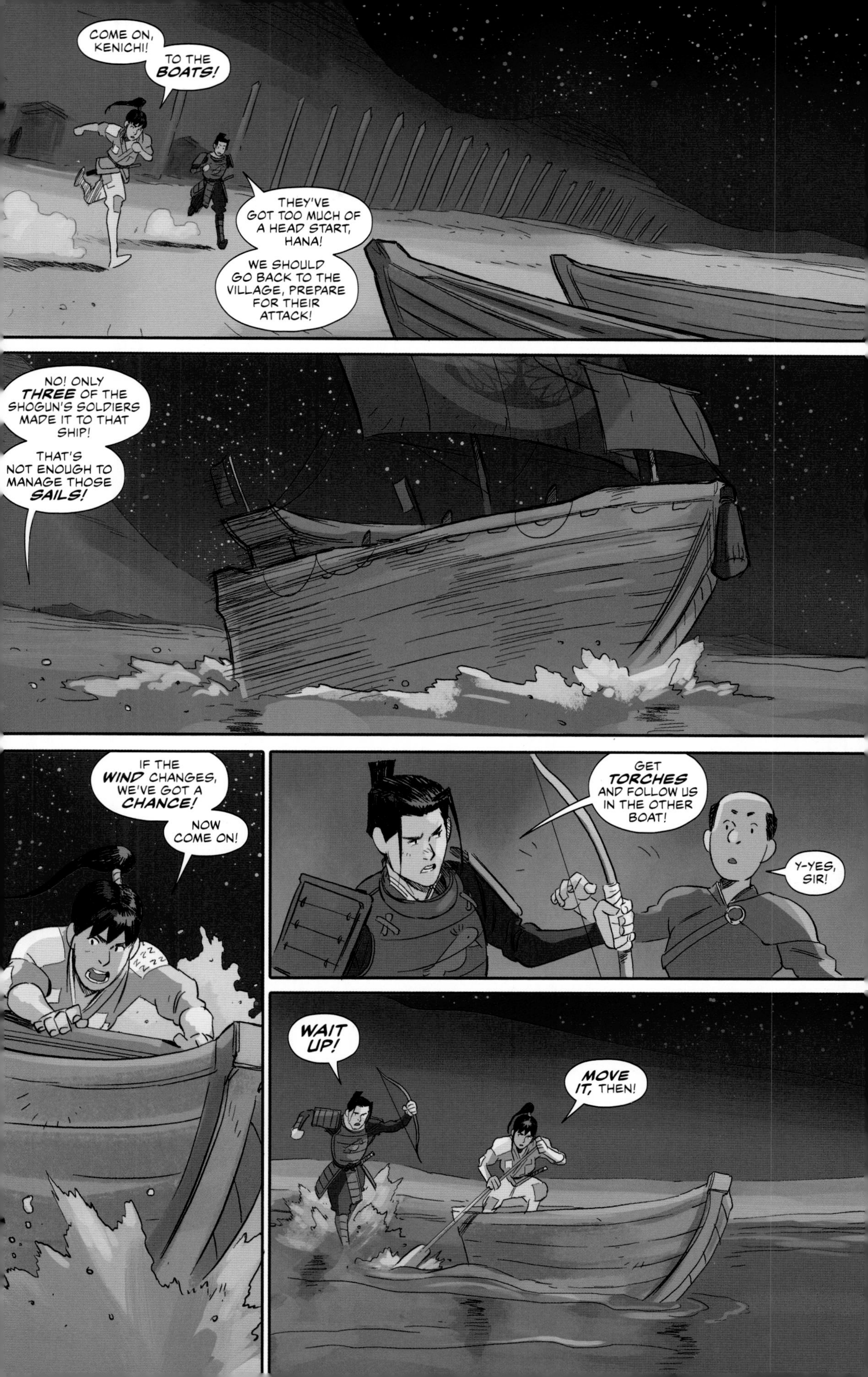
COME ON, KENICHI!
TO THE BOATS!
THEY'VE GOT TOO MUCH OF A HEAD START, HANA!
WE SHOULD GO BACK TO THE VILLAGE, PREPARE FOR THEIR ATTACK!
NO! ONLY THREE OF THE SHOGUN'S SOLDIERS MADE IT TO THAT SHIP!
THAT'S NOT ENOUGH TO MANAGE THOSE SAILS!
IF THE WIND CHANGES, WE'VE GOT A CHANCE!
NOW COME ON!
GET TORCHES AND FOLLOW US IN THE OTHER BOAT!
Y-YES, SIR!
WAIT UP!
MOVE IT, THEN!

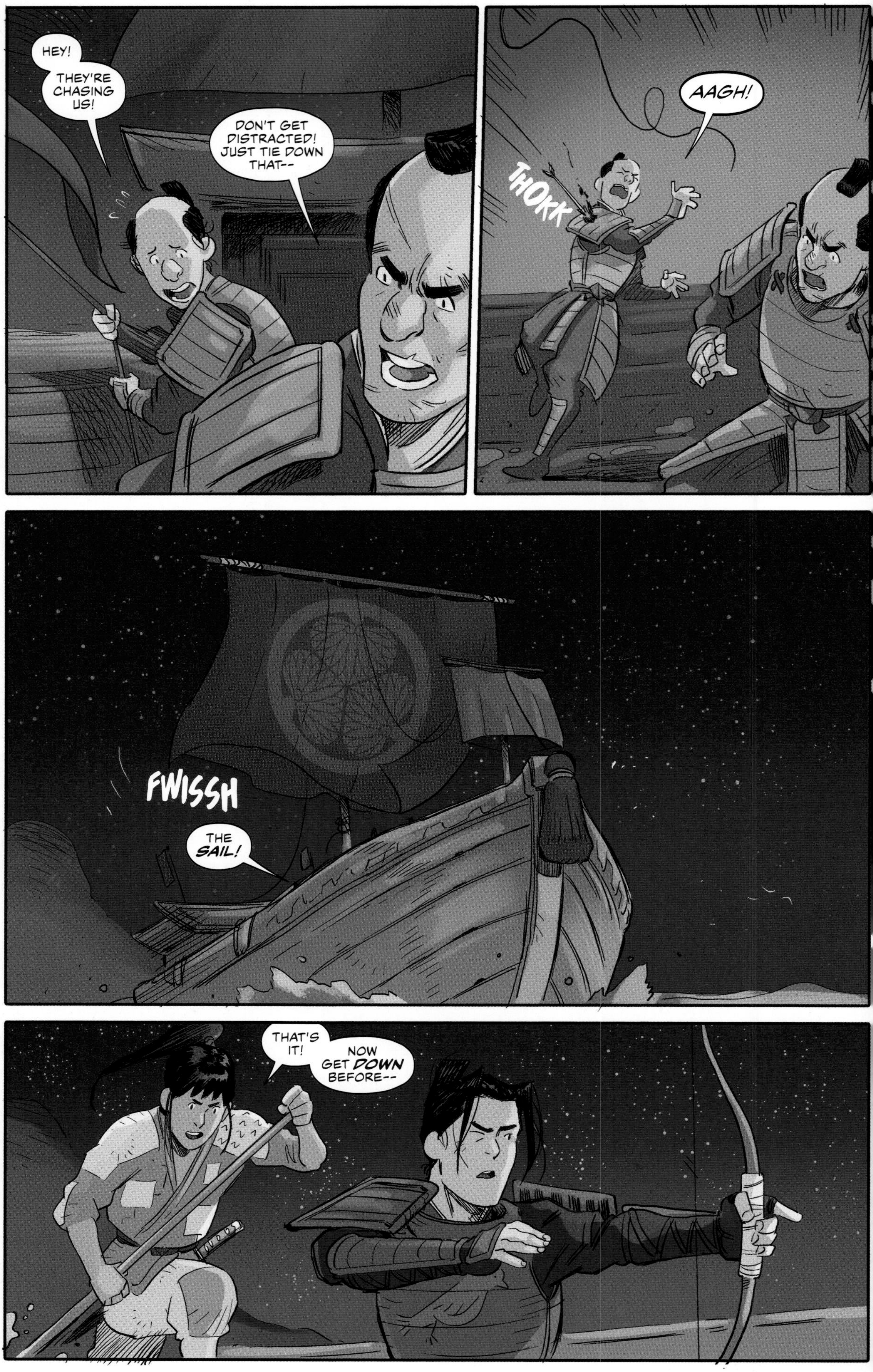
HEY!
THEY'RE CHASING US!
DON'T GET DISTRACTED! JUST TIE DOWN THAT--
THOKK
AAGH!
FWISSH
THE SAIL!
THAT'S IT!
NOW GET DOWN BEFORE--

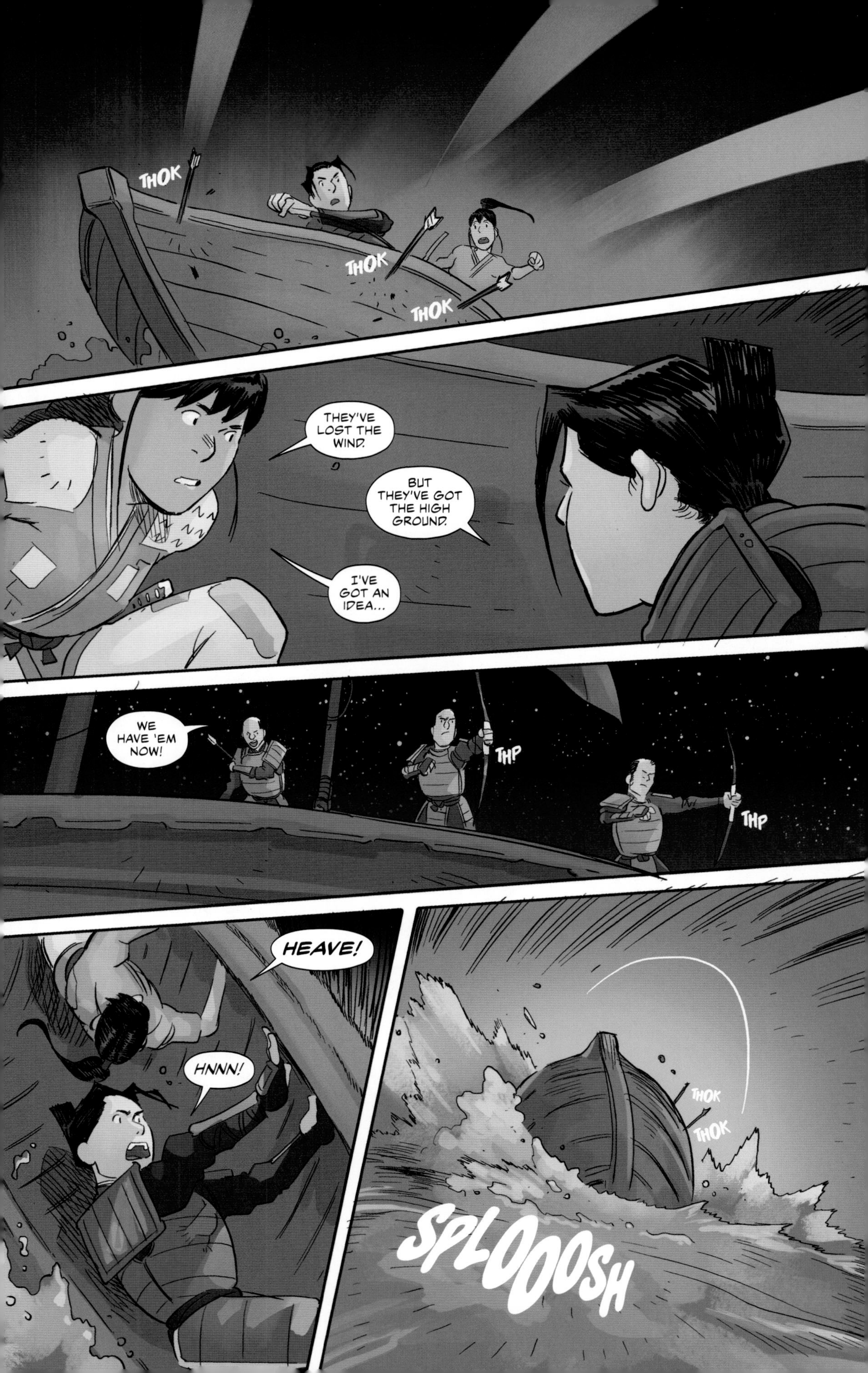
THOK
THOK
THOK
THEY'VE LOST THE WIND.
BUT THEY'VE GOT THE HIGH GROUND.
I'VE GOT AN IDEA...
WE HAVE 'EM NOW!
THP
THP
HEAVE!
HNNN!
THOK
THOK
SPLOOOSH

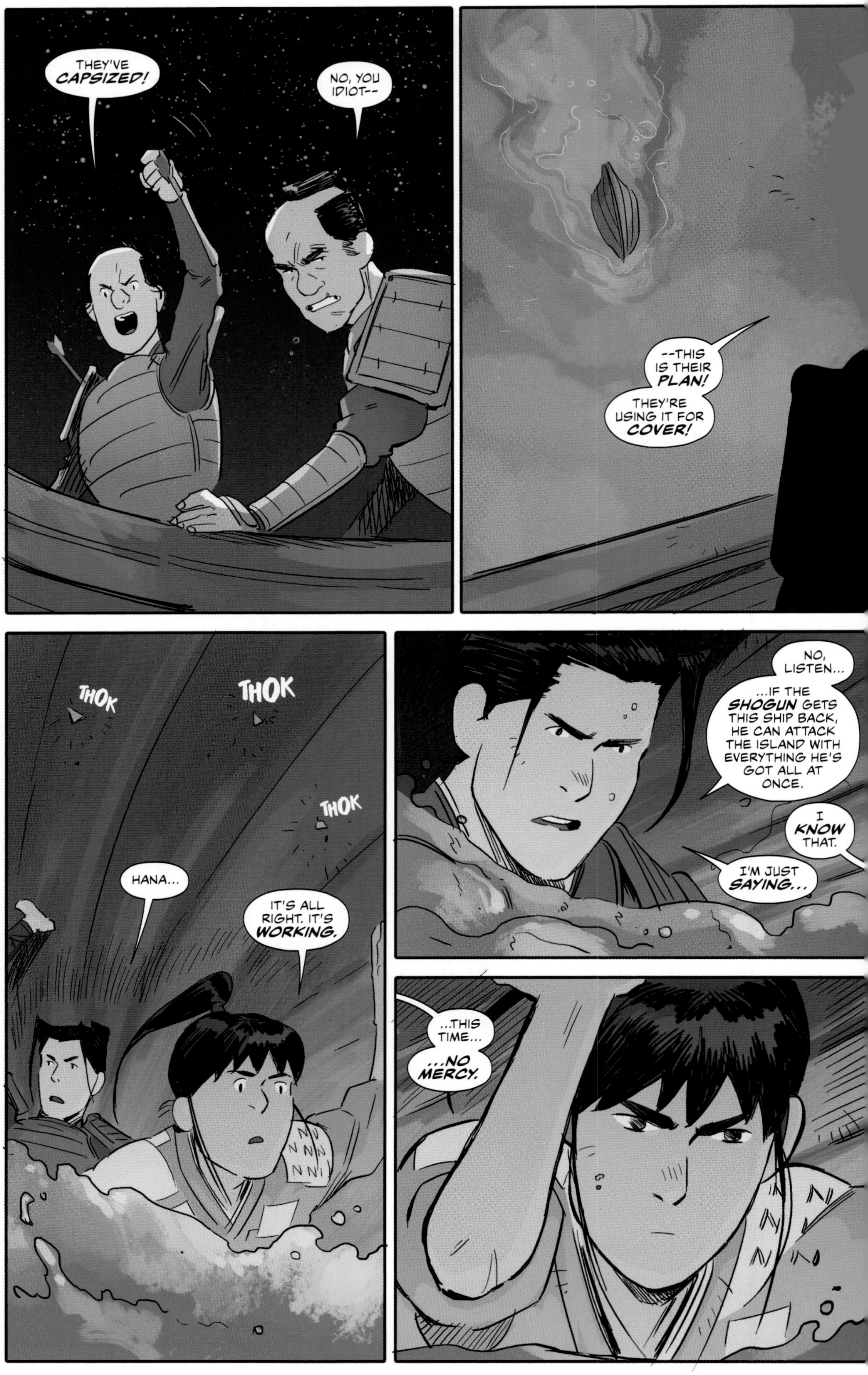
THEY'VE CAPSIZED!
NO, YOU IDIOT--
--THIS IS THEIR PLAN!
THEY'RE USING IT FOR COVER!
THOK
THOK
THOK
HANA...
IT'S ALL RIGHT. IT'S WORKING.
NO, LISTEN...
...IF THE SHOGUN GETS THIS SHIP BACK, HE CAN ATTACK THE ISLAND WITH EVERYTHING HE'S GOT ALL AT ONCE.
I KNOW THAT.
I'M JUST SAYING...
...THIS TIME...
...NO MERCY.

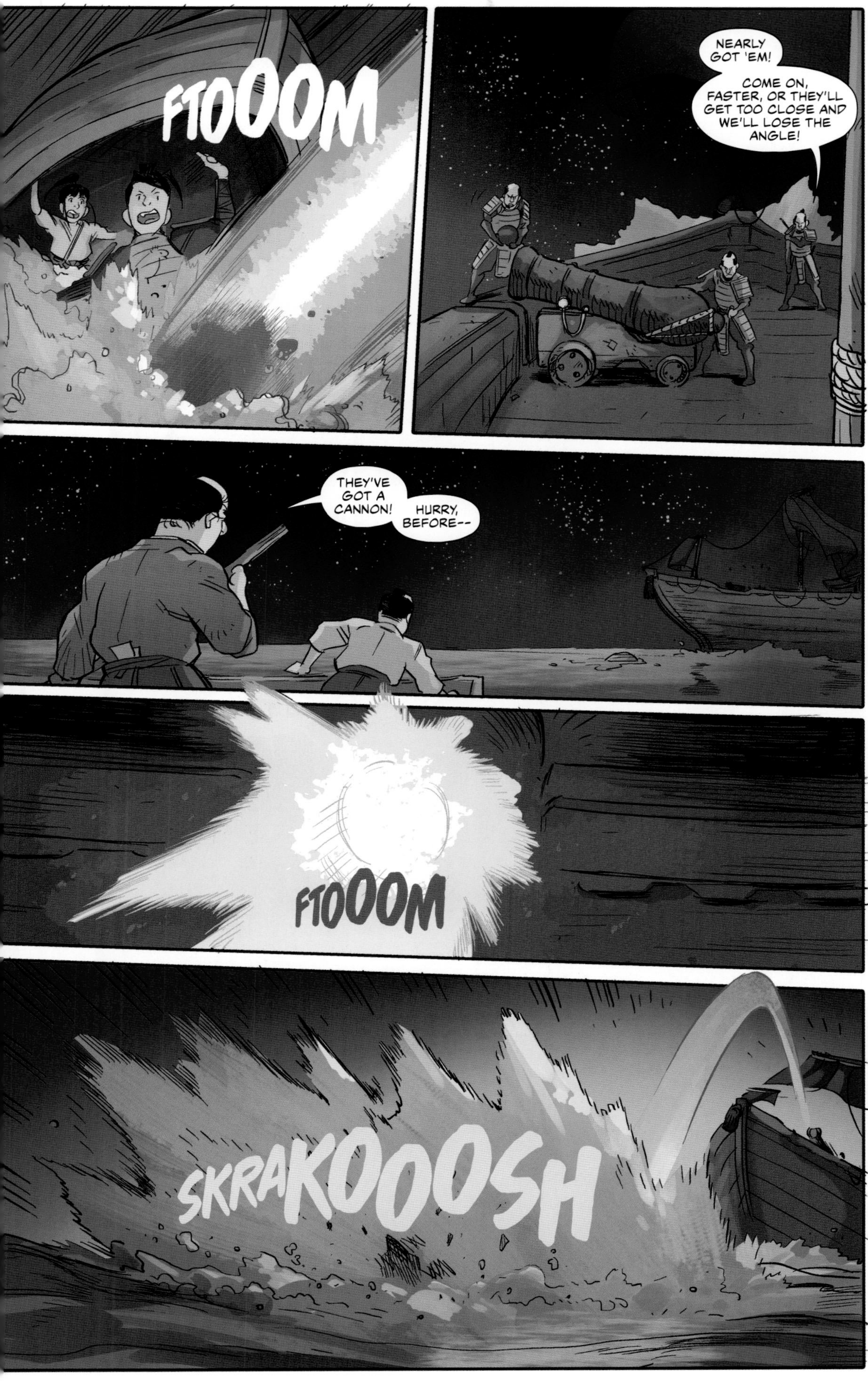
FTOOOM
NEARLY GOT 'EM!
COME ON, FASTER, OR THEY'LL GET TOO CLOSE AND WE'LL LOSE THE ANGLE!
THEY'VE GOT A CANNON!
HURRY, BEFORE--
FTOOOM
SKRAKOOOOSH

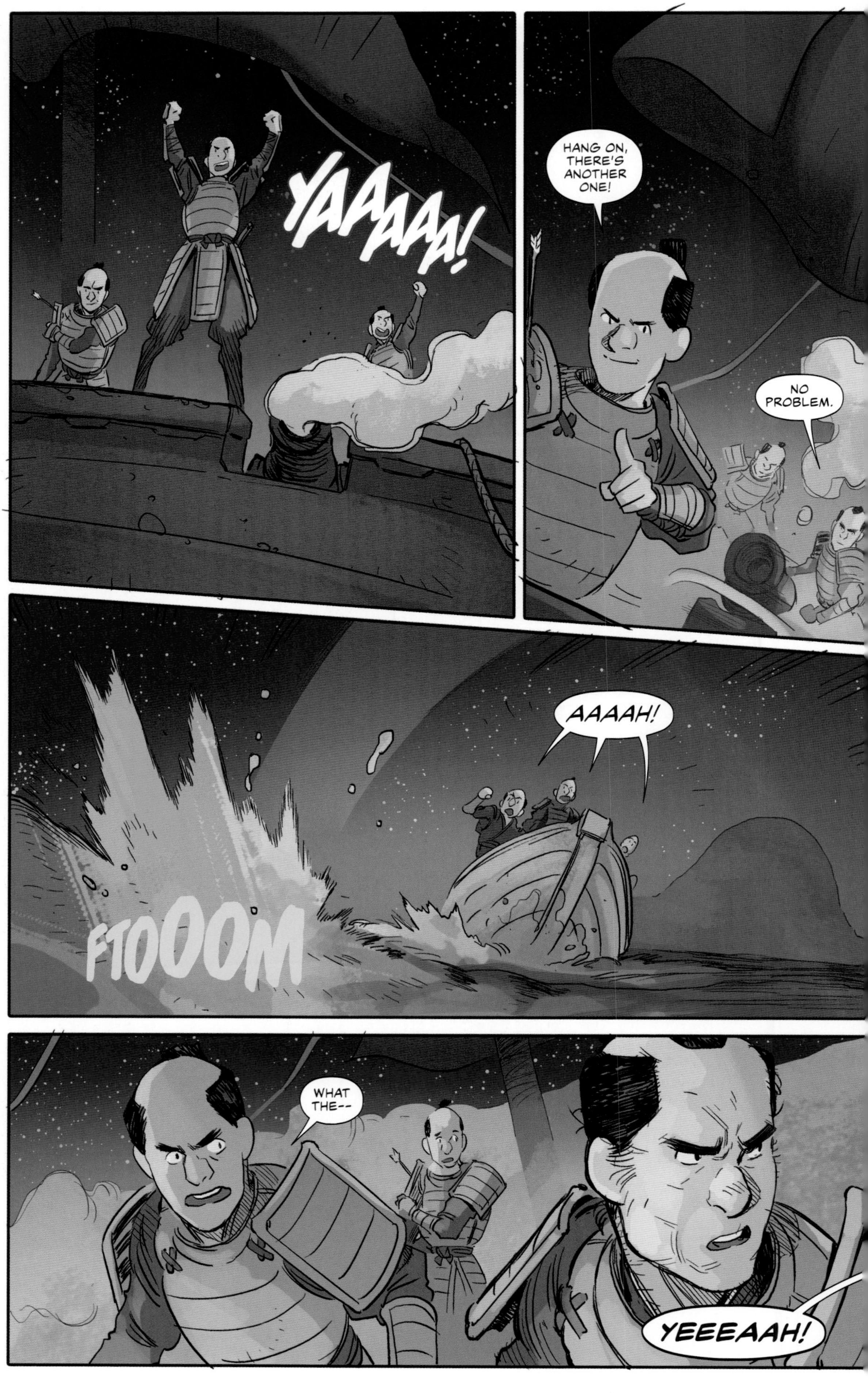
YAAAAA!
HANG ON, THERE'S ANOTHER ONE!
NO PROBLEM.
AAAAH!
FTOOOM
WHAT THE--
YEEEAAH!

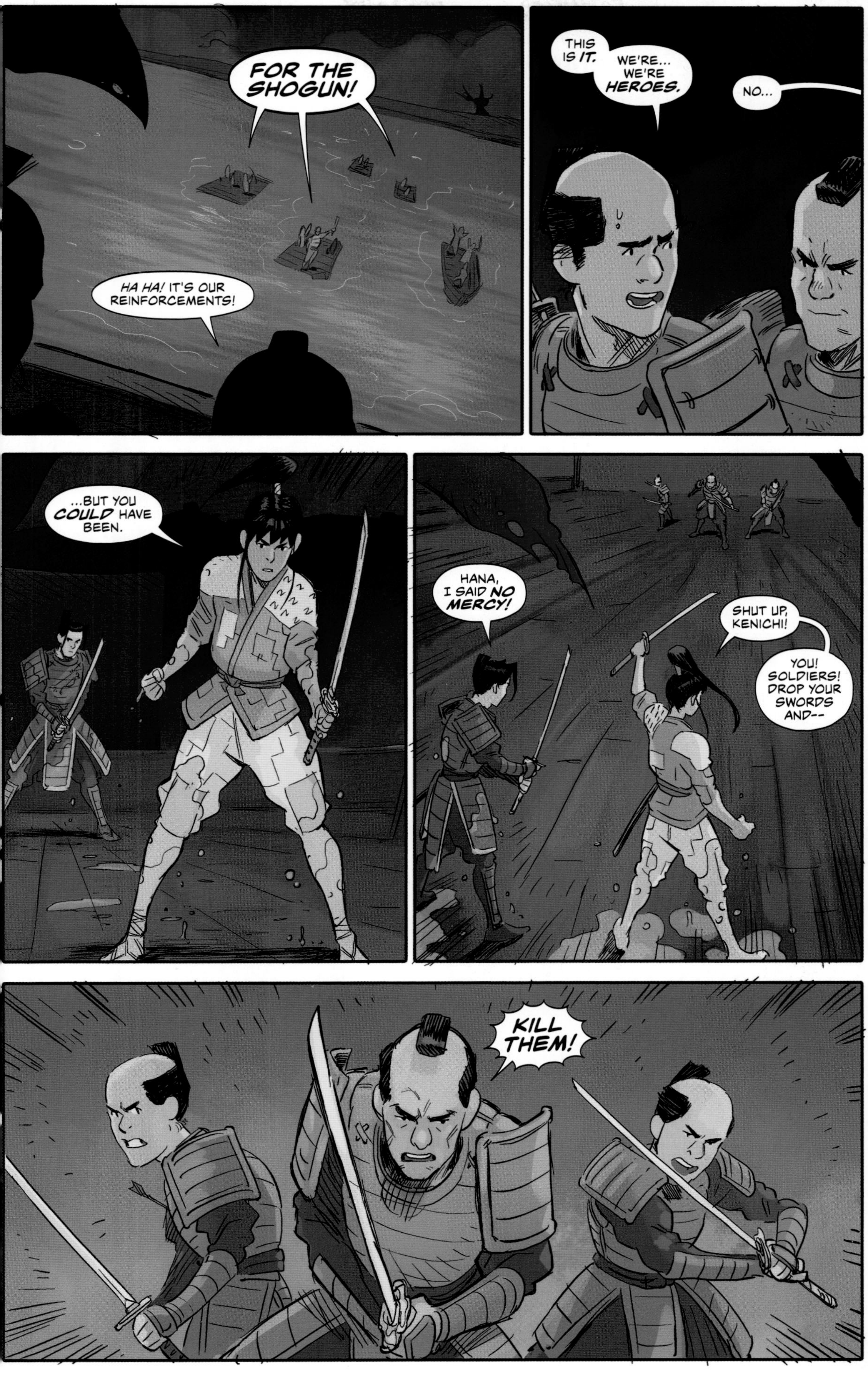
FOR THE SHOGUN!
HA HA! IT'S OUR REINFORCEMENTS!
THIS IS IT.
WE'RE... WE'RE HEROES.
NO...
...BUT YOU COULD HAVE BEEN.
HANA, I SAID NO MERCY!
SHUT UP, KENICHI!
YOU! SOLDIERS! DROP YOUR SWORDS AND--
KILL THEM!

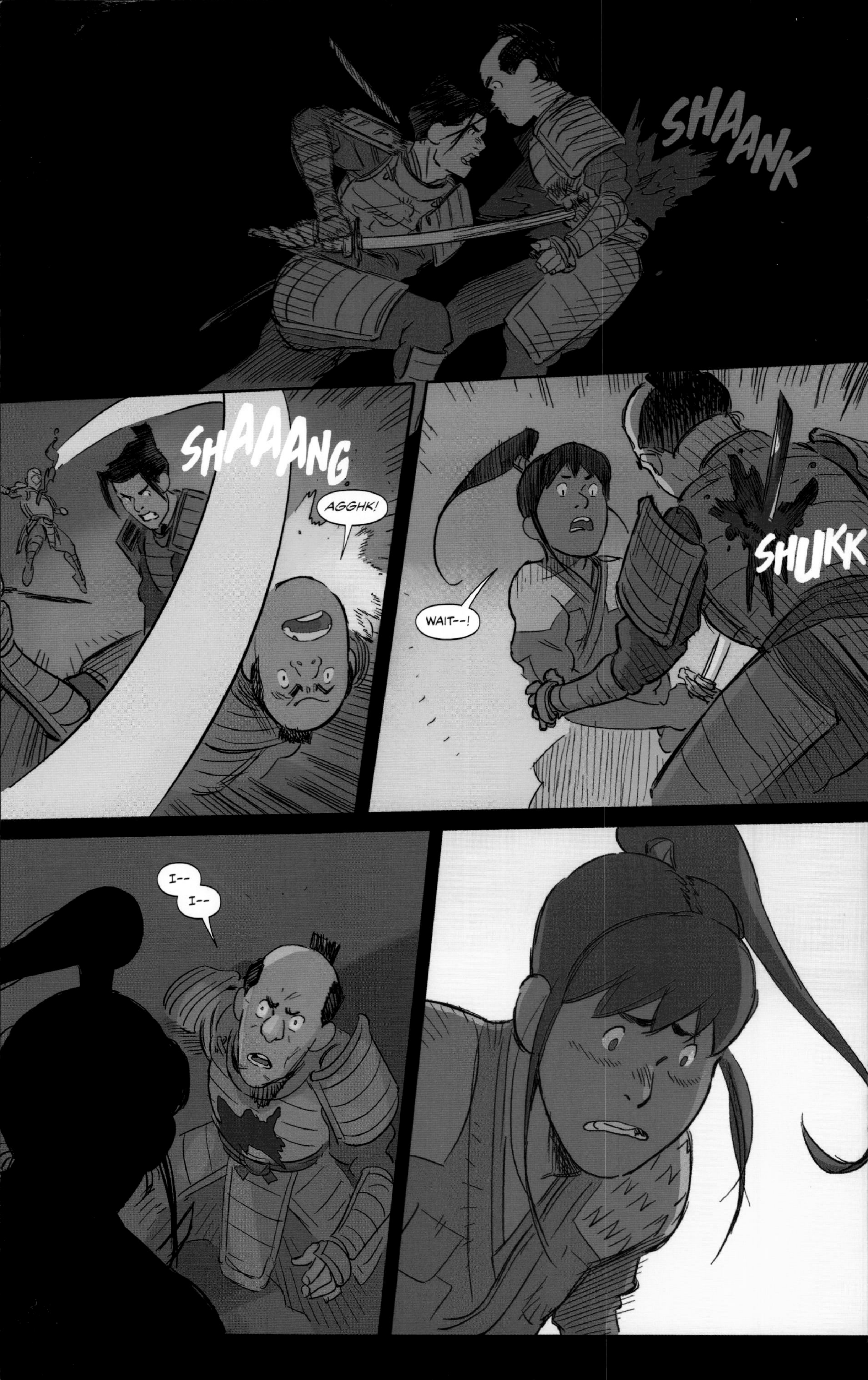
SHAANK
SHAAAANG
AGGHK!
WAIT--!
SHUKK
I--
I--

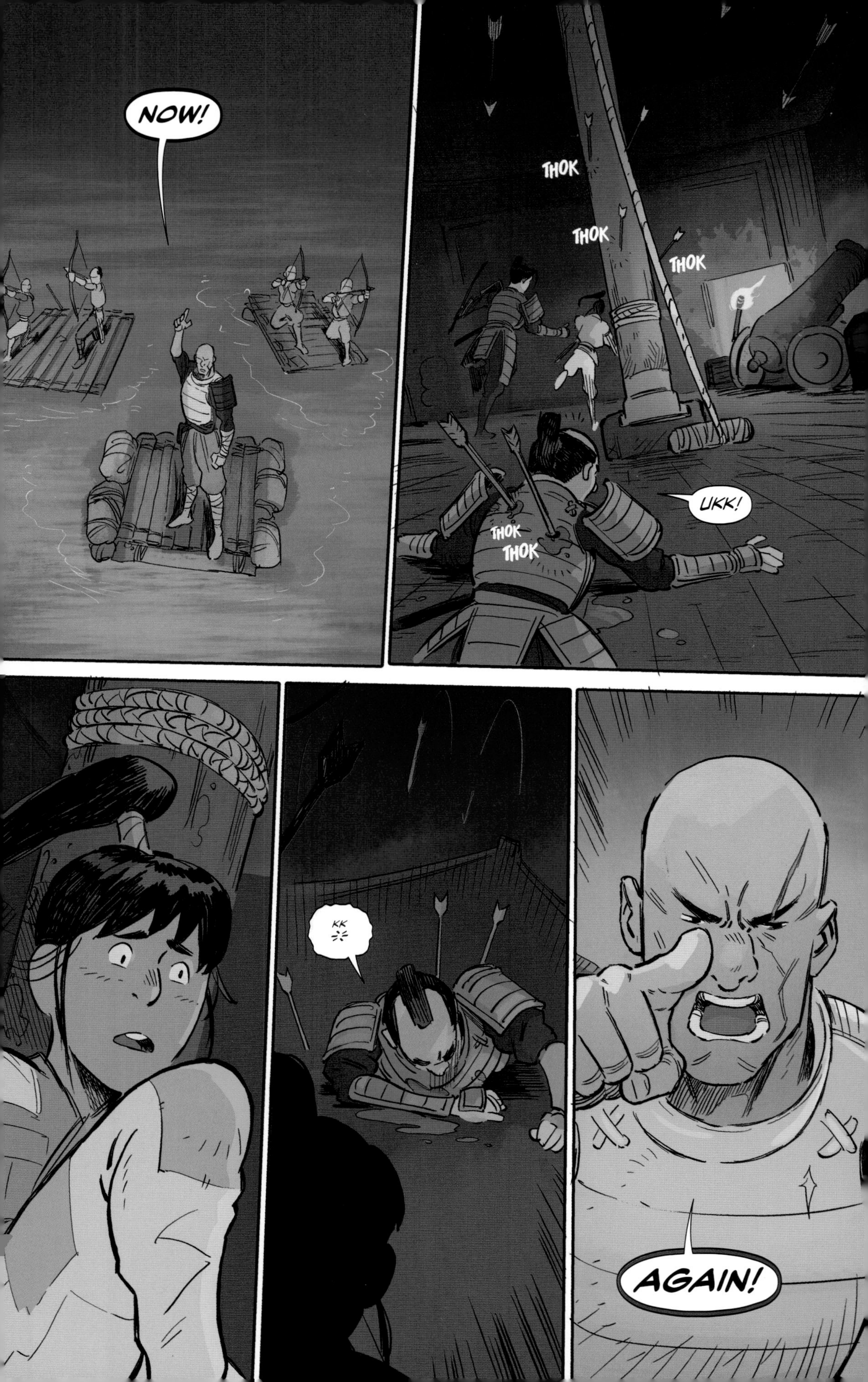
NOW!
THOK
THOK
THOK
THOK
THOK
UKK!
KK
AGAIN!

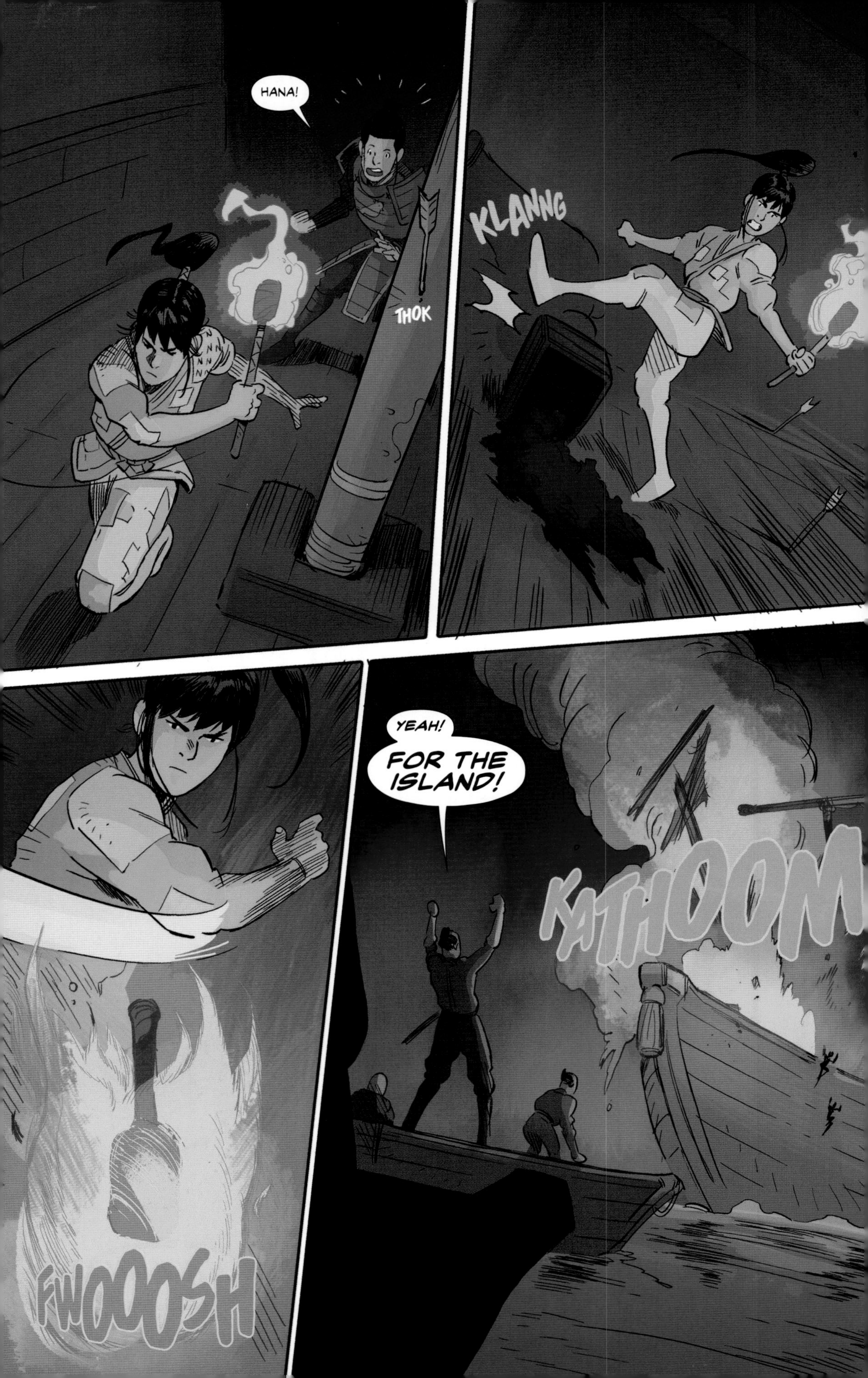
HANA!
THOK
KLANNG
FWOOOSH
YEAH!
FOR THE ISLAND!
KATHOOM

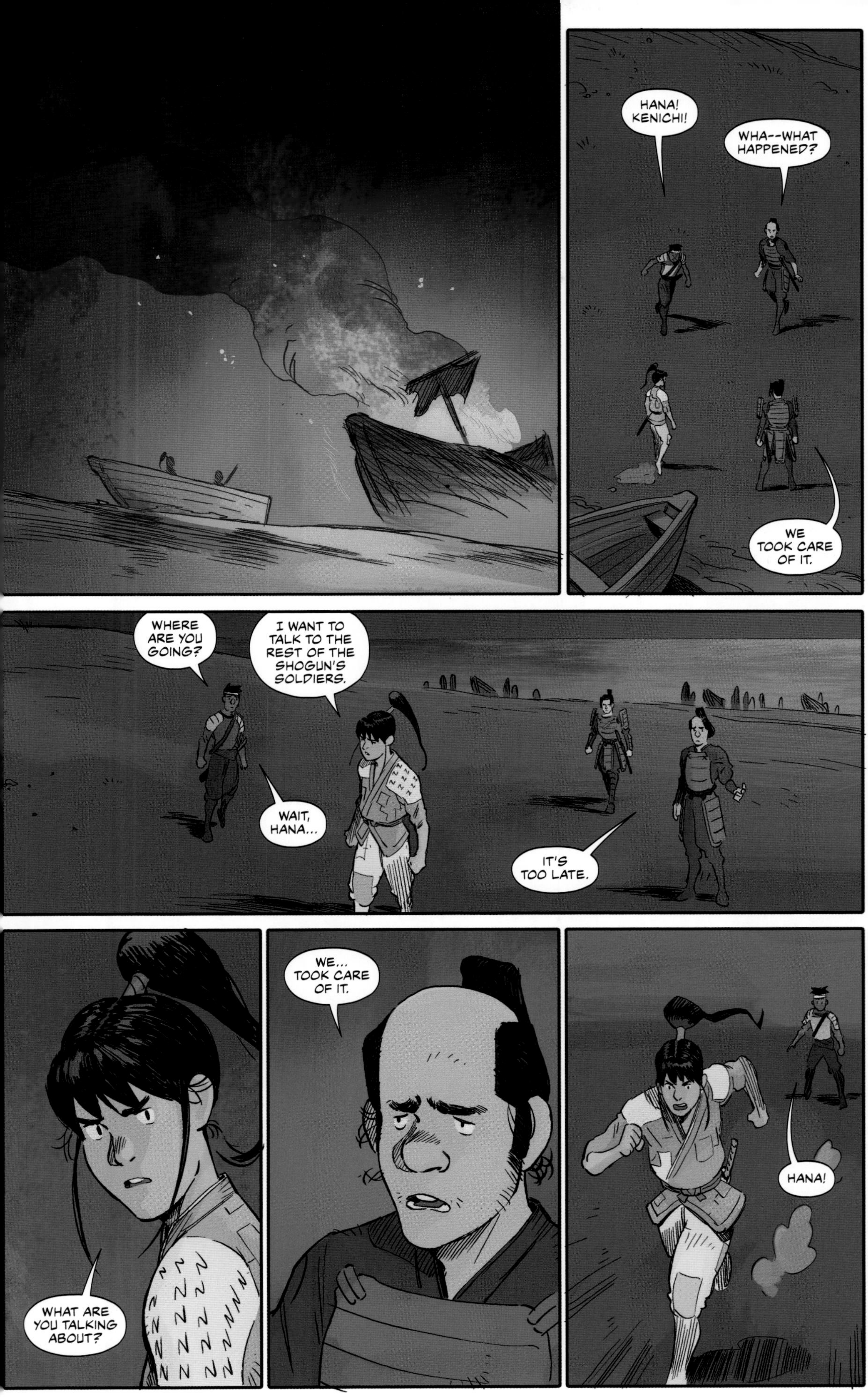
HANA! KENICHI!
WHA--WHAT HAPPENED?
WE TOOK CARE OF IT.
WHERE ARE YOU GOING?
I WANT TO TALK TO THE REST OF THE SHOGUN'S SOLDIERS.
WAIT, HANA...
IT'S TOO LATE.
WHAT ARE YOU TALKING ABOUT?
WE... TOOK CARE OF IT.
HANA!

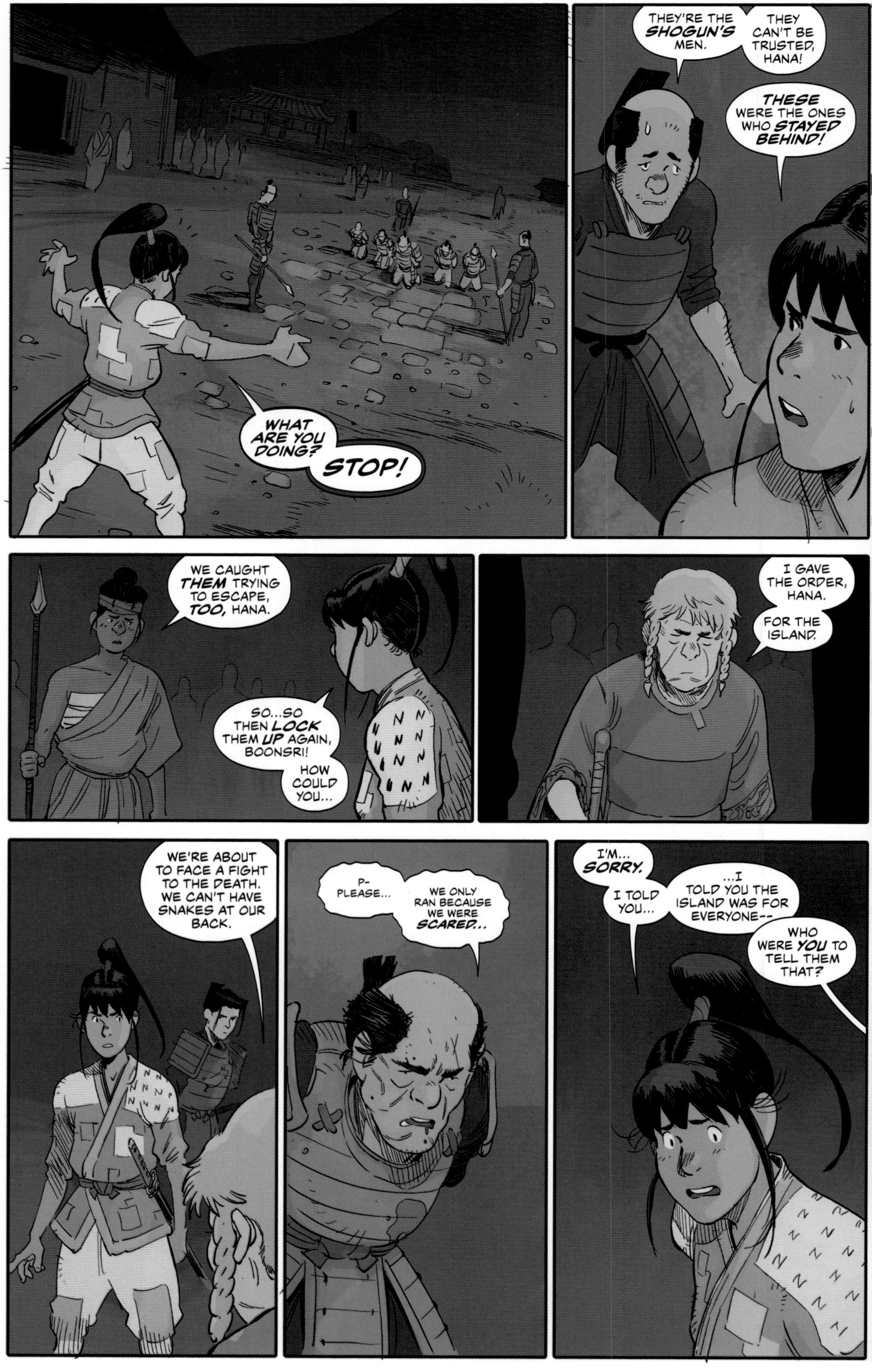
WHAT ARE YOU DOING? STOP!
THEY'RE THE SHOGUN'S MEN.
THEY CAN'T BE TRUSTED, HANA!
THESE WERE THE ONES WHO STAYED BEHIND!
WE CAUGHT THEM TRYING TO ESCAPE, TOO, HANA.
SO...SO THEN LOCK THEM UP AGAIN, BOONSRI!
HOW COULD YOU...
I GAVE THE ORDER, HANA.
FOR THE ISLAND.
WE'RE ABOUT TO FACE A FIGHT TO THE DEATH. WE CAN'T HAVE SNAKES AT OUR BACK.
P-PLEASE...
WE ONLY RAN BECAUSE WE WERE SCARED...
I'M... SORRY.
I TOLD YOU...
...I TOLD YOU THE ISLAND WAS FOR EVERYONE--
WHO WERE YOU TO TELL THEM THAT?

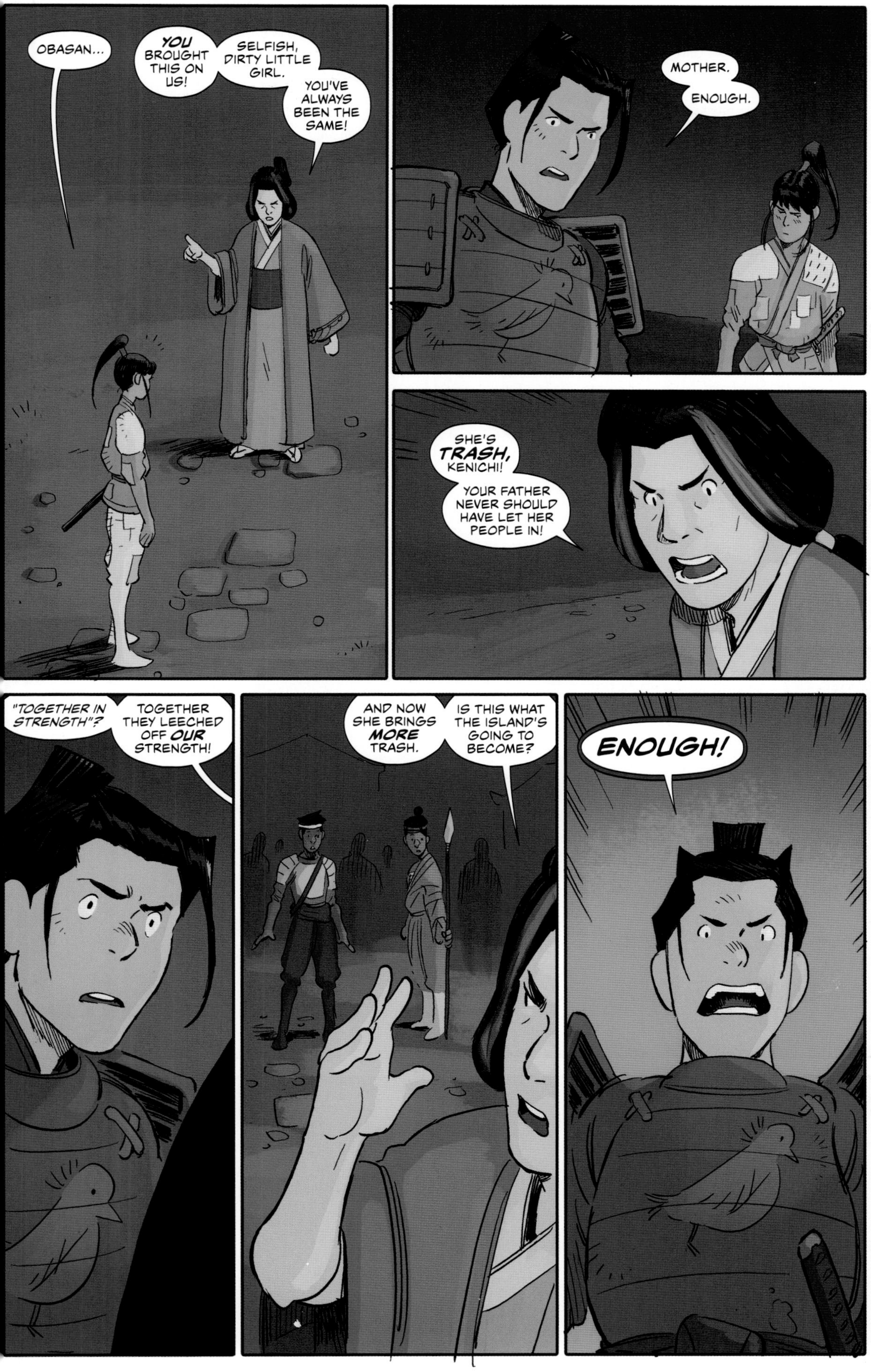
OBASAN...
YOU BROUGHT THIS ON US!
SELFISH, DIRTY LITTLE GIRL.
YOU'VE ALWAYS BEEN THE SAME!
MOTHER.
ENOUGH.
SHE'S TRASH, KENICHI!
YOUR FATHER NEVER SHOULD HAVE LET HER PEOPLE IN!
"TOGETHER IN STRENGTH"?
TOGETHER THEY LEECHED OFF OUR STRENGTH!
AND NOW SHE BRINGS MORE TRASH.
IS THIS WHAT THE ISLAND'S GOING TO BECOME?
ENOUGH!

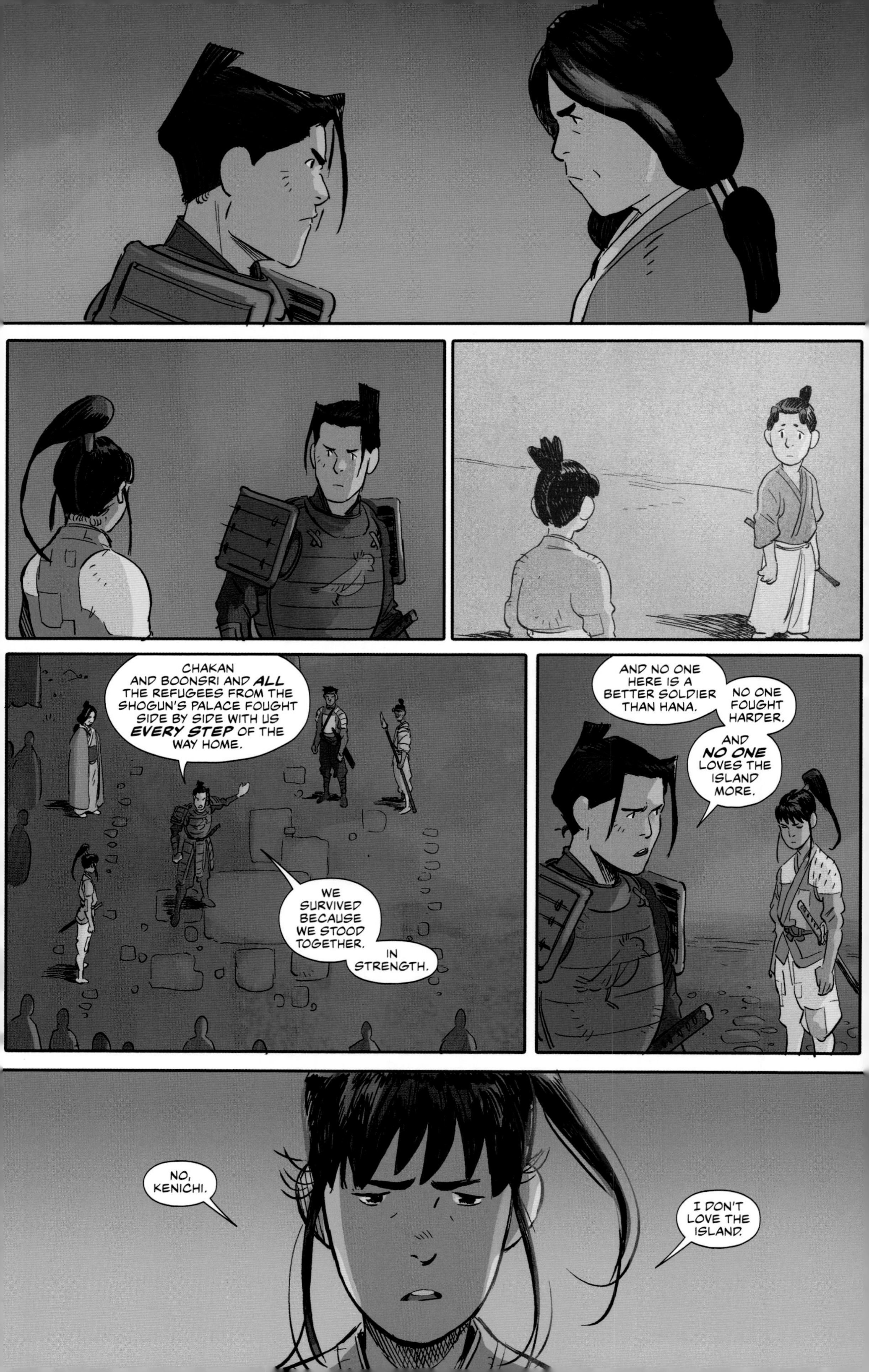
CHAKAN AND BOONSRI AND ALL THE REFUGEES FROM THE SHOGUN'S PALACE FOUGHT SIDE BY SIDE WITH US EVERY STEP OF THE WAY HOME.
WE SURVIVED BECAUSE WE STOOD TOGETHER.
IN STRENGTH.
AND NO ONE HERE IS A BETTER SOLDIER THAN HANA.
NO ONE FOUGHT HARDER.
AND NO ONE LOVES THE ISLAND MORE.
NO, KENICHI.
I DON'T LOVE THE ISLAND.

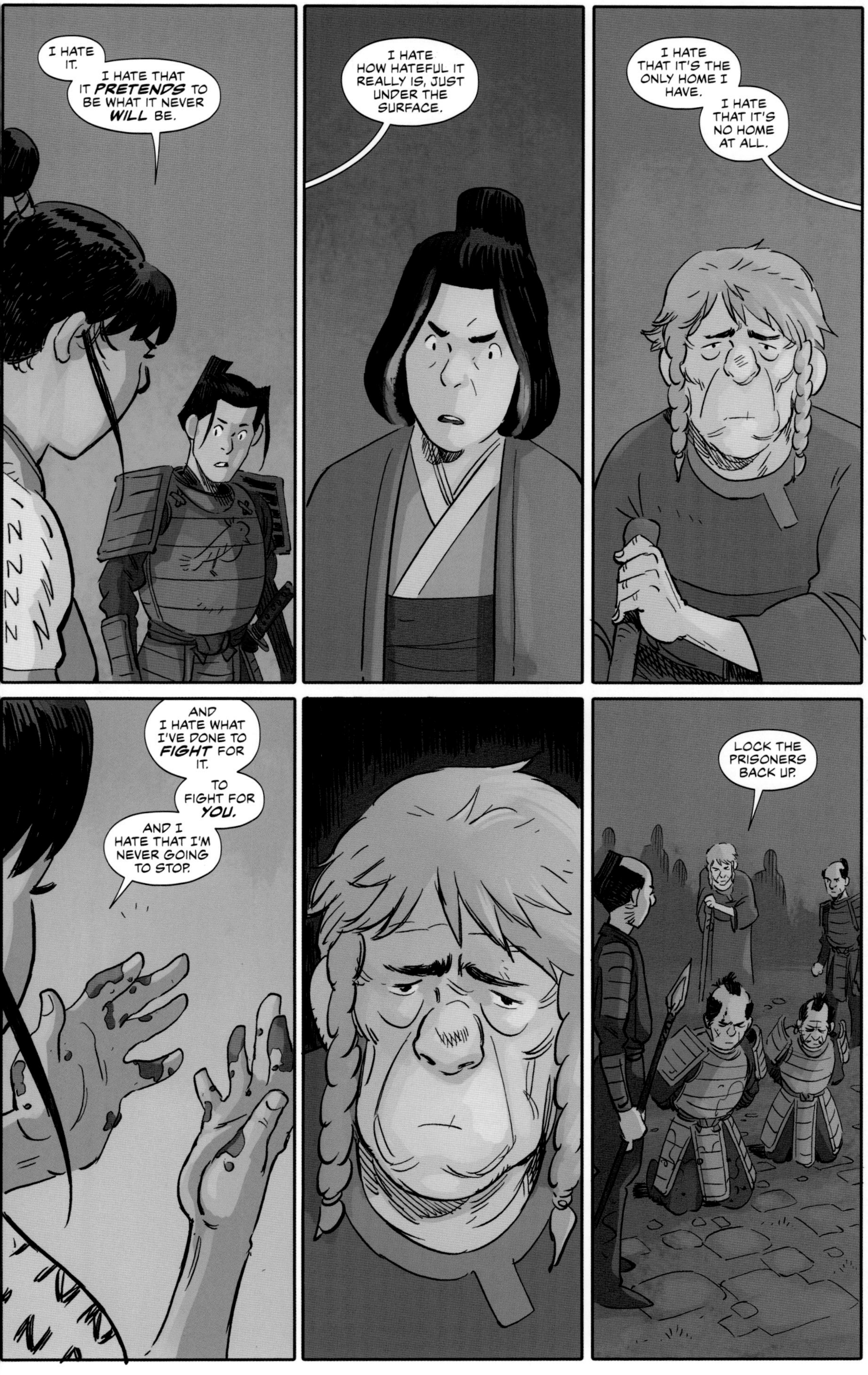
I HATE IT.
I HATE THAT IT PRETENDS TO BE WHAT IT NEVER WILL BE.
I HATE HOW HATEFUL IT REALLY IS, JUST UNDER THE SURFACE.
I HATE THAT IT'S THE ONLY HOME I HAVE.
I HATE THAT IT'S NO HOME AT ALL.
AND I HATE WHAT I'VE DONE TO FIGHT FOR IT.
TO FIGHT FOR YOU.
AND I HATE THAT I'M NEVER GOING TO STOP.
LOCK THE PRISONERS BACK UP.

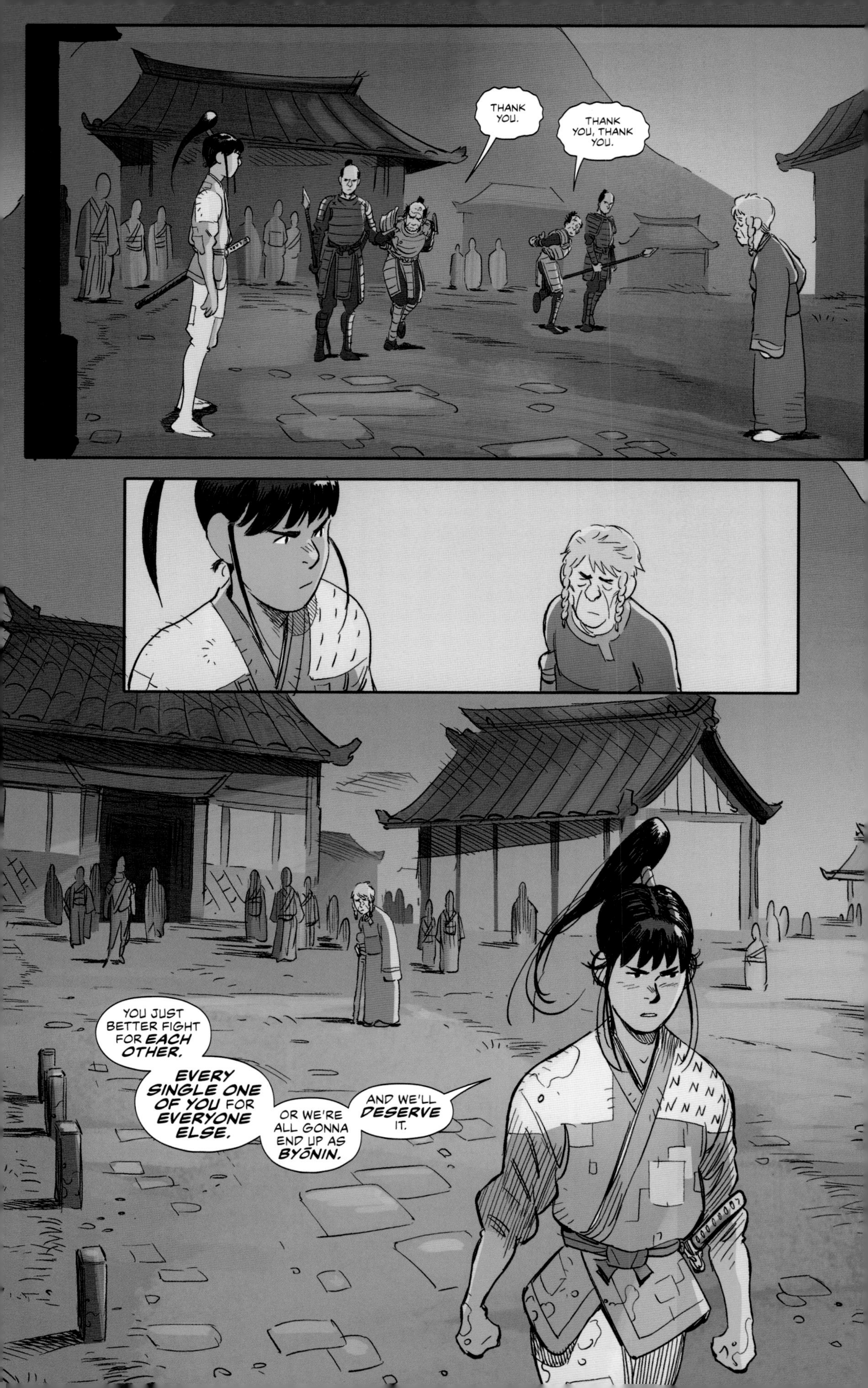
THANK YOU.
THANK YOU, THANK YOU.
YOU JUST BETTER FIGHT FOR **EACH OTHER.**
EVERY SINGLE ONE OF YOU FOR **EVERYONE ELSE.**
OR WE'RE ALL GONNA END UP AS **BYŌNIN.**
AND WE'LL **DESERVE** IT.

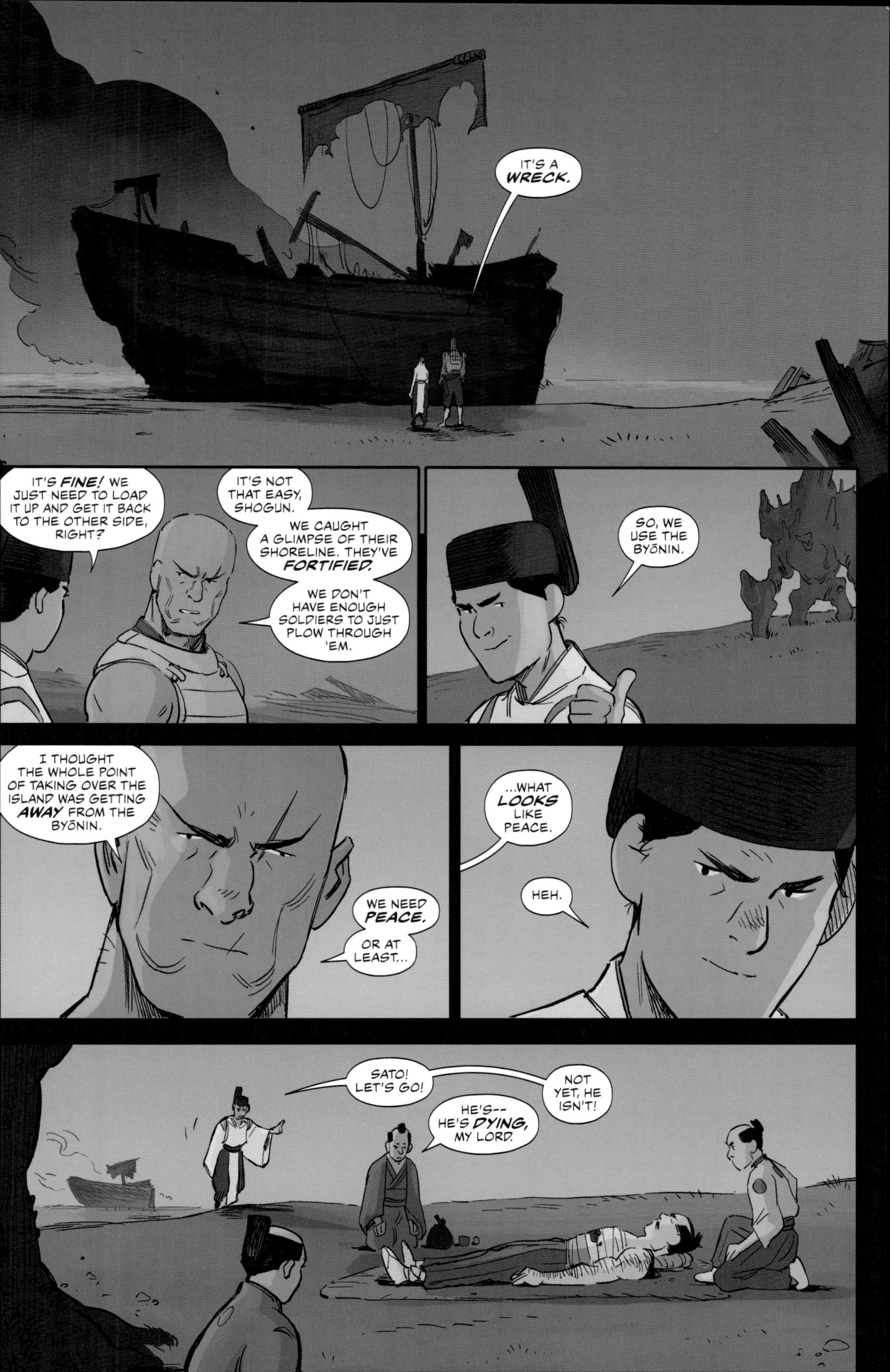
IT'S A WRECK.
IT'S FINE! WE JUST NEED TO LOAD IT UP AND GET IT BACK TO THE OTHER SIDE, RIGHT?
IT'S NOT THAT EASY, SHOGUN.
WE CAUGHT A GLIMPSE OF THEIR SHORELINE. THEY'VE FORTIFIED.
WE DON'T HAVE ENOUGH SOLDIERS TO JUST PLOW THROUGH 'EM.
SO, WE USE THE BYŌNIN.
I THOUGHT THE WHOLE POINT OF TAKING OVER THE ISLAND WAS GETTING AWAY FROM THE BYŌNIN.
WE NEED PEACE.
OR AT LEAST...
...WHAT LOOKS LIKE PEACE.
HEH.
SATO! LET'S GO!
HE'S-- HE'S DYING, MY LORD.
NOT YET, HE ISN'T!

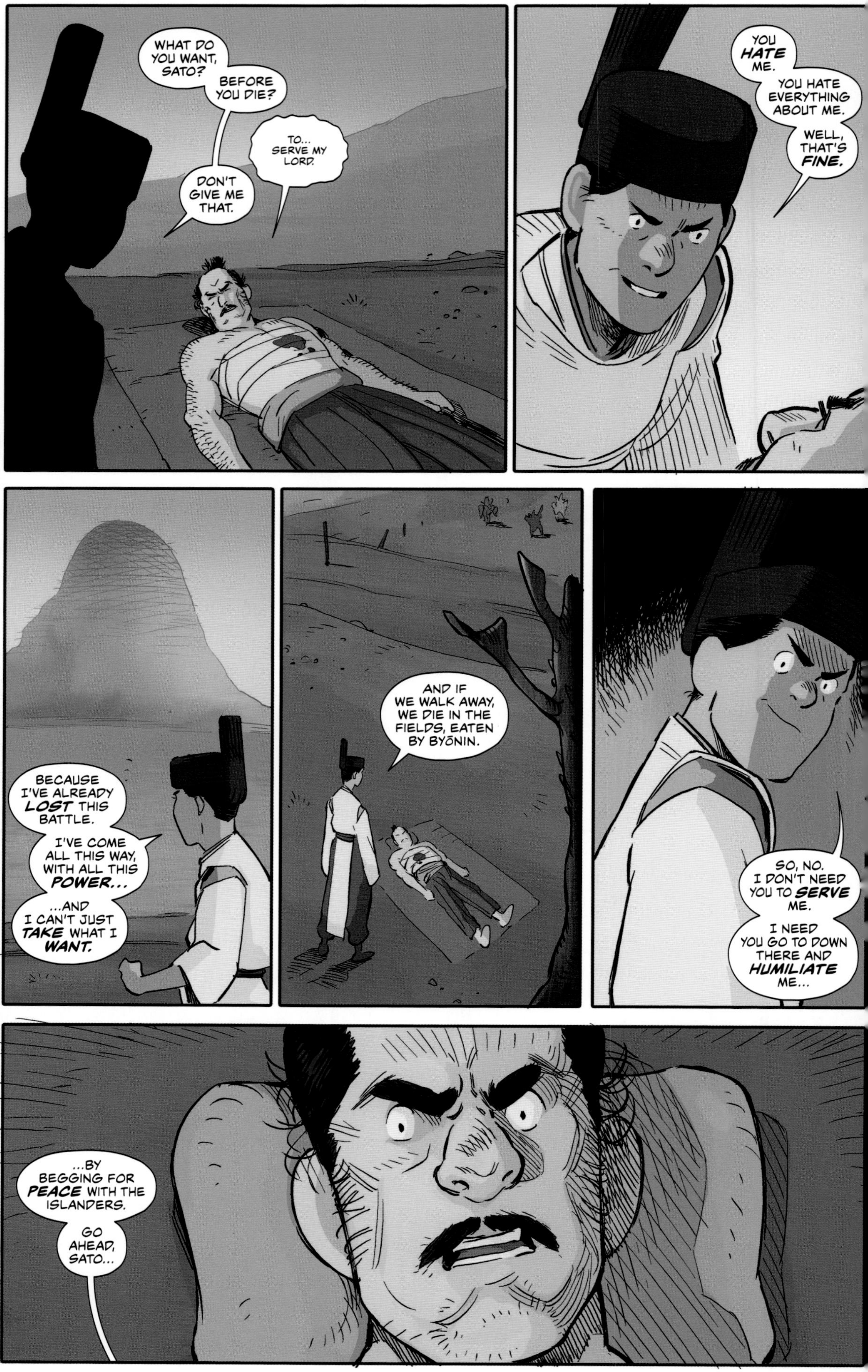
WHAT DO YOU WANT, SATO?
BEFORE YOU DIE?
TO... SERVE MY LORD.
DON'T GIVE ME THAT.
YOU HATE ME.
YOU HATE EVERYTHING ABOUT ME.
WELL, THAT'S FINE.
BECAUSE I'VE ALREADY LOST THIS BATTLE.
I'VE COME ALL THIS WAY, WITH ALL THIS POWER...
...AND I CAN'T JUST TAKE WHAT I WANT.
AND IF WE WALK AWAY, WE DIE IN THE FIELDS, EATEN BY BYŌNIN.
SO, NO. I DON'T NEED YOU TO SERVE ME.
I NEED YOU GO TO DOWN THERE AND HUMILIATE ME...
...BY BEGGING FOR PEACE WITH THE ISLANDERS.
GO AHEAD, SATO...

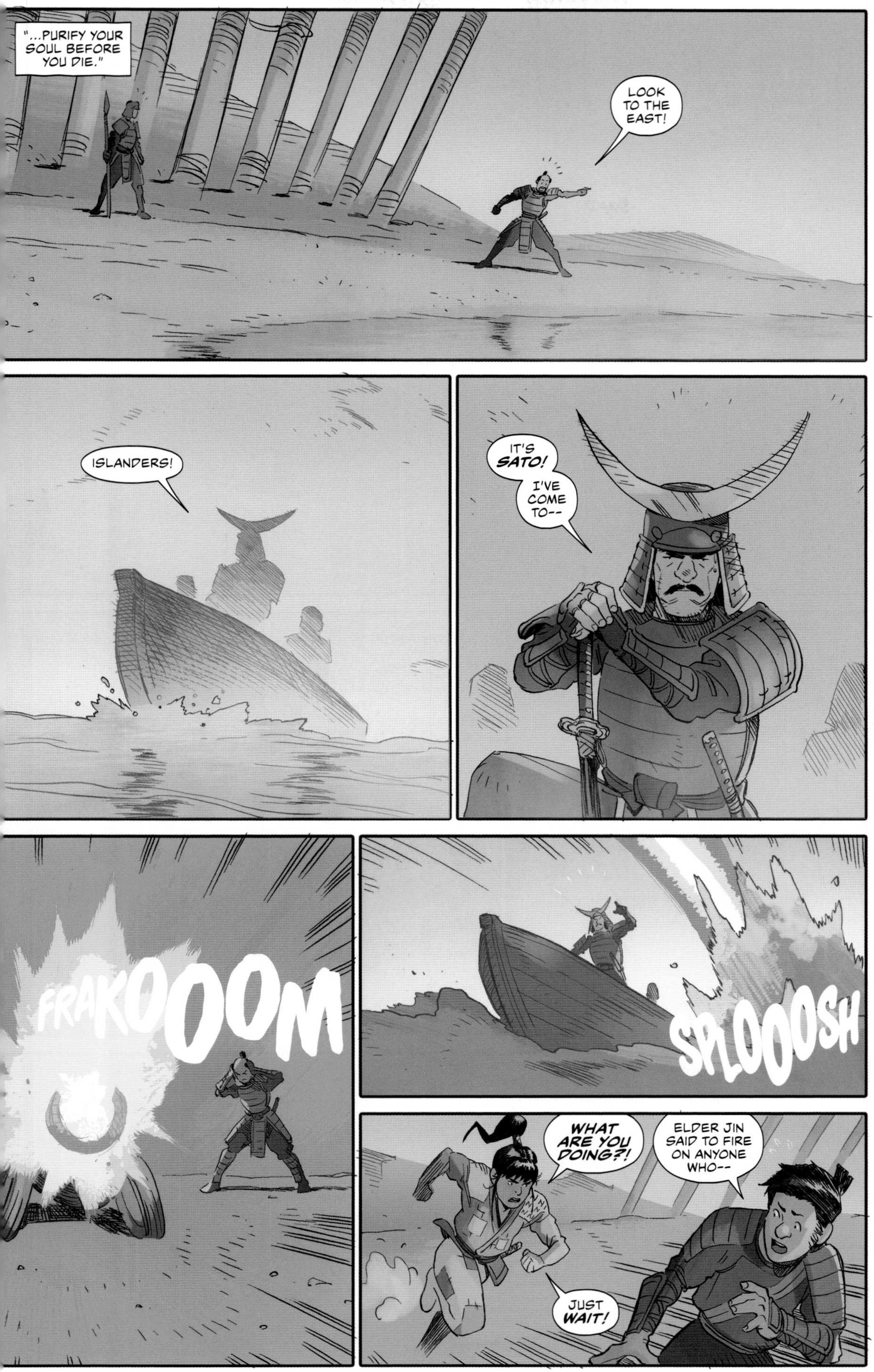
"...PURIFY YOUR SOUL BEFORE YOU DIE."
LOOK TO THE EAST!
ISLANDERS!
IT'S SATO!
I'VE COME TO--
FRAKOOOM
SPLOOOSH
WHAT ARE YOU DOING?!
ELDER JIN SAID TO FIRE ON ANYONE WHO--
JUST WAIT!

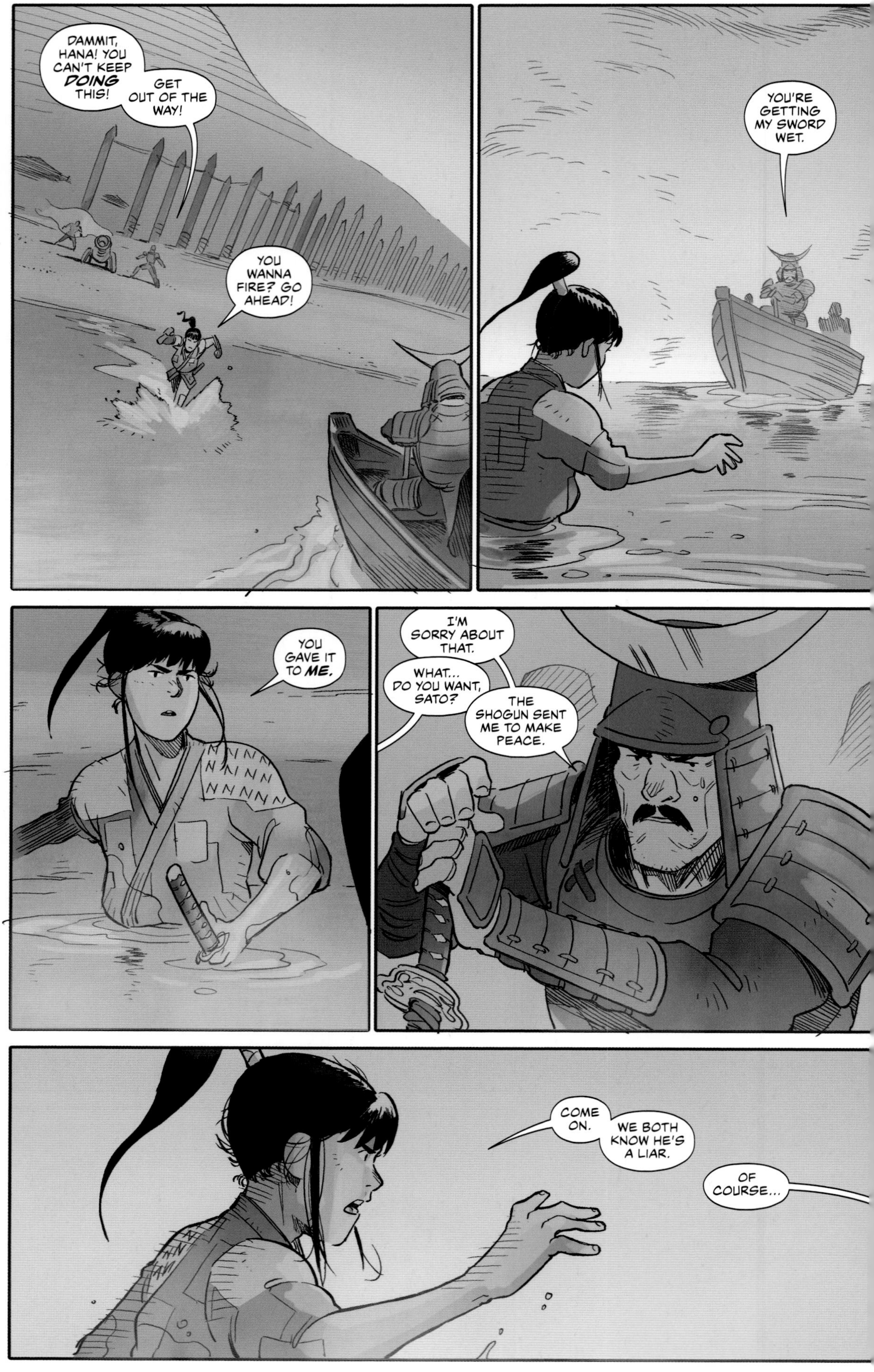
DAMMIT, HANA! YOU CAN'T KEEP ***DOING*** THIS!
GET OUT OF THE WAY!
YOU WANNA FIRE? GO AHEAD!
YOU'RE GETTING MY SWORD WET.
YOU GAVE IT TO ***ME.***
I'M SORRY ABOUT THAT.
WHAT... DO YOU WANT, SATO?
THE SHOGUN SENT ME TO MAKE PEACE.
COME ON.
WE BOTH KNOW HE'S A LIAR.
OF COURSE...

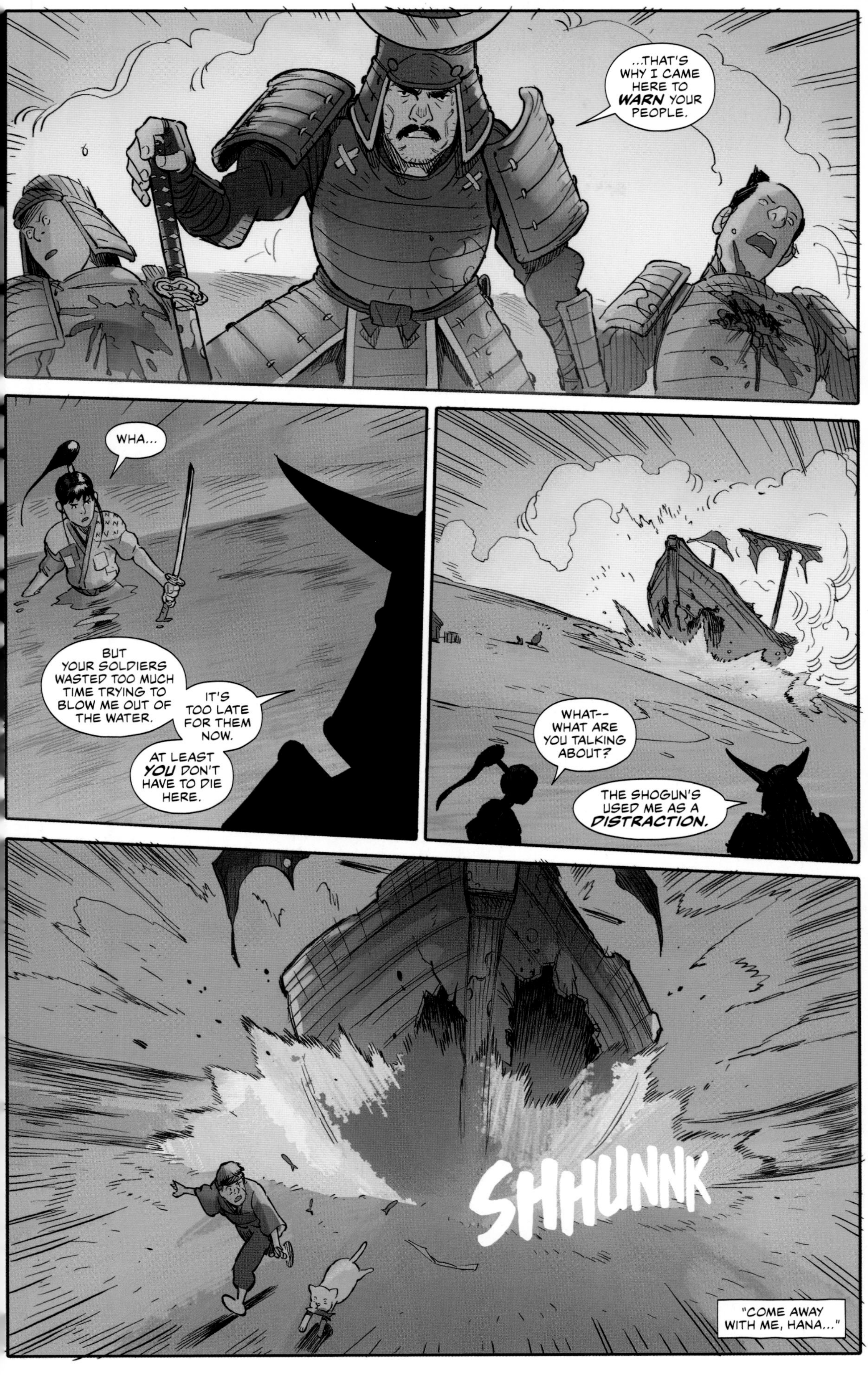
...THAT'S WHY I CAME HERE TO WARN YOUR PEOPLE.
WHA...
BUT YOUR SOLDIERS WASTED TOO MUCH TIME TRYING TO BLOW ME OUT OF THE WATER.
IT'S TOO LATE FOR THEM NOW.
AT LEAST YOU DON'T HAVE TO DIE HERE.
WHAT-- WHAT ARE YOU TALKING ABOUT?
THE SHOGUN'S USED ME AS A DISTRACTION.
SHHUNNK
"COME AWAY WITH ME, HANA..."

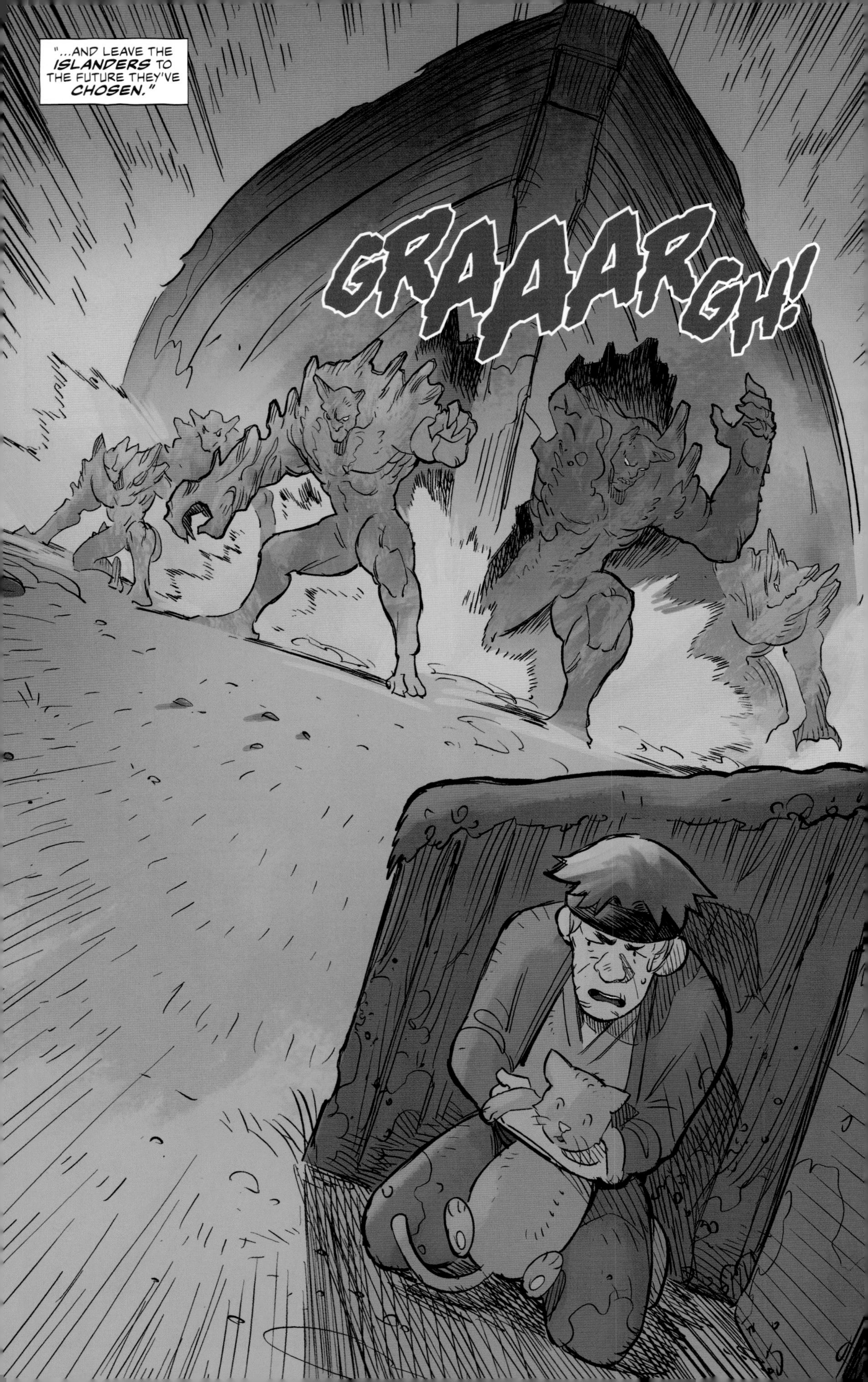
"...AND LEAVE THE ISLANDERS TO THE FUTURE THEY'VE CHOSEN."
GRAAARGH!

Issue Eleven Cover by **Ethan Young**

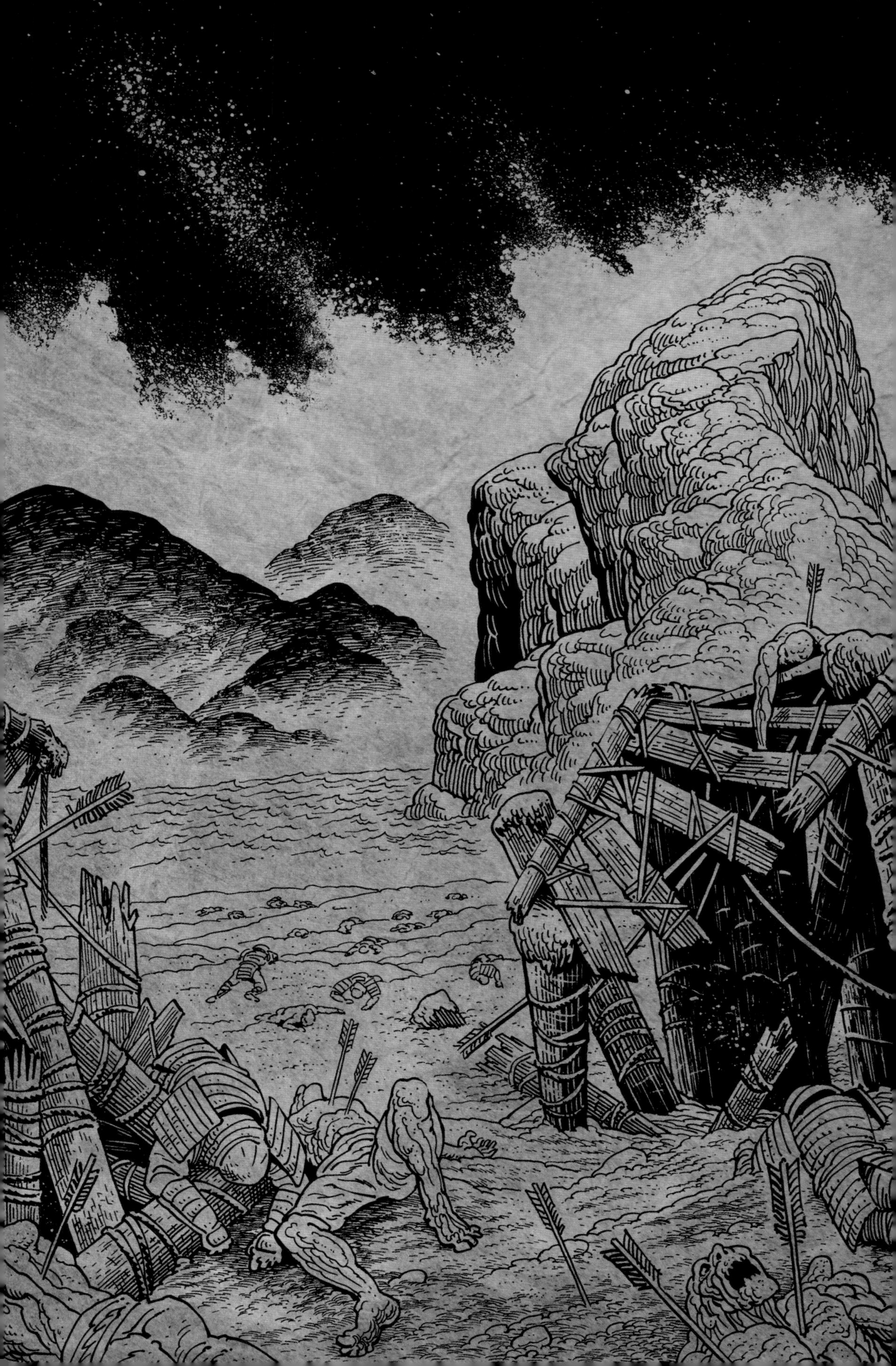

CHAPTER TWELVE

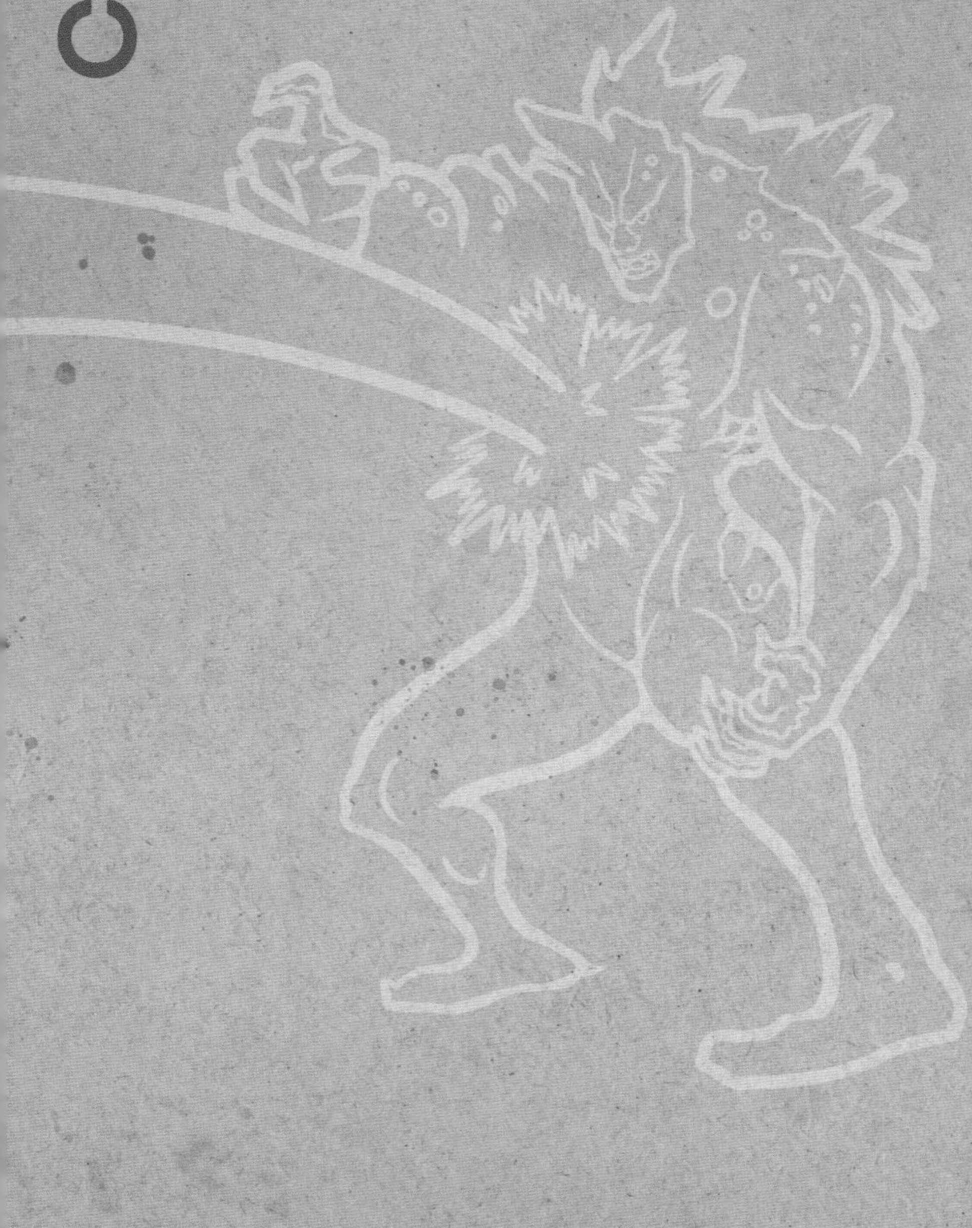

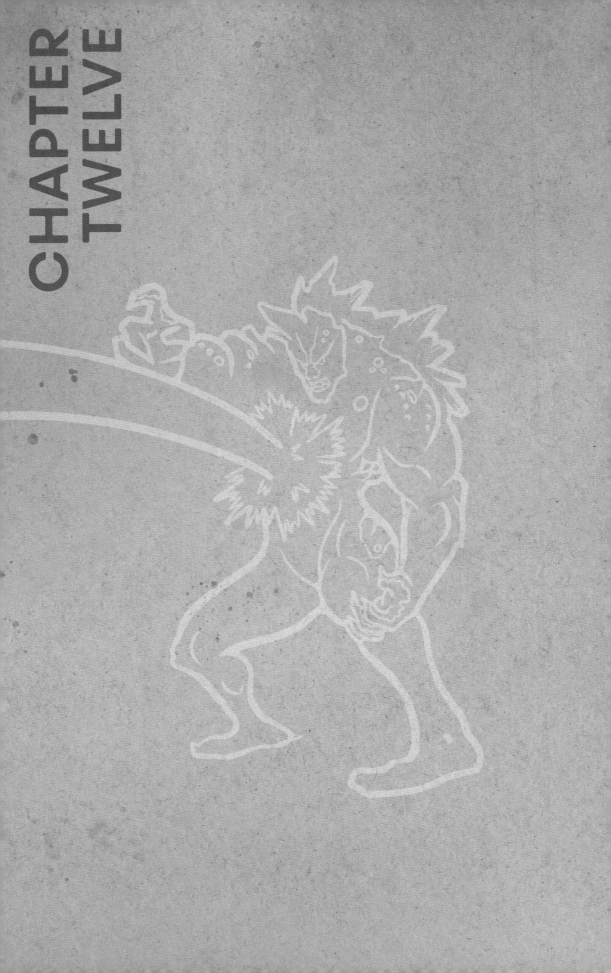

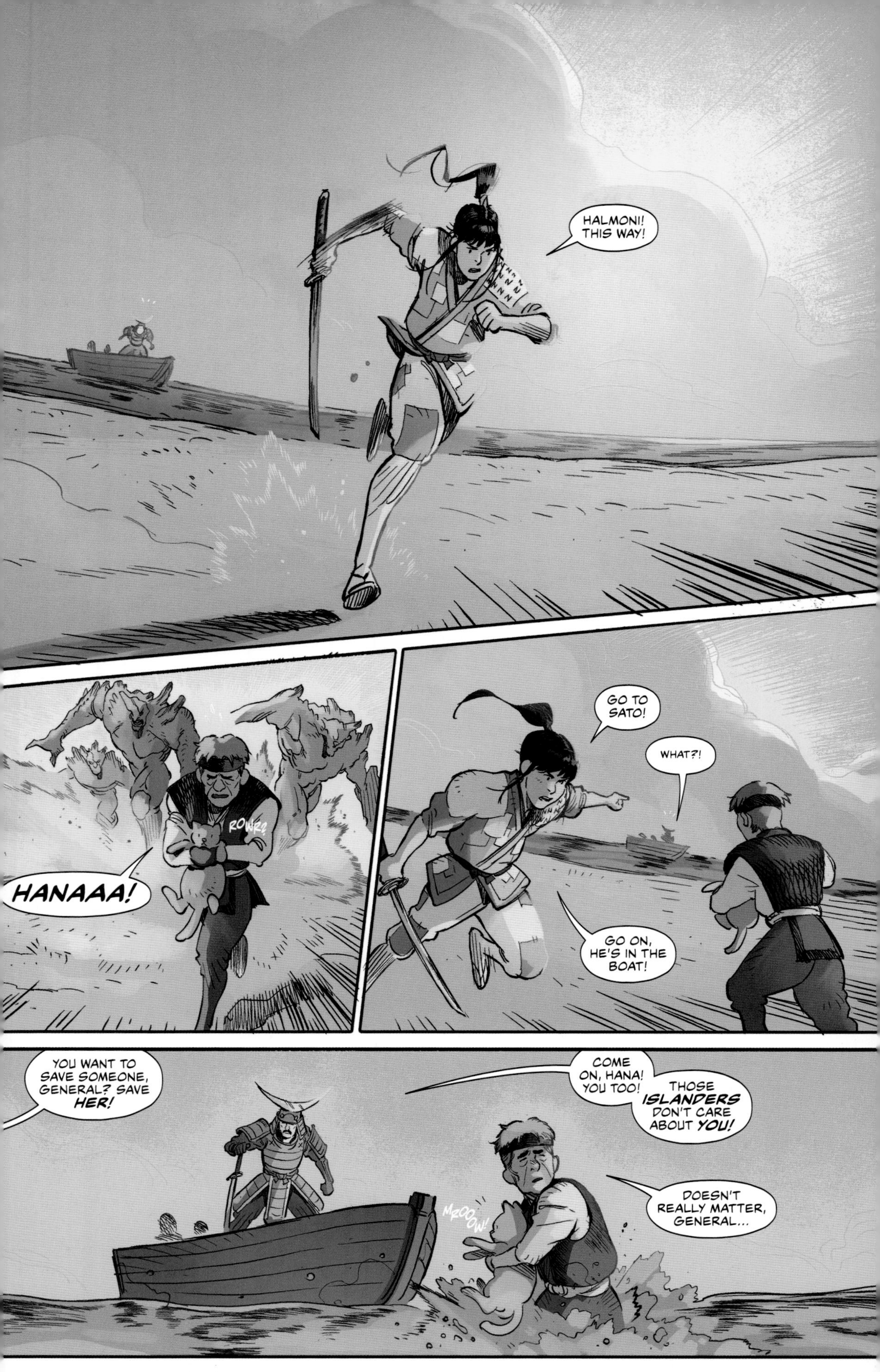
HALMONI! THIS WAY!
ROWR?
HANAAA!
GO TO SATO!
WHAT?!
GO ON, HE'S IN THE BOAT!
YOU WANT TO SAVE SOMEONE, GENERAL? SAVE HER!
COME ON, HANA! YOU TOO!
THOSE ISLANDERS DON'T CARE ABOUT YOU!
MROOOW!
DOESN'T REALLY MATTER, GENERAL...

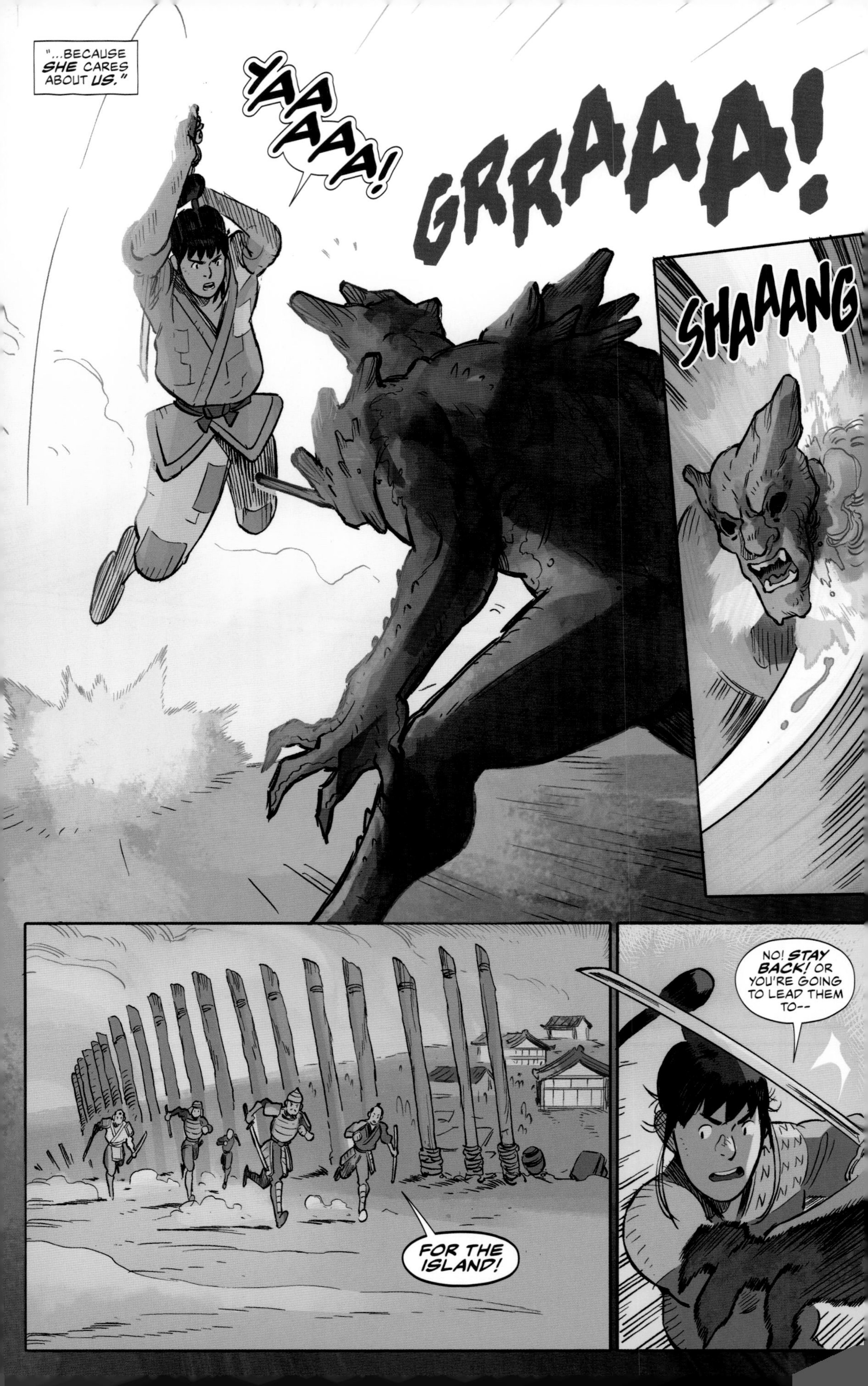
"...BECAUSE SHE CARES ABOUT US."
YAAAAA!
GRRAAAA!
SHAAANG
FOR THE ISLAND!
NO! STAY BACK! OR YOU'RE GOING TO LEAD THEM TO--

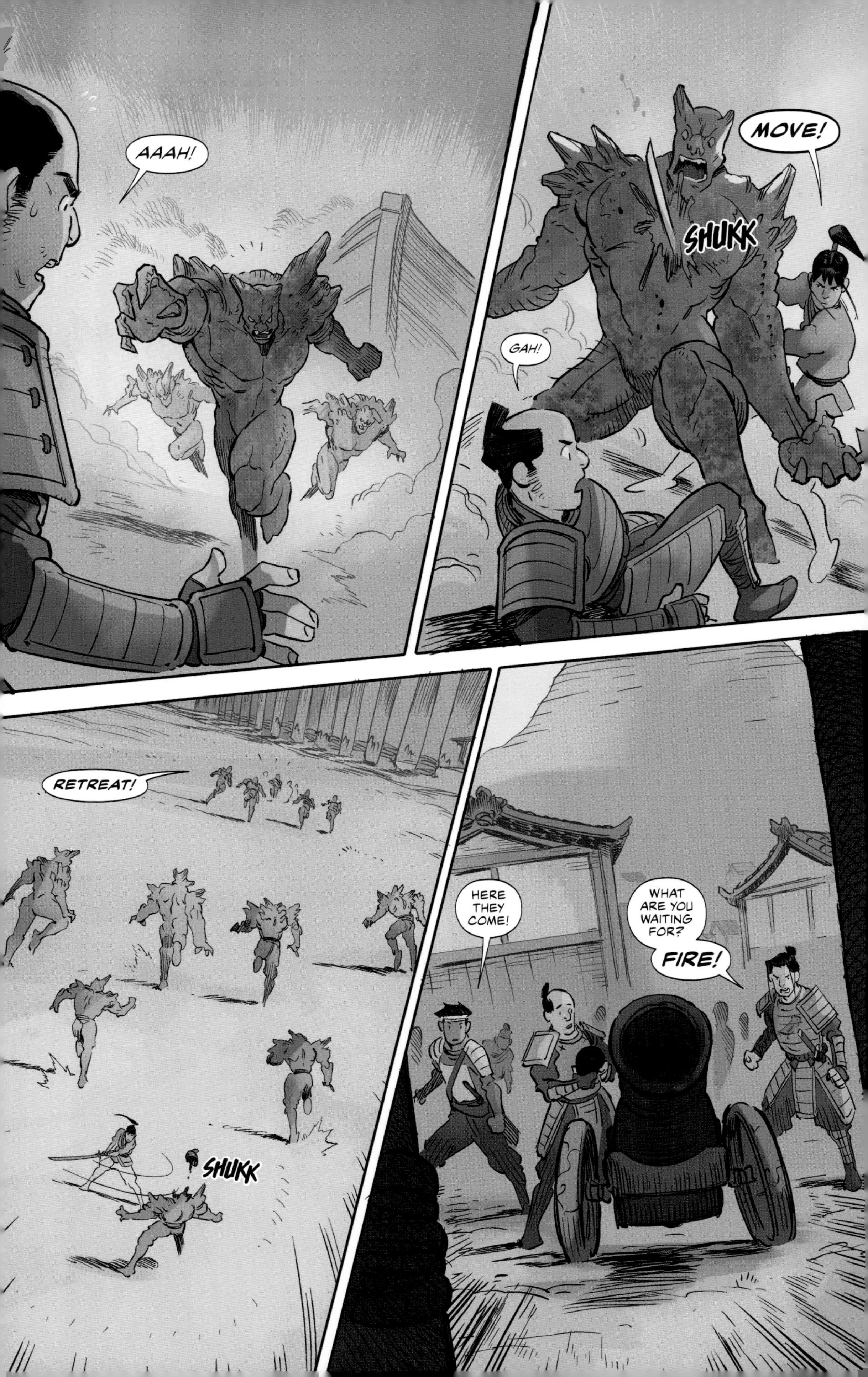
AAAH!
MOVE!
SHUKK
GAH!
RETREAT!
SHUKK
HERE THEY COME!
WHAT ARE YOU WAITING FOR?
FIRE!

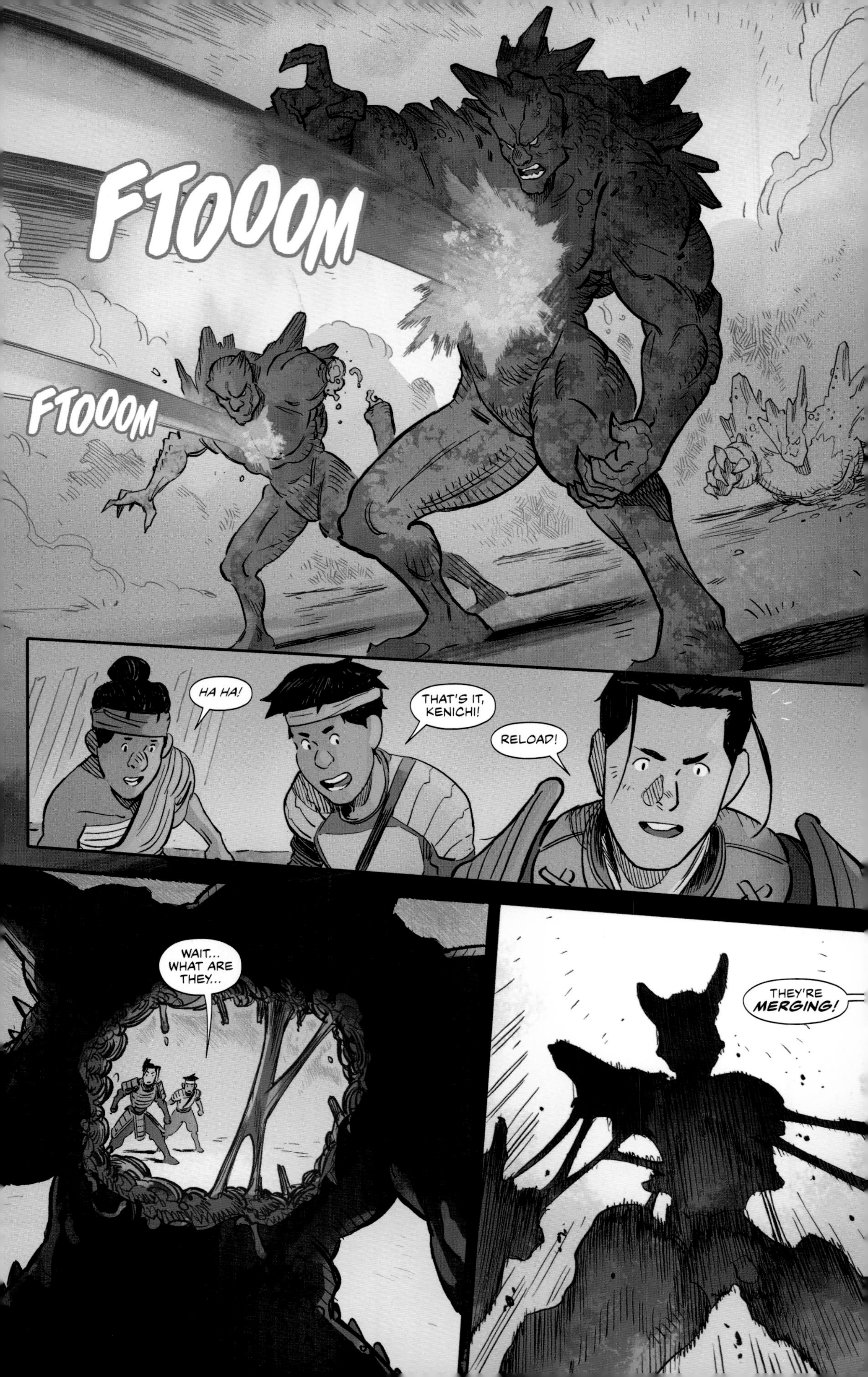
FTOOOM
FTOOOM
HA HA!
THAT'S IT, KENICHI!
RELOAD!
WAIT... WHAT ARE THEY...
THEY'RE *MERGING!*

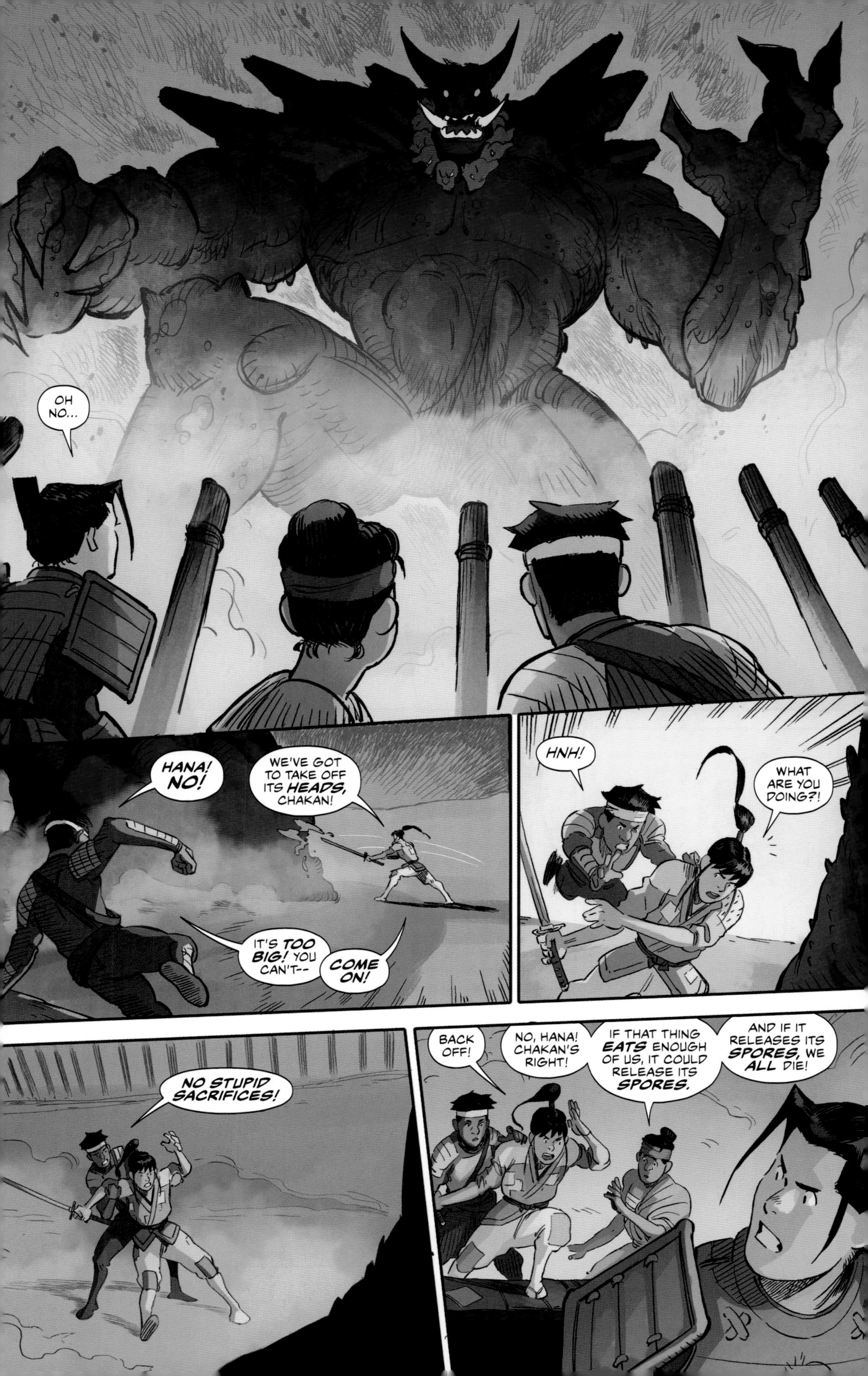
OH NO...
HANA! NO!
WE'VE GOT TO TAKE OFF ITS HEADS, CHAKAN!
IT'S TOO BIG! YOU CAN'T--
COME ON!
HNH!
WHAT ARE YOU DOING?!
NO STUPID SACRIFICES!
BACK OFF!
NO, HANA! CHAKAN'S RIGHT!
IF THAT THING EATS ENOUGH OF US, IT COULD RELEASE ITS SPORES.
AND IF IT RELEASES ITS SPORES, WE ALL DIE!

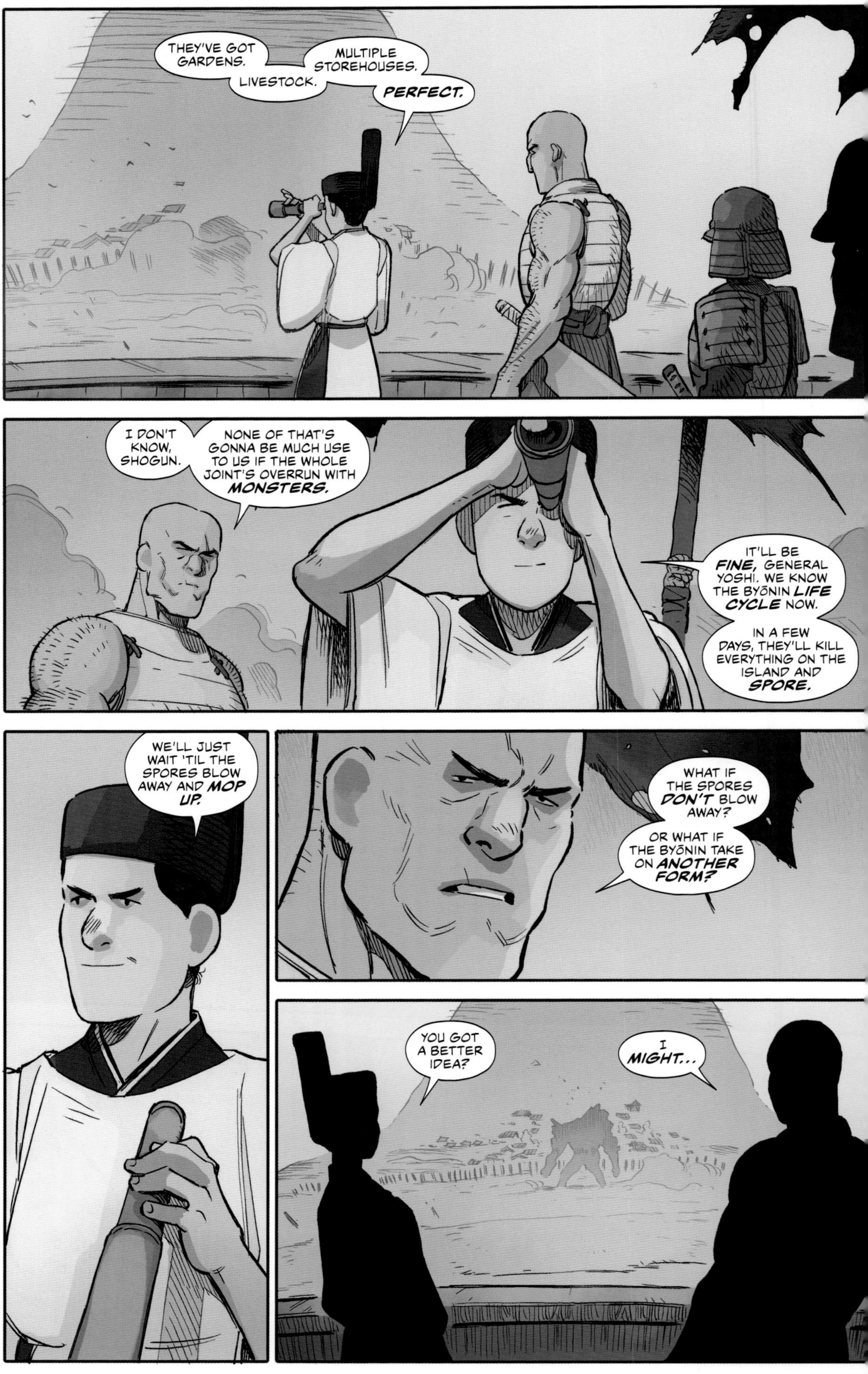

THEY'VE GOT GARDENS.
LIVESTOCK.
MULTIPLE STOREHOUSES.
PERFECT.
I DON'T KNOW, SHOGUN.
NONE OF THAT'S GONNA BE MUCH USE TO US IF THE WHOLE JOINT'S OVERRUN WITH MONSTERS.
IT'LL BE FINE, GENERAL YOSHI. WE KNOW THE BYŌNIN LIFE CYCLE NOW.
IN A FEW DAYS, THEY'LL KILL EVERYTHING ON THE ISLAND AND SPORE.
WE'LL JUST WAIT 'TIL THE SPORES BLOW AWAY AND MOP UP.
WHAT IF THE SPORES DON'T BLOW AWAY?
OR WHAT IF THE BYŌNIN TAKE ON ANOTHER FORM?
YOU GOT A BETTER IDEA?
I MIGHT...

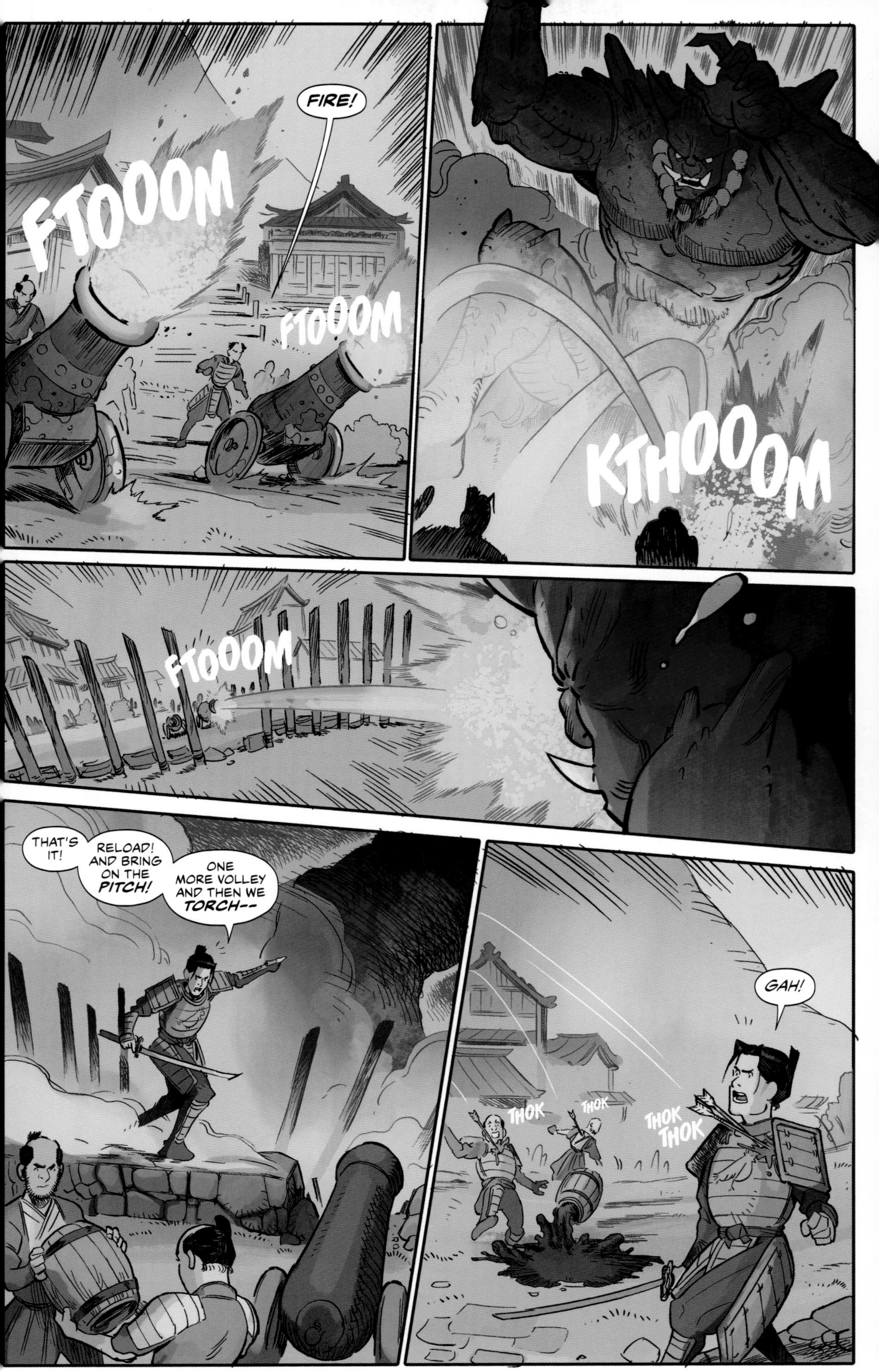
FIRE!
FTOOOM
FTOOOM
KTHOOOOM
FTOOOM
THAT'S IT!
RELOAD! AND BRING ON THE PITCH!
ONE MORE VOLLEY AND THEN WE TORCH--
GAH!
THOK
THOK
THOK THOK

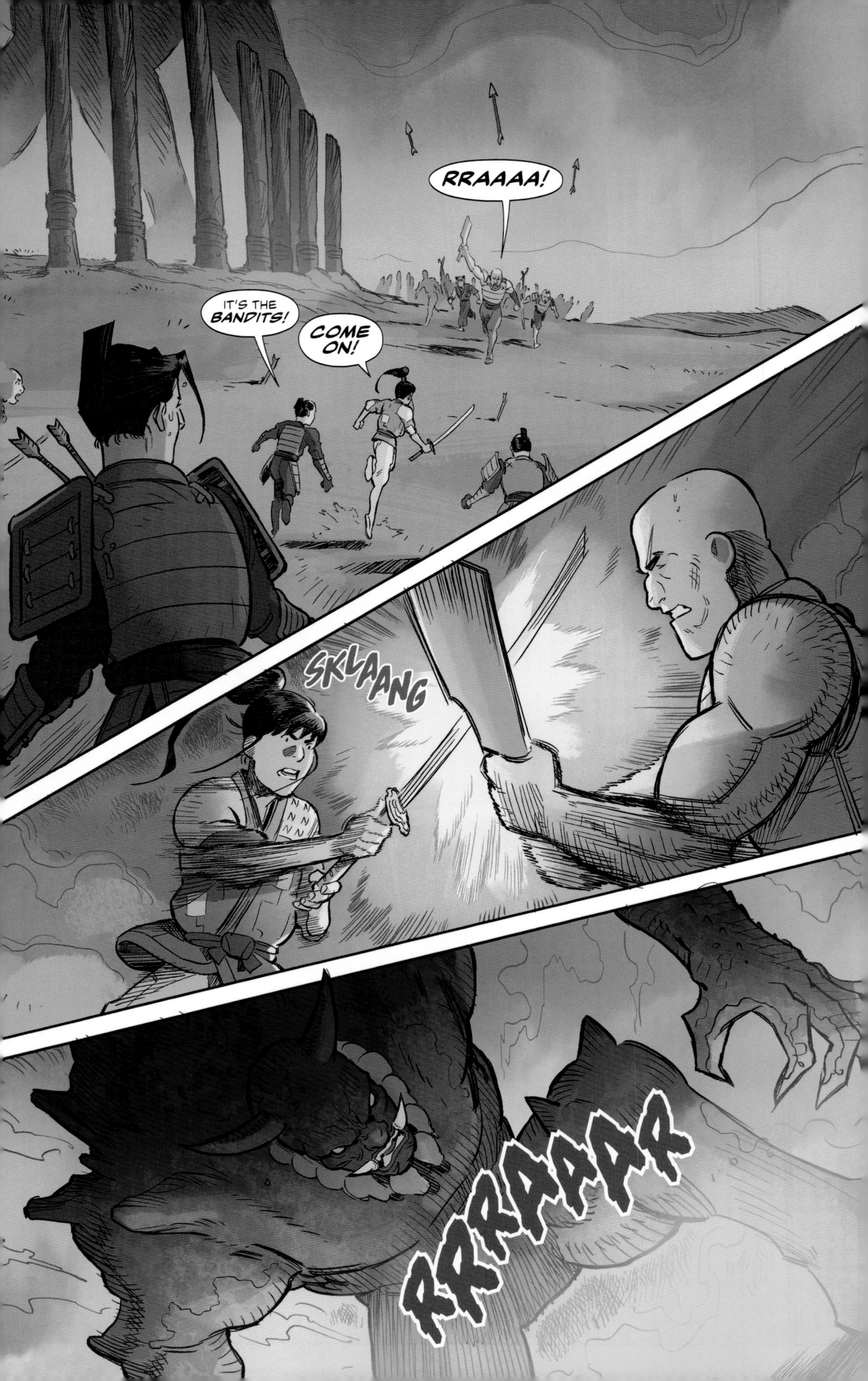
RRAAAA!
IT'S THE BANDITS!
COME ON!
SKLAAANG
RRRAAAAR

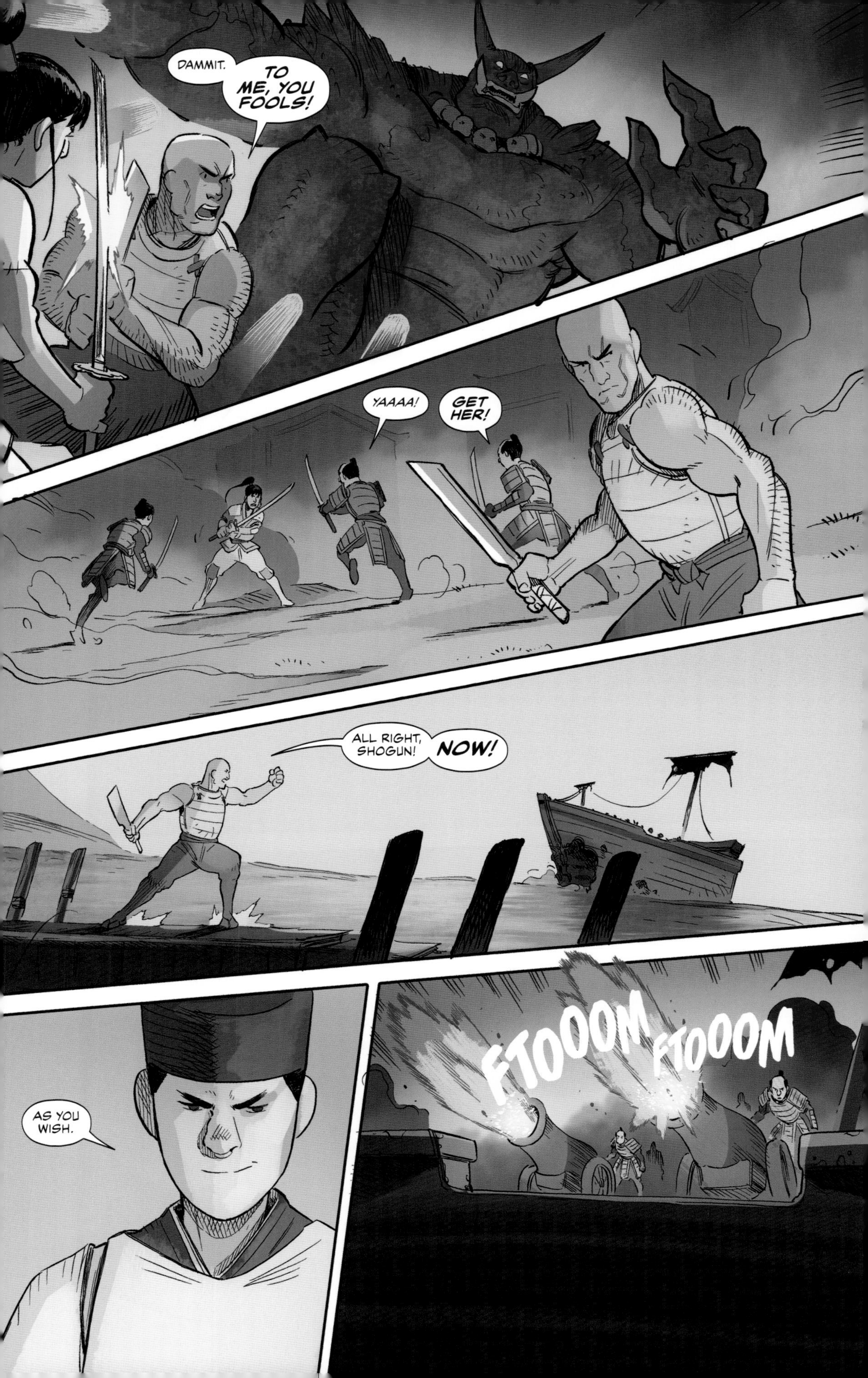
DAMMIT.
TO ME, YOU FOOLS!
YAAAA!
GET HER!
ALL RIGHT, SHOGUN!
NOW!
AS YOU WISH.
FTOOOM
FTOOOM

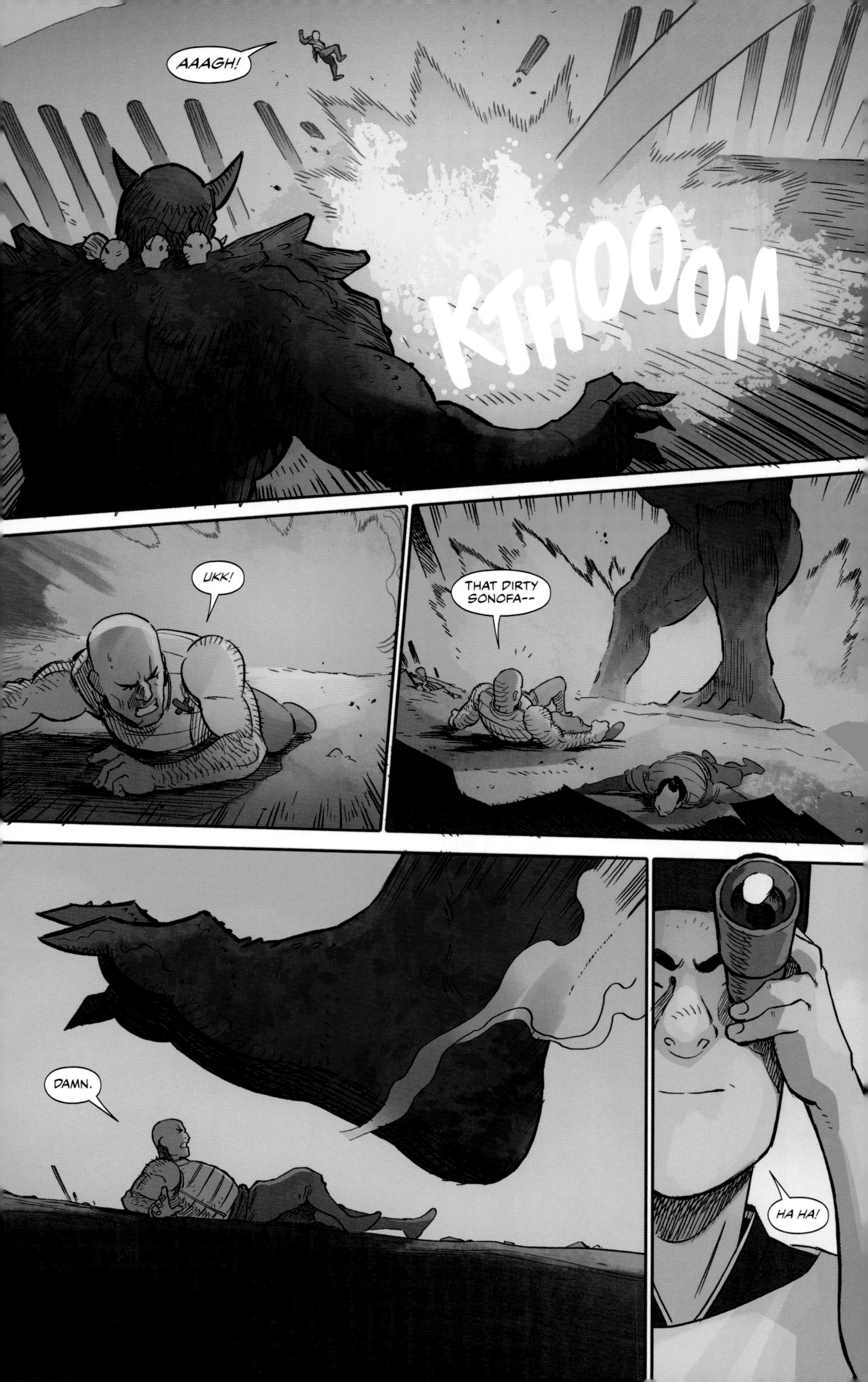
AAAGH!
KTHOOOOM
UKK!
THAT DIRTY SONOFA--
DAMN.
HA HA!

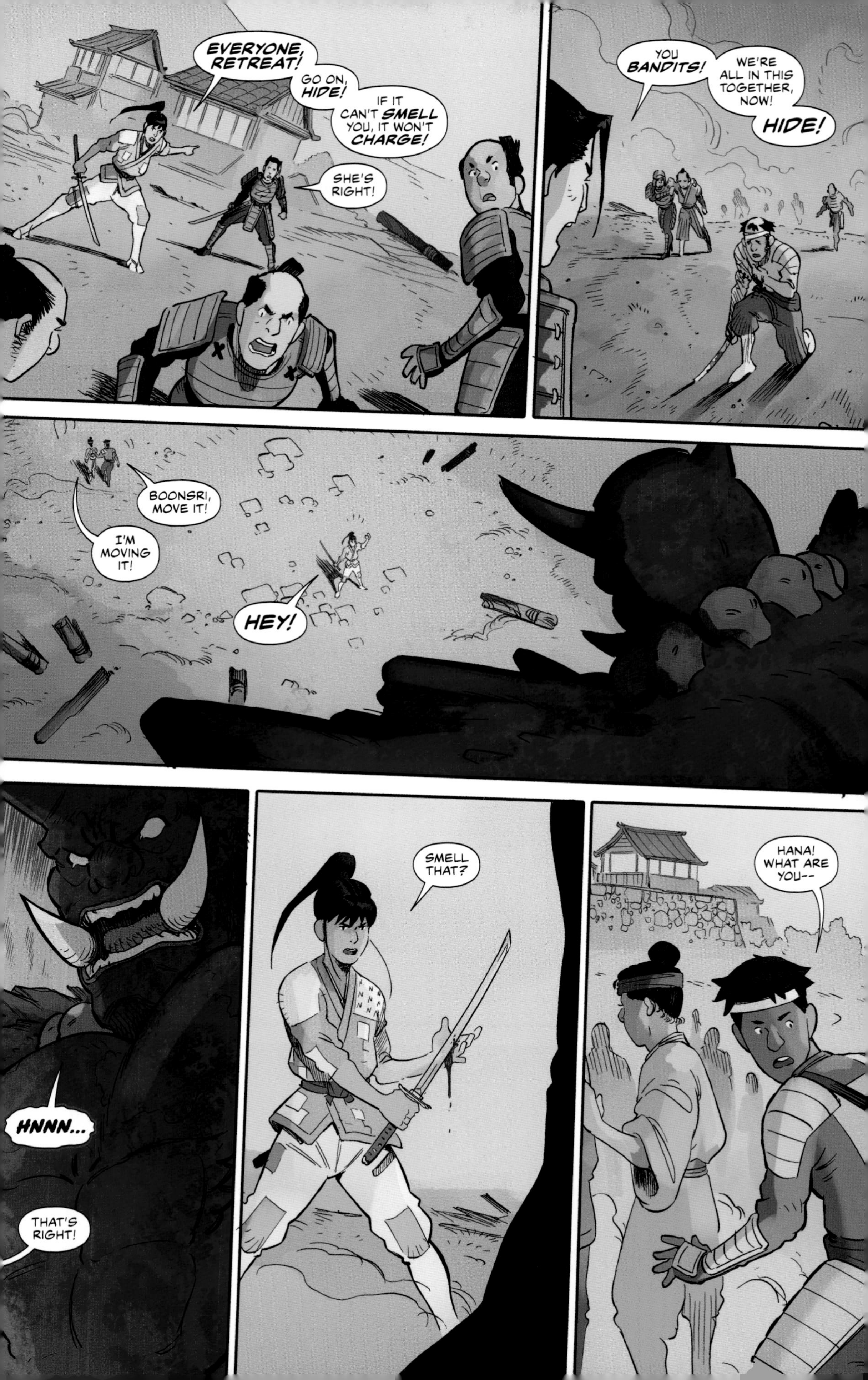
EVERYONE, RETREAT!
GO ON, HIDE!
IF IT CAN'T SMELL YOU, IT WON'T CHARGE!
SHE'S RIGHT!
YOU BANDITS!
WE'RE ALL IN THIS TOGETHER, NOW!
HIDE!
BOONSRI, MOVE IT!
I'M MOVING IT!
HEY!
HNNN...
THAT'S RIGHT!
SMELL THAT?
HANA! WHAT ARE YOU--

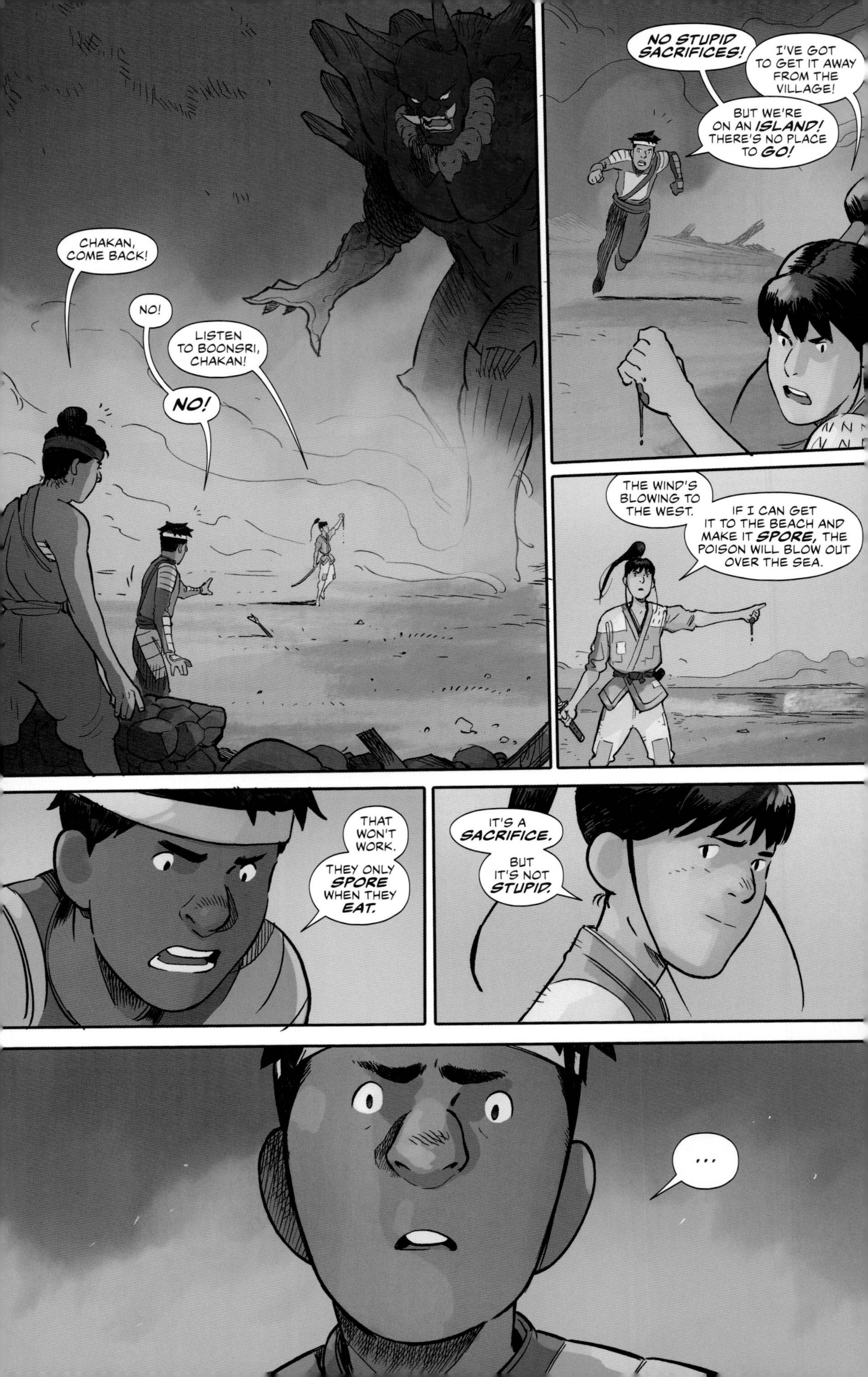
CHAKAN, COME BACK!
NO!
LISTEN TO BOONSRI, CHAKAN!
NO!
NO STUPID SACRIFICES!
I'VE GOT TO GET IT AWAY FROM THE VILLAGE!
BUT WE'RE ON AN ISLAND! THERE'S NO PLACE TO GO!
THE WIND'S BLOWING TO THE WEST.
IF I CAN GET IT TO THE BEACH AND MAKE IT SPORE, THE POISON WILL BLOW OUT OVER THE SEA.
THAT WON'T WORK.
THEY ONLY SPORE WHEN THEY EAT.
IT'S A SACRIFICE.
BUT IT'S NOT STUPID.
...

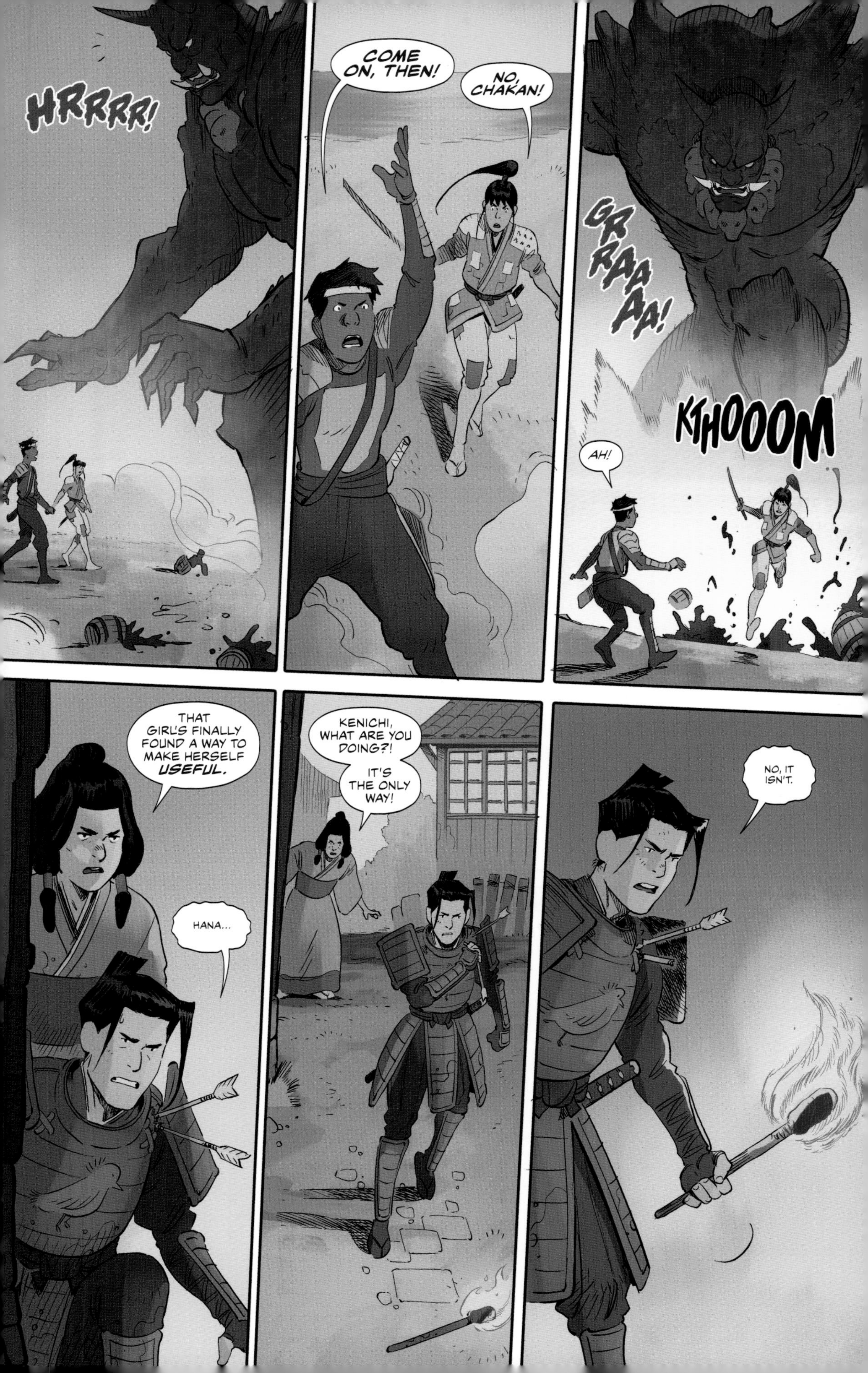
HRRRR!
COME ON, THEN!
NO, CHAKAN!
GRRAAAA!
KTHOOOM
AH!
THAT GIRL'S FINALLY FOUND A WAY TO MAKE HERSELF USEFUL.
HANA...
KENICHI, WHAT ARE YOU DOING?!
IT'S THE ONLY WAY!
NO, IT ISN'T.

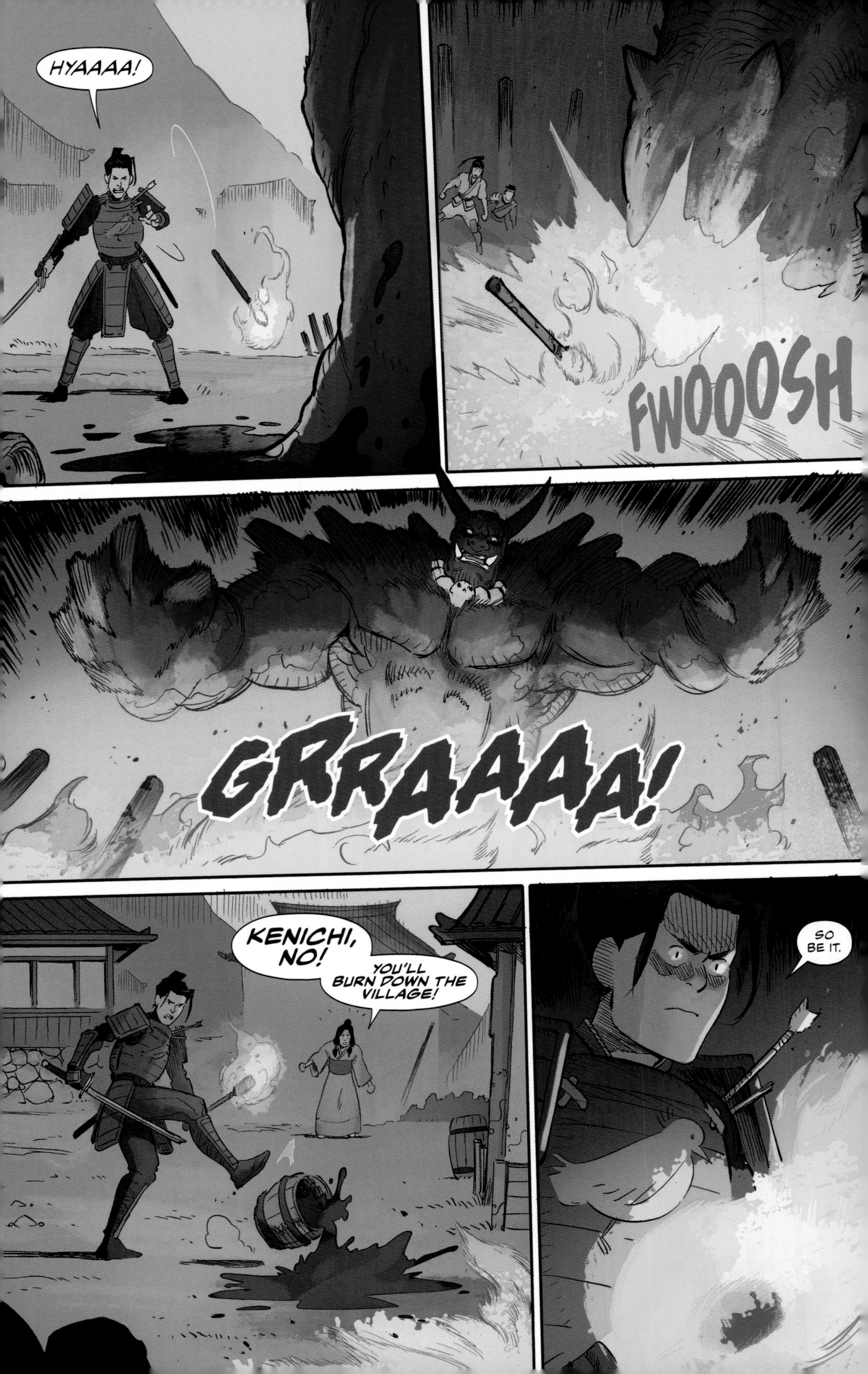
HYAAAA!
FWOOOSH
GRRAAAA!
KENICHI, NO!
YOU'LL BURN DOWN THE VILLAGE!
SO BE IT.

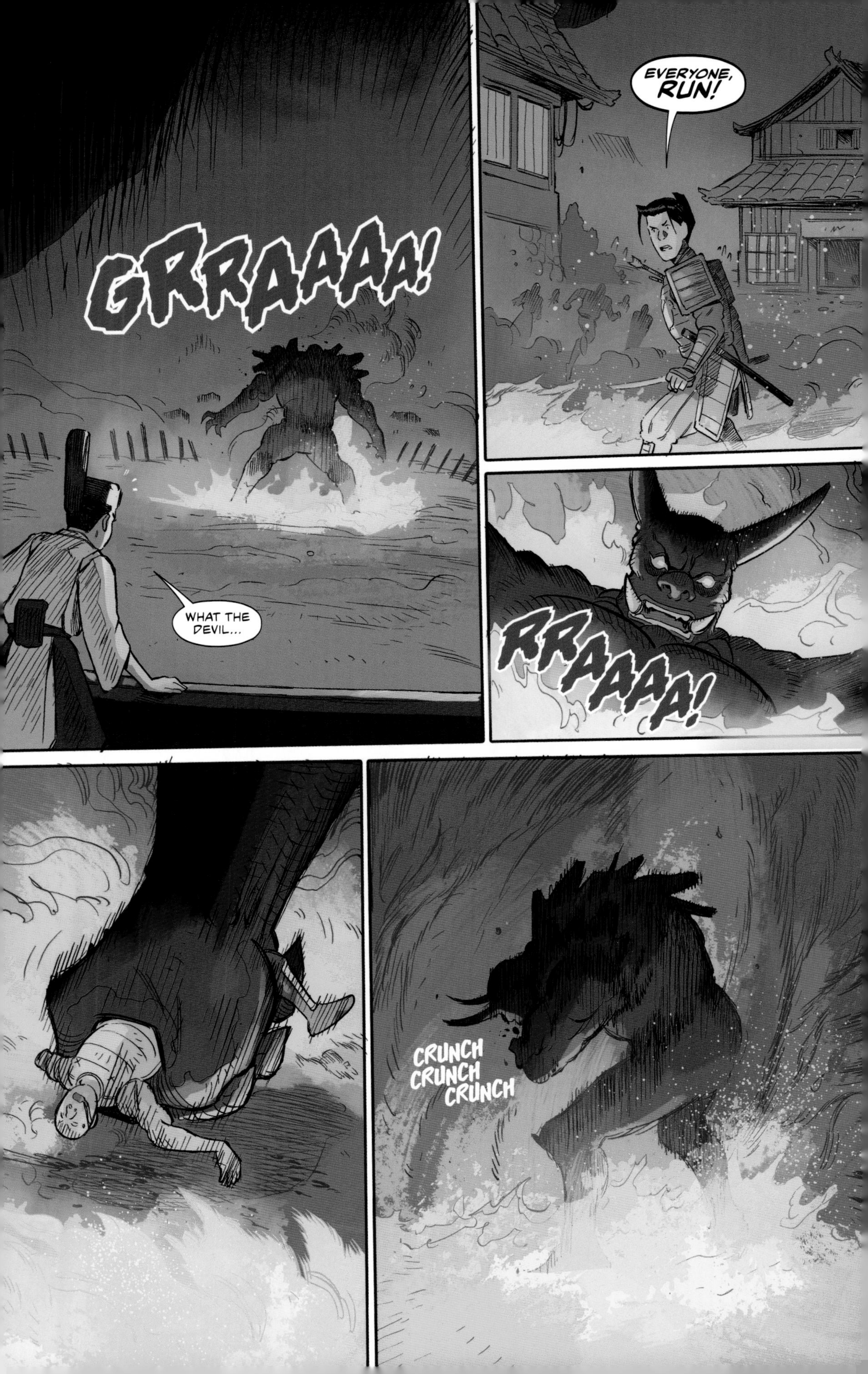
GRRAAAA!
WHAT THE DEVIL...
EVERYONE, RUN!
RRAAAAA!
CRUNCH CRUNCH CRUNCH

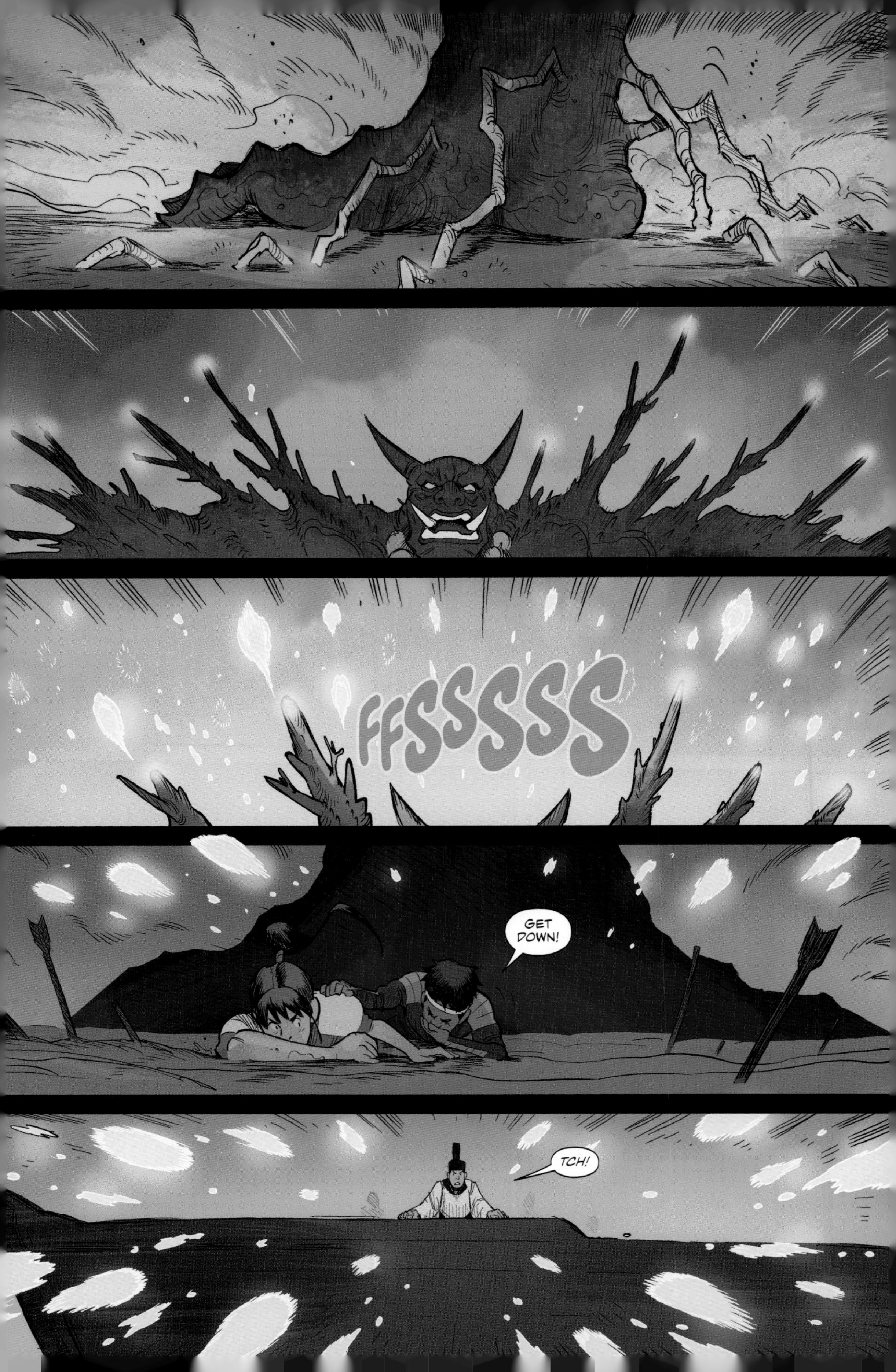
FFSSSSSS
GET DOWN!
TCH!

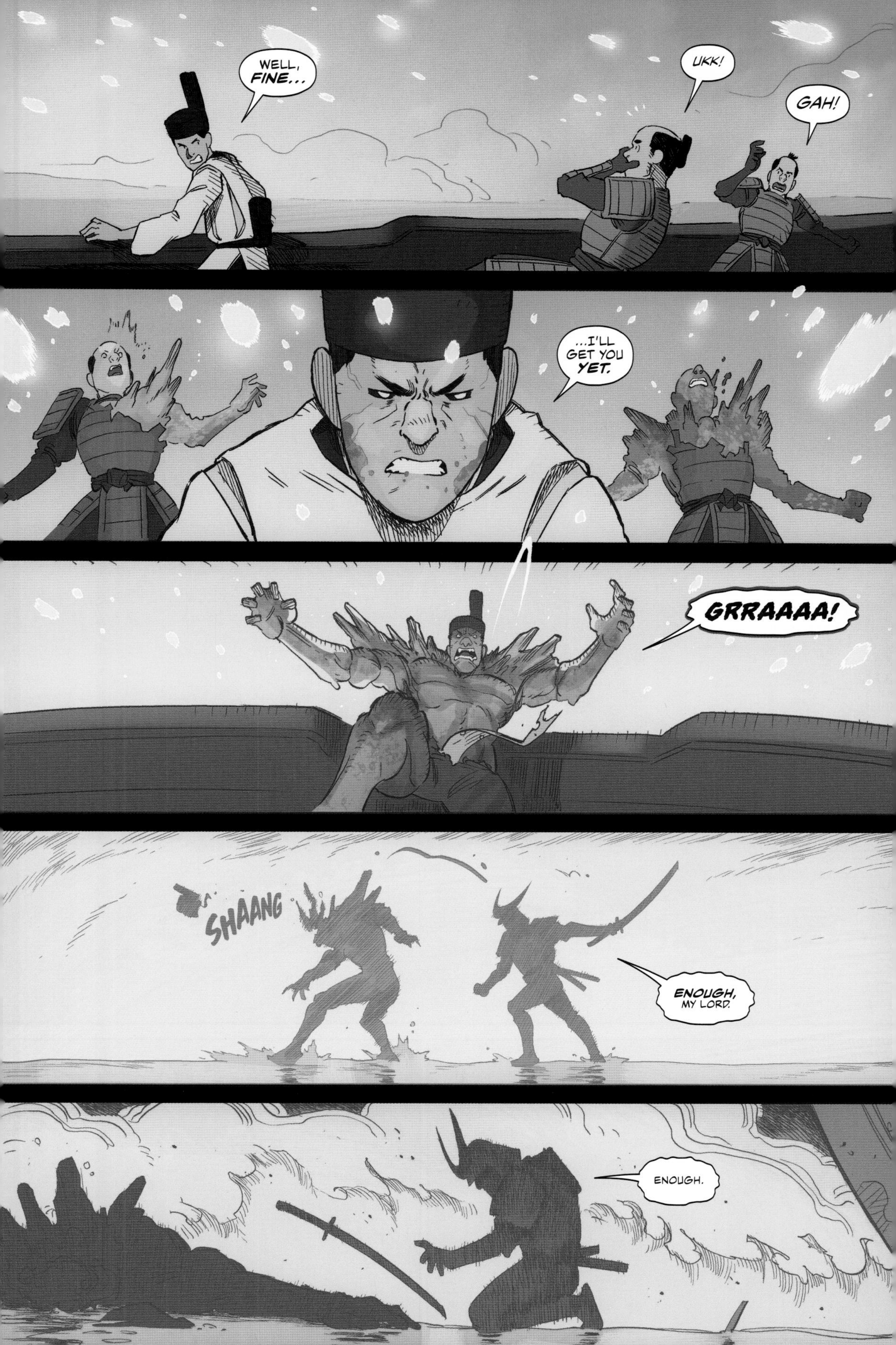
WELL, FINE...
UKK!
GAH!
...I'LL GET YOU YET.
GRRAAAA!
SHAANG
ENOUGH, MY LORD.
ENOUGH.

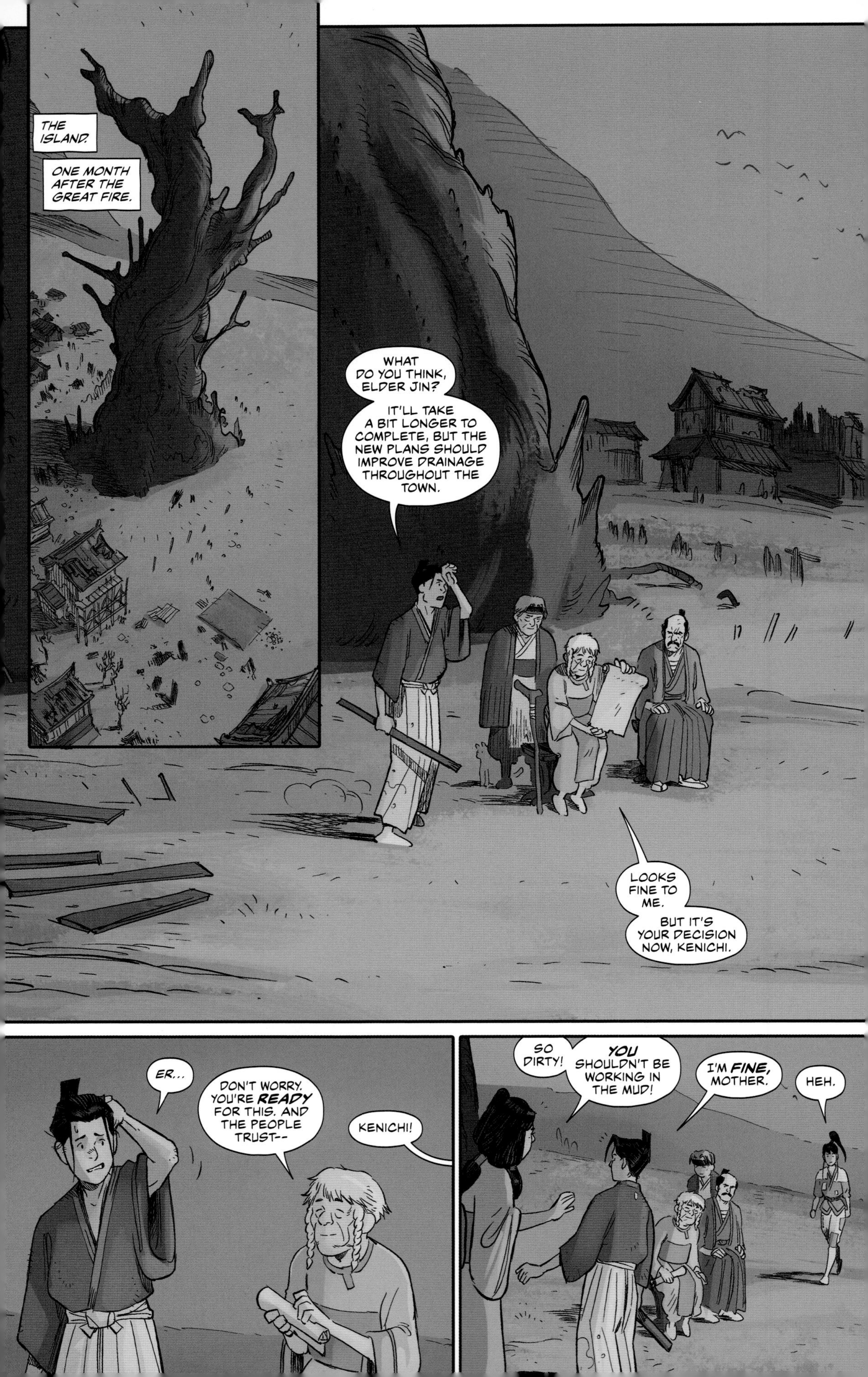
THE ISLAND.
ONE MONTH AFTER THE GREAT FIRE.
WHAT DO YOU THINK, ELDER JIN?
IT'LL TAKE A BIT LONGER TO COMPLETE, BUT THE NEW PLANS SHOULD IMPROVE DRAINAGE THROUGHOUT THE TOWN.
LOOKS FINE TO ME.
BUT IT'S YOUR DECISION NOW, KENICHI.
ER...
DON'T WORRY. YOU'RE READY FOR THIS. AND THE PEOPLE TRUST--
KENICHI!
SO DIRTY!
YOU SHOULDN'T BE WORKING IN THE MUD!
I'M FINE, MOTHER.
HEH.

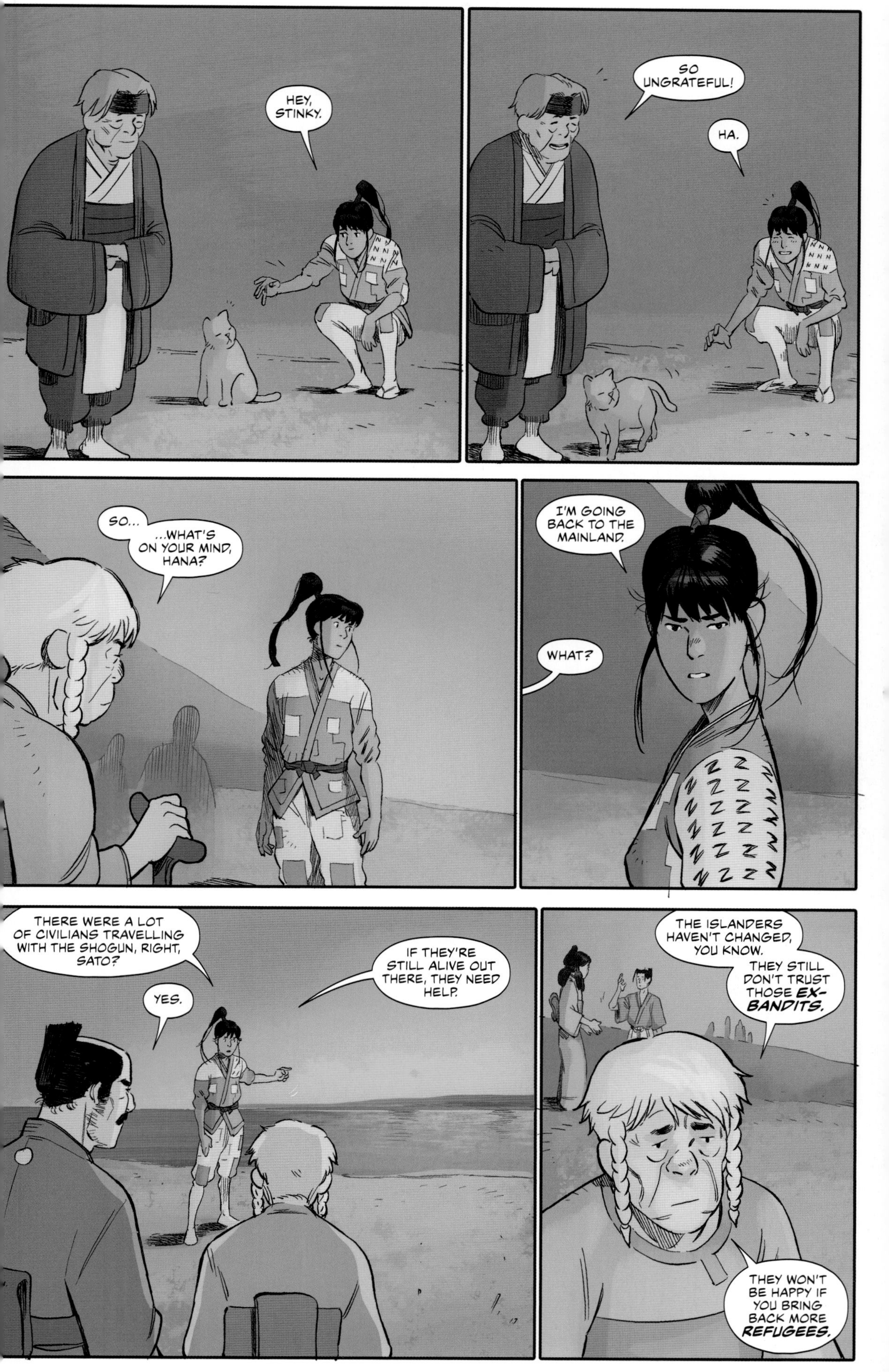
HEY, STINKY.
SO UNGRATEFUL!
HA.
SO...
...WHAT'S ON YOUR MIND, HANA?
I'M GOING BACK TO THE MAINLAND.
WHAT?
THERE WERE A LOT OF CIVILIANS TRAVELLING WITH THE SHOGUN, RIGHT, SATO?
YES.
IF THEY'RE STILL ALIVE OUT THERE, THEY NEED HELP.
THE ISLANDERS HAVEN'T CHANGED, YOU KNOW.
THEY STILL DON'T TRUST THOSE EX-BANDITS.
THEY WON'T BE HAPPY IF YOU BRING BACK MORE REFUGEES.

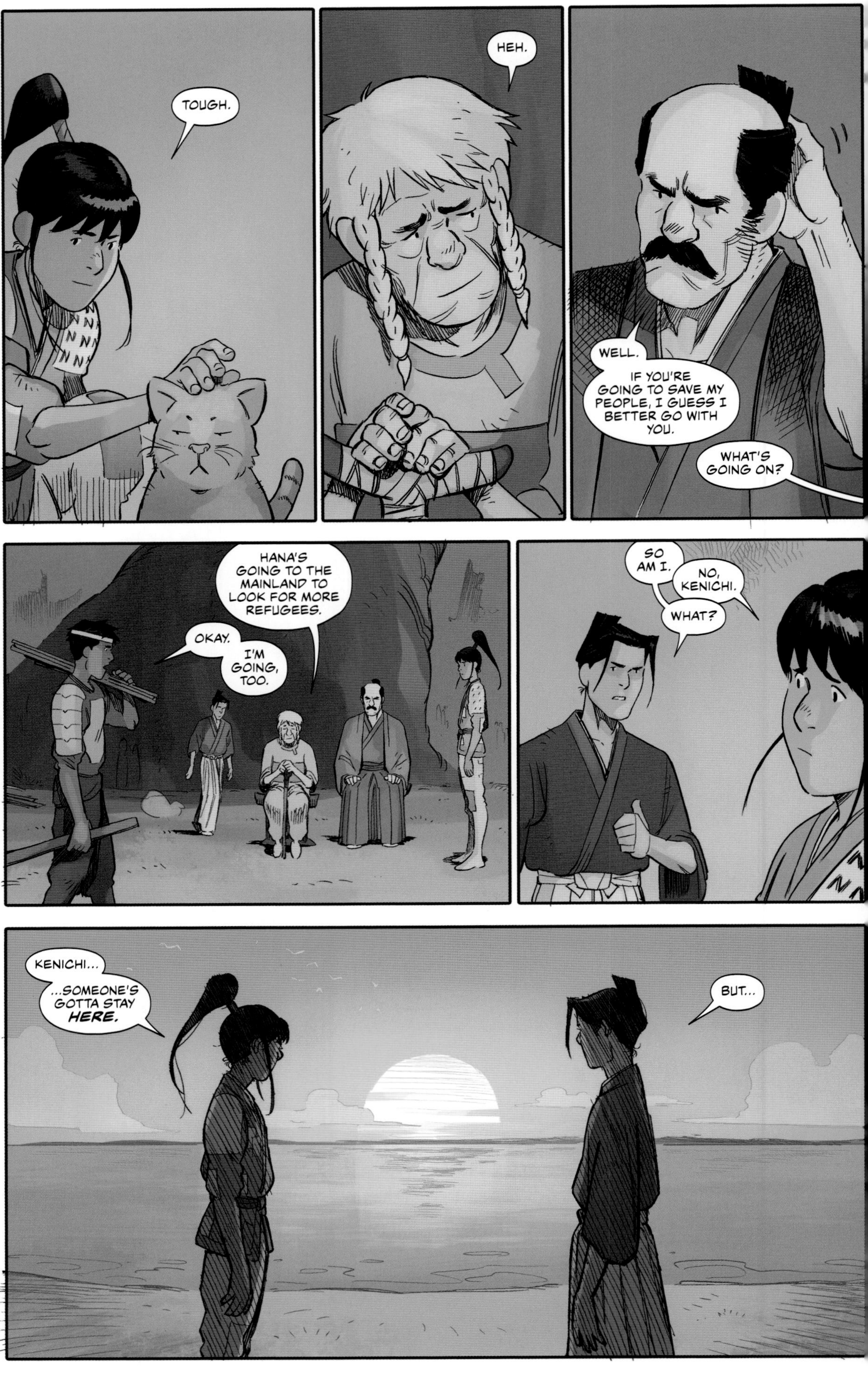
TOUGH.
HEH.
WELL.
IF YOU'RE GOING TO SAVE MY PEOPLE, I GUESS I BETTER GO WITH YOU.
WHAT'S GOING ON?
HANA'S GOING TO THE MAINLAND TO LOOK FOR MORE REFUGEES.
OKAY.
I'M GOING, TOO.
SO AM I.
WHAT?
NO, KENICHI.
KENICHI...
...SOMEONE'S GOTTA STAY HERE.
BUT...

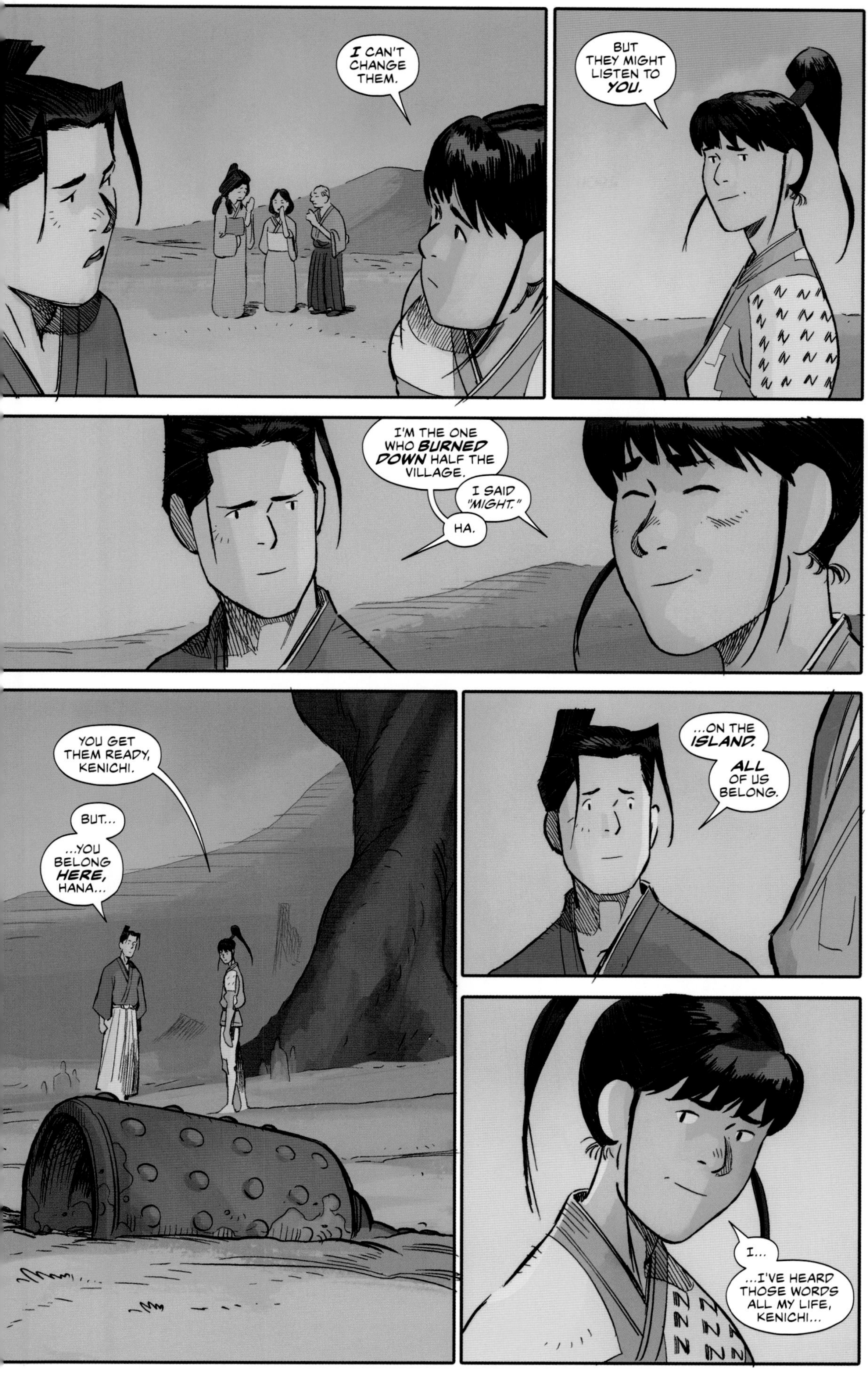
I CAN'T CHANGE THEM.
BUT THEY MIGHT LISTEN TO YOU.
I'M THE ONE WHO BURNED DOWN HALF THE VILLAGE.
I SAID "MIGHT."
HA.
YOU GET THEM READY, KENICHI.
BUT...
...YOU BELONG HERE, HANA...
...ON THE ISLAND.
ALL OF US BELONG.
I...
...I'VE HEARD THOSE WORDS ALL MY LIFE, KENICHI...

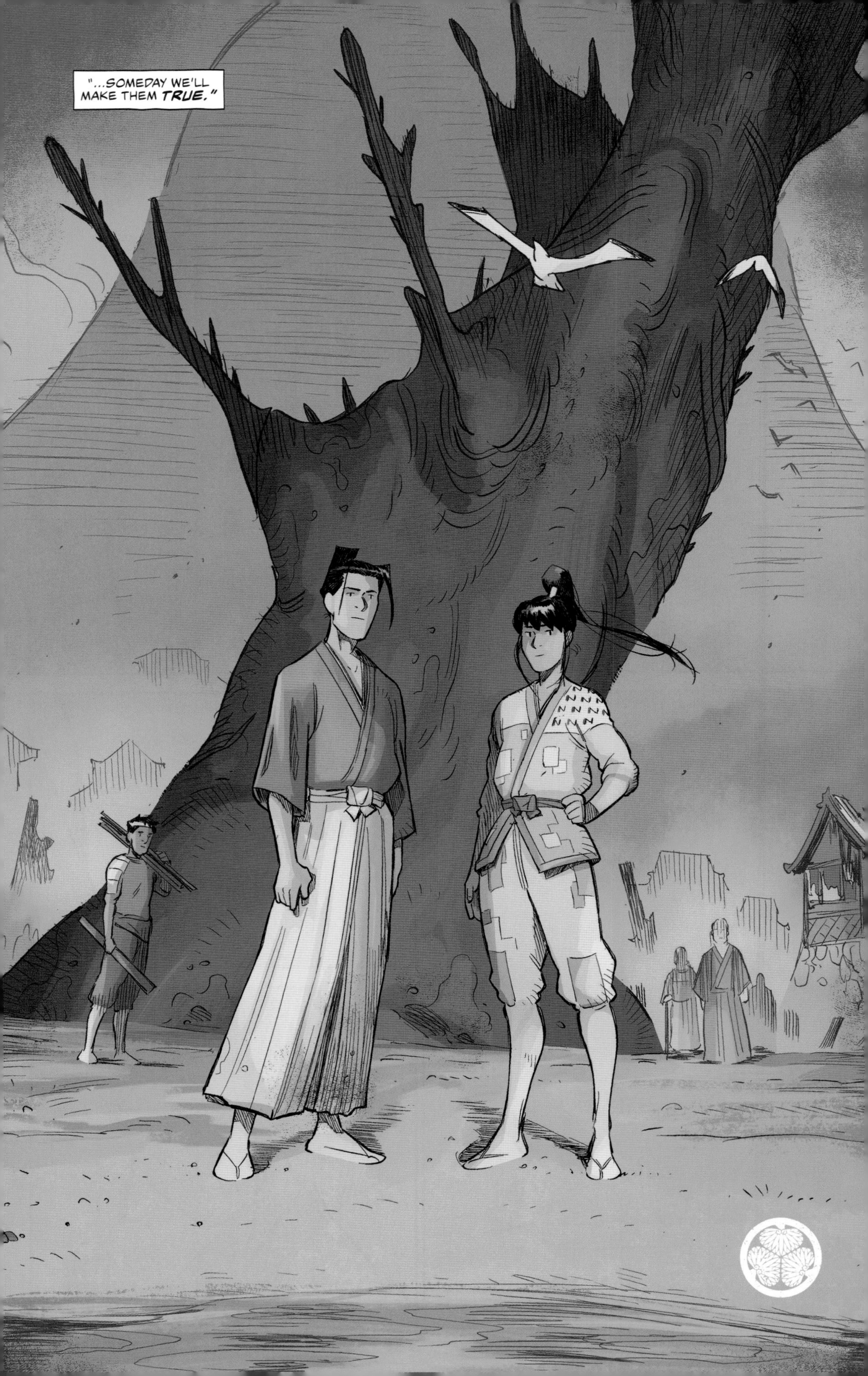
"...SOMEDAY WE'LL MAKE THEM TRUE."

Issue Twelve Cover by **Ethan Young**

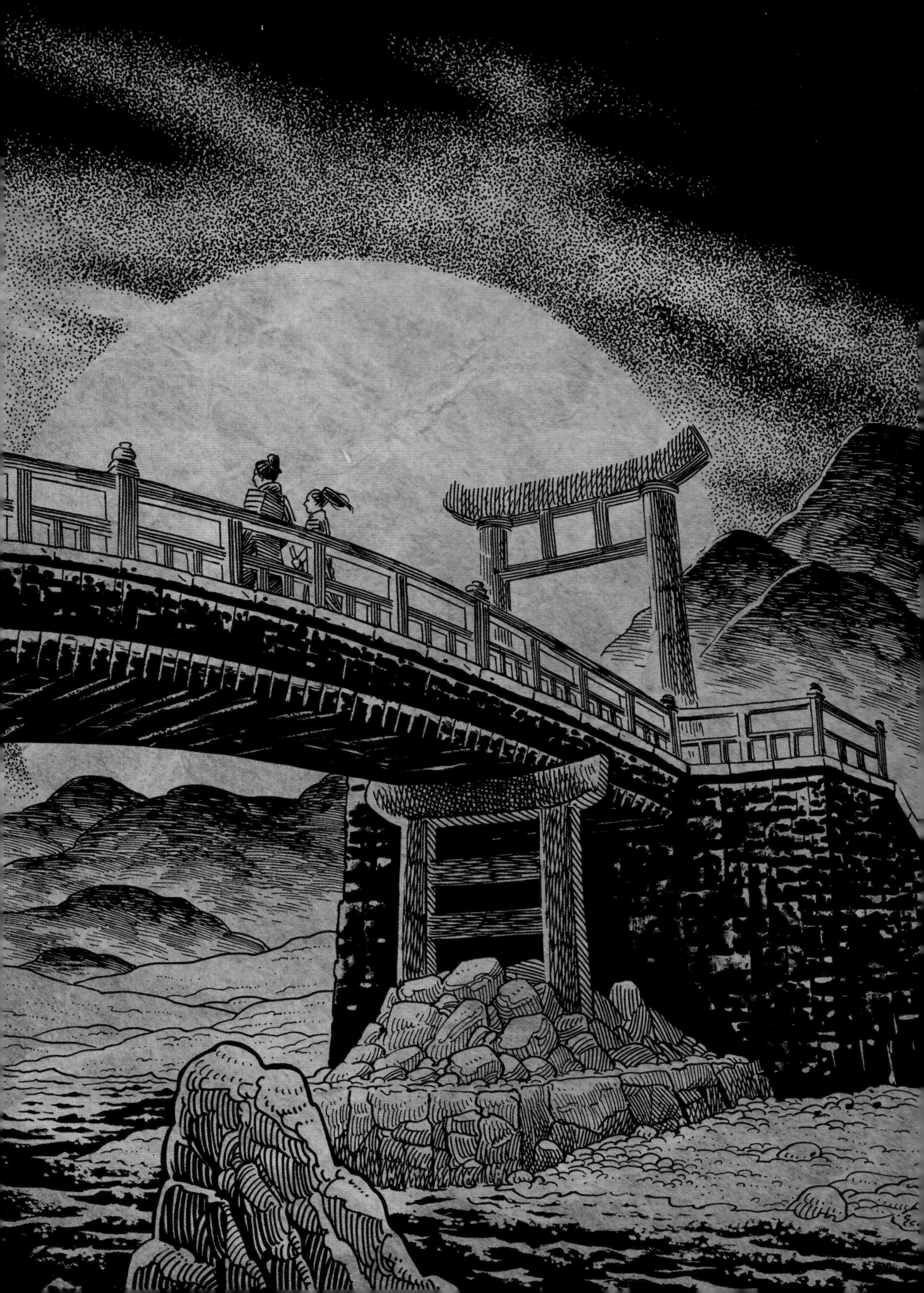

COVER GALLERY

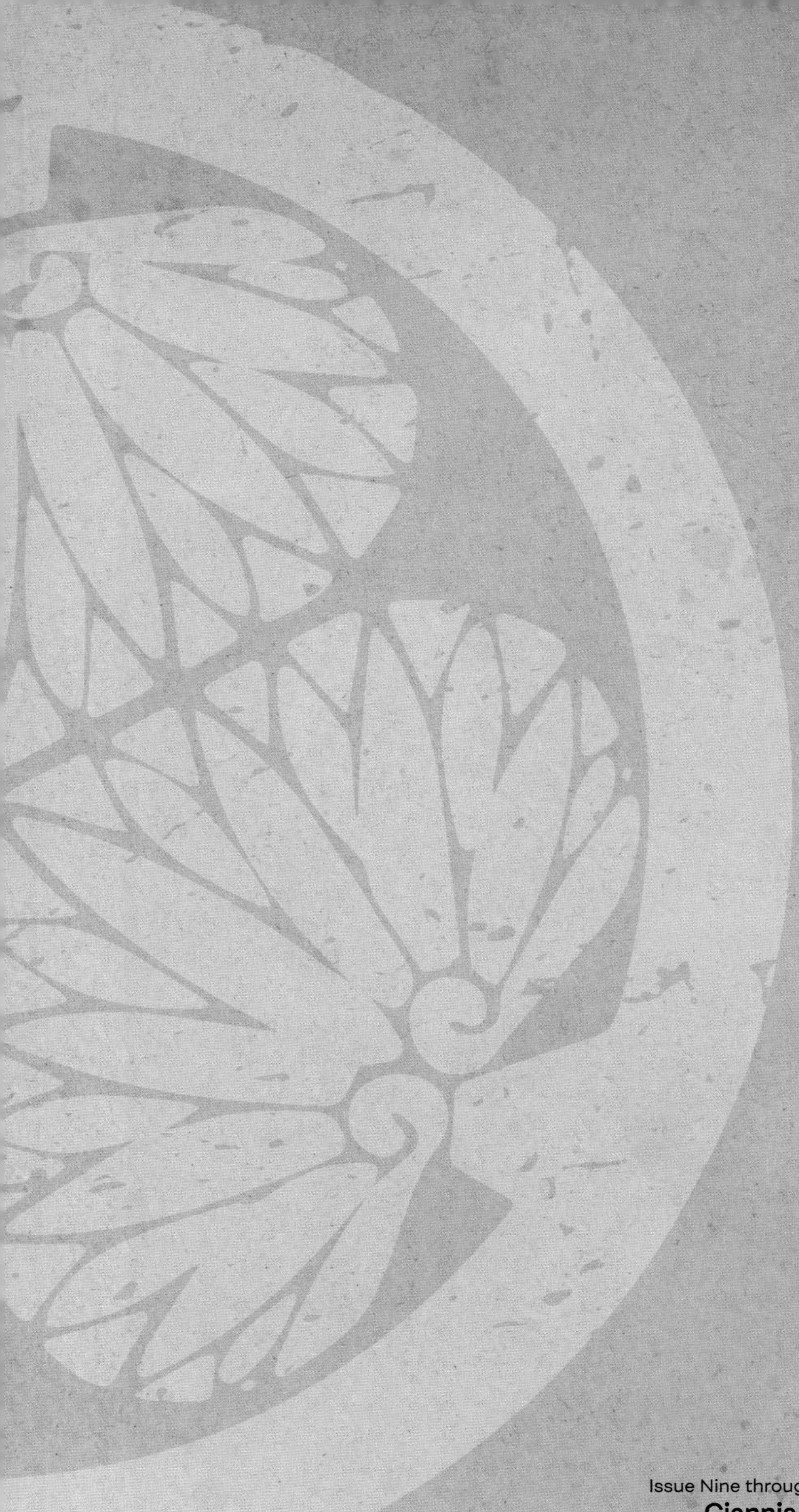

Issue Nine through Twelve Covers by
Giannis Milonogiannis
with colors by **MSASSYK**

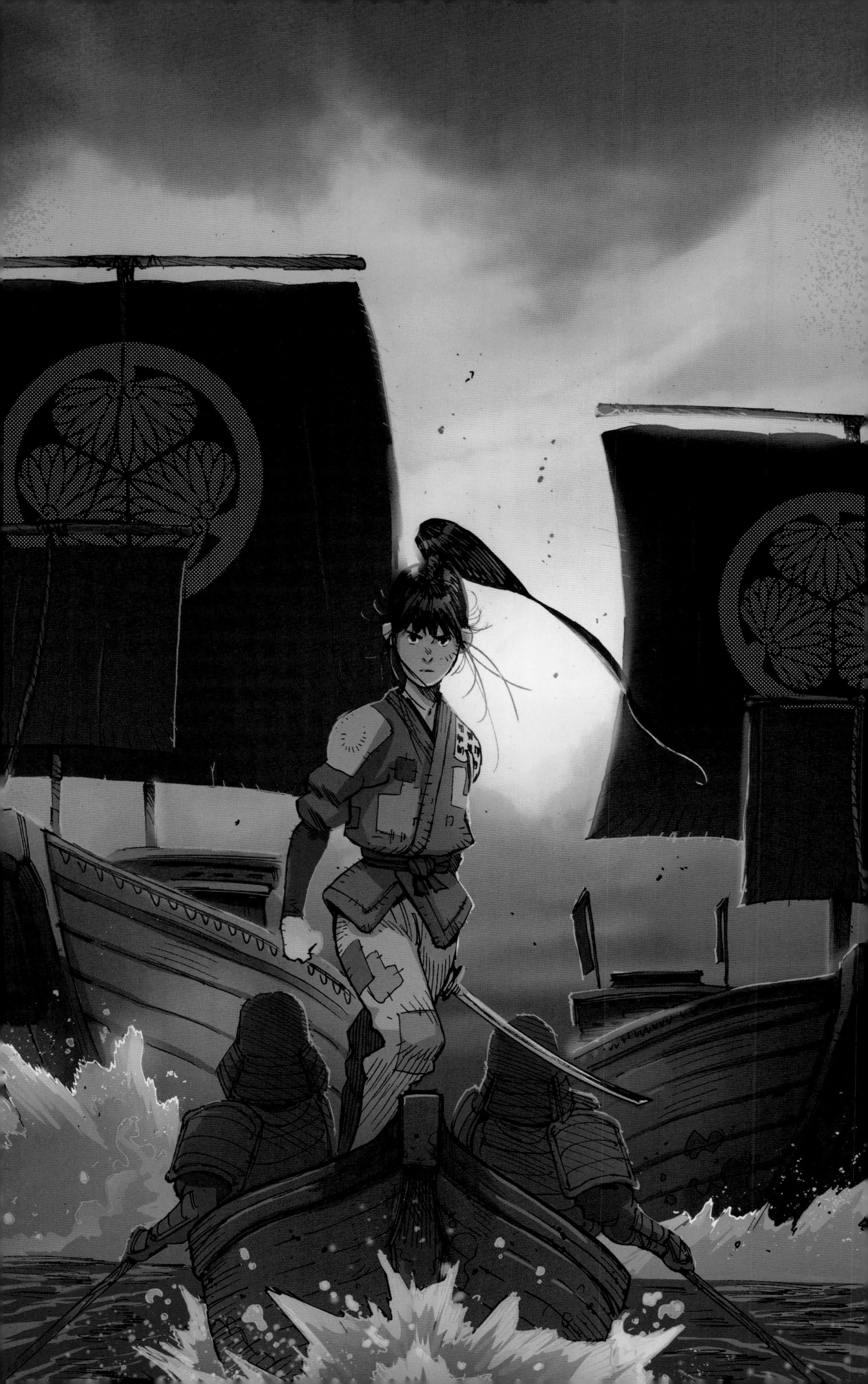

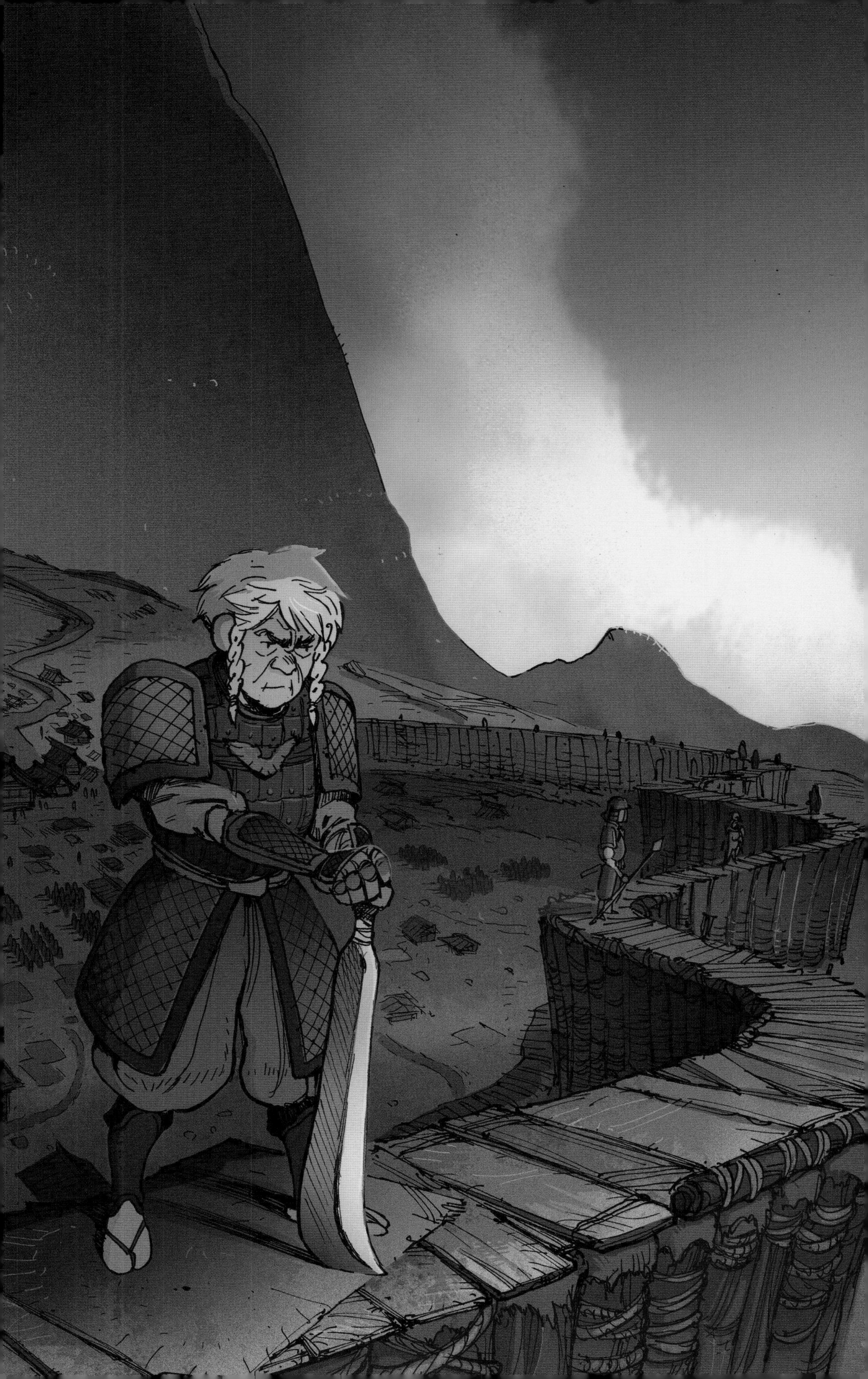

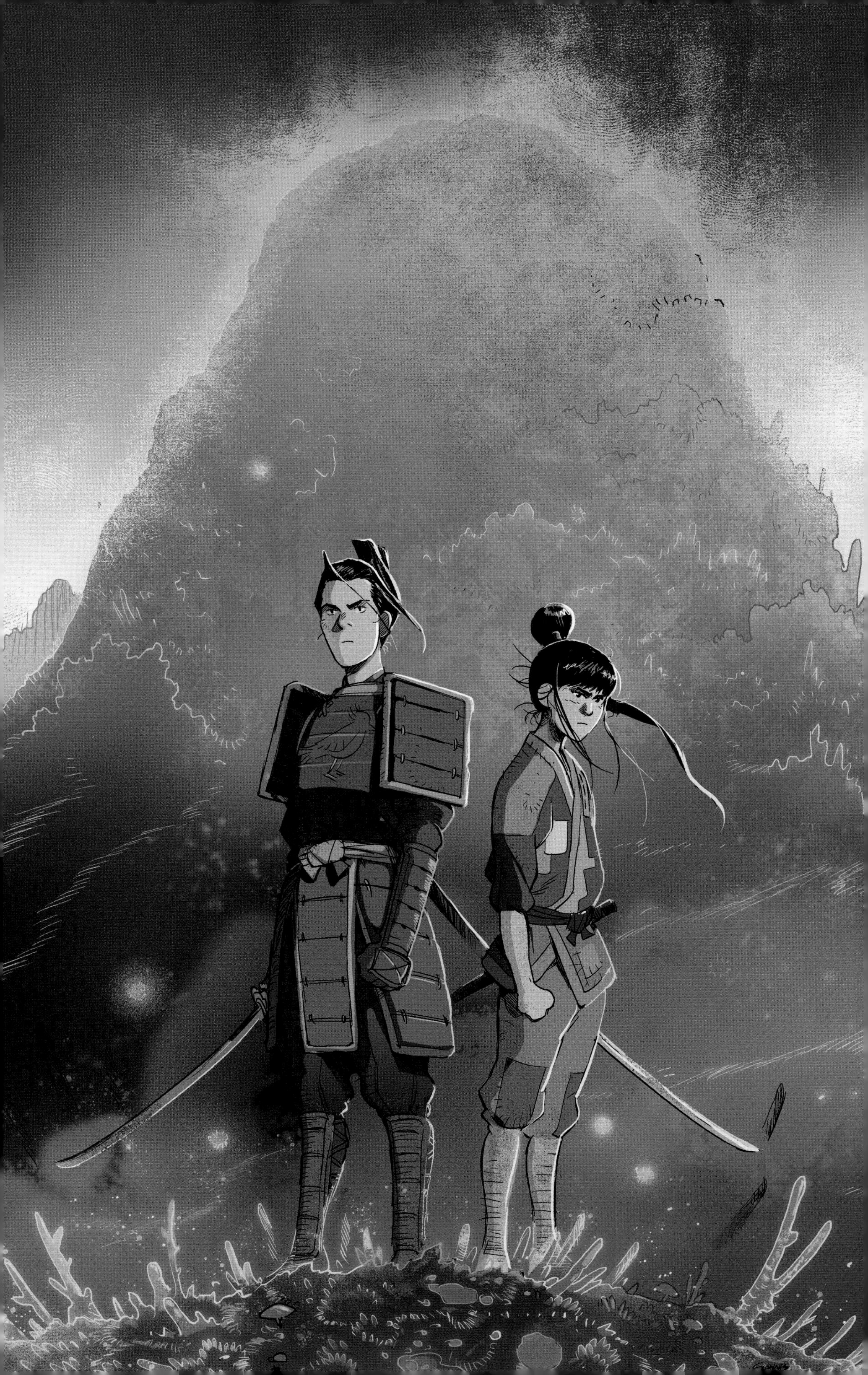

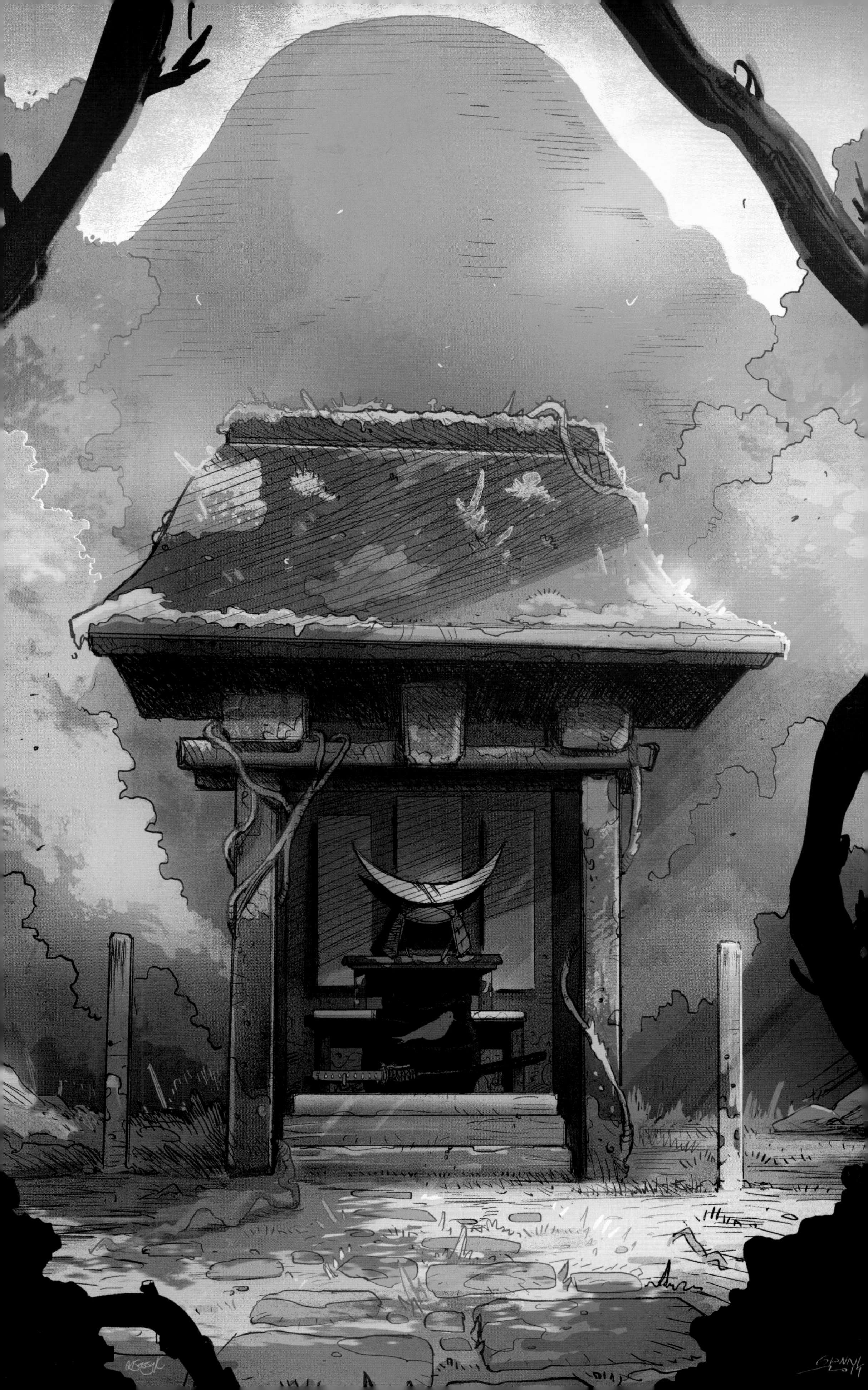

RETROSPECTIVES

A little over two years ago, BOOM! editor Cameron Chittock and I began a series of conversations about our next original project, and somehow we kept coming back to samurai.

I grew watching all kinds of outdoor adventure stories—from Westerns to epic fantasy to space opera. But samurai movies have always had a special place in my heart. I was a half-Korean kid living in the Dallas suburbs in the '70s and '80s. Kurosawa movies and samurai comics were some of the only places I saw wildly exciting, non-stereotypical depictions of Asian heroes in any kind of media.

But ironically, when I became a professional writer, I always shied away from tackling martial arts stories. Even as a kid, while I found solace and inspiration in martial arts fiction, I was painfully aware of the ways racists used martial arts stereotypes against Asians in real life. So even after fifteen years of writing adventure comics of all kinds, I was a bit leery of trying to write in this genre that I loved and knew so well.

But in 2018, it felt like it was time to reclaim this genre that had meant so much to me all my life, and to try to contribute something that felt personal and real and vital. The pan-Asian community of RONIN ISLAND, with all its virtues and flaws, gave me a new way to explore some of the big questions of the Asian diaspora that I've grappled with for decades. And the very specific ways our two main heroes tackle those questions and challenges, with the story giving both points of view equal respect and weight, felt both honest and aspirational at the same time.

Working on RONIN ISLAND has been one of the most gratifying experiences in my sixteen years of working in comics. Along with Cameron, my editors Eric Harburn and Amanda LaFranco have been an absolute dream. They were totally committed to the vision and story from page one and have challenged me in all the right ways to make every script as good as it could be. Giannis Milonogiannis's line art, Irma Kniivila's colors, Simon Bowland's letters, and the variant covers from tremendous artists like Ethan Young came together every issue with the kind of gorgeous seamlessness that only comes from tremendous sensitivity and care. I love this creative team with all my heart and send them all my thanks.

I've also been overwhelmed by the response from readers and retailers and reviewers. This story is so very personal to me. The fact that so many people embraced it—allowing us to expand from a five-issue mini to a twelve-issue epic—has been astounding and hugely gratifying.

Thank you so much for coming along for the ride. May we all find and fight for our own islands in our own time.

Together in strength,
Greg Pak
April 2020, New York City

Drawing a series set in feudal Japan has been a dream of mine for nearly a decade. When I was asked to be part of a new book called RONIN ISLAND, I was drawn to the setting and the chance to play with sword fights. What I didn't realize was that I was about to meet Hana and Kenichi—two characters who, by the end, feel like part of my family.

Thanks to our series getting extended, I was given the rare chance to keep working on the same characters for twelve entire issues. As I got to know them better, the way they were drawn changed dramatically, and most of my time was spent making sure their expressions helped communicate the moral dilemmas Greg had the two of them facing. As the book ended, I wondered where they'd go next and realized—whatever situation they might face, they'll make good choices. They're two genuinely good people, and I'm glad to have met them.

Thanks to the entire team for the hard work and great collaboration—and thank you for reading RONIN ISLAND.

Giannis Milonogiannis

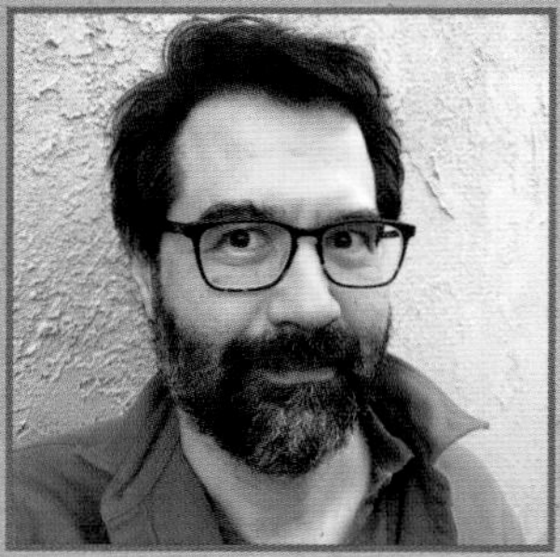

GREG PAK is a Korean American filmmaker and comic book writer best known for his award-winning feature film *Robot Stories*, his blockbuster comic book series like *Planet Hulk* and *World War Hulk*, and his record-breaking Kickstarter publishing projects with Jonathan Coulton, *Code Monkey Save World* and *The Princess Who Saved Herself*.

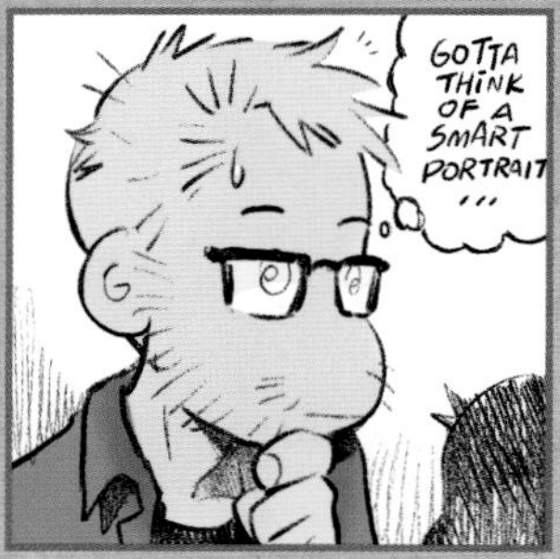
GOTTA THINK OF A SMART PORTRAIT...

GIANNIS MILONOGIANNIS was born in 1988 and has been writing and drawing comics since 2010. Works include *Old City Blues*, *Prophet*, *All-New Ultimates*, *Ghost in the Shell: Global Neural Network*, and others.

IRMA KNIIVILA lives and works out of Toronto, Canada. Her credits include BOOM! Studios, Marvel Inc., Skybound Entertainment, and she has illustrated for The Globe and Mail, Reader's Digest, Penguin Random House, and more. See more at IRMAILLUSTRATION.COM

SIMON BOWLAND has been lettering comics for over fifteen years and is currently working for BOOM!, 2000AD, DC, Marvel, and Image, amongst others. Born and bred in England, Simon still lives there today alongside his wife, Pippa, and their rescue cat, Jess.

DISCOVER
VISIONARY CREATORS

THE WOODS
JAMES TYNION IV • MICHAEL DIALYNAS
VOL. 1
THE ARROW

"The Spire is fantastic! My kind of genre free-for-all."
—BRIAN K. VAUGHAN (Saga)
THE SPIRE
SIMON SPURRIER
JEFF STOKELY
ANDRÉ MAY

MARK WAID · PETER KRAUSE
IRREDEEMABLE
AFTERWORD BY GRANT MORRISON

MARK WAID · JEAN DIAZ
INCORRUPTIBLE

MICHAEL ALAN NELSON
DAN MORA
GABRIEL CASSATA
HEXED
THE HARLOT & THE THIEF VOLUME ONE

ABNETT & CULBARD
WILD'S END
FIRST LIGHT
"IT'S REALLY GREAT!"
JEFF LEMIRE

AVAILABLE AT YOUR LOCAL COMICS SHOP AND BOOKSTORE

To find a comics shop in your area, visit www.comicshoplocator.com

WWW.**BOOM-STUDIOS**.COM

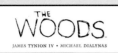

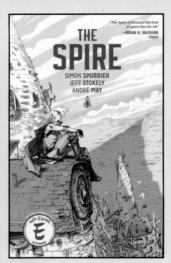

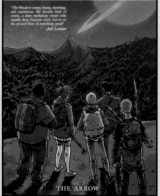

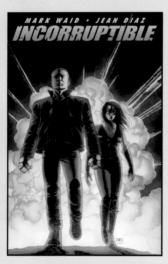

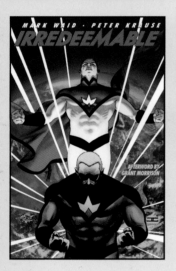

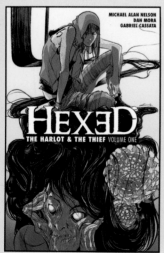

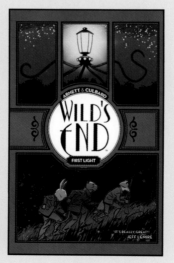

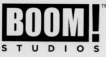

James Tynion IV

The Woods

Volume 1
ISBN: 978-1-60886-454-6 | $9.99 US
Volume 2
ISBN: 978-1-60886-495-9 | $14.99 US
Volume 3
ISBN: 978-1-60886-773-8 | $14.99 US

The Backstagers

Volume 1
ISBN: 978-1-60886-993-0 | $14.99 US

Simon Spurrier

Six-Gun Gorilla

ISBN: 978-1-60886-390-7 | $19.99 US

The Spire

ISBN: 978-1-60886-913-8 | $29.99 US

Weavers

ISBN: 978-1-60886-963-3 | $19.99 US

Mark Waid

Irredeemable

Volume 1
ISBN: 978-1-93450-690-5 | $16.99 US
Volume 2
ISBN: 978-1-60886-000-5 | $16.99 US

Incorruptible

Volume 1
ISBN: 978-1-60886-015-9 | $16.99 US
Volume 2
ISBN: 978-1-60886-028-9 | $16.99 US

Michael Alan Nelson

Hexed The Harlot & The Thief

Volume 1
ISBN: 978-1-60886-718-9 | $14.99 US
Volume 2
ISBN: 978-1-60886-816-2 | $14.99 US

Day Men

Volume 1
ISBN: 978-1-60886-393-8 | $9.99 US
Volume 2
ISBN: 978-1-60886-852-0 | $9.99 US

Dan Abnett

Wild's End

Volume 1: First Light
ISBN: 978-1-60886-735-6 | $19.99 US
Volume 2: The Enemy Within
ISBN: 978-1-60886-877-3 | $19.99 US

Hypernaturals

Volume 1
ISBN: 978-1-60886-298-6 | $16.99 US
Volume 2
ISBN: 978-1-60886-319-8 | $19.99 US